Implementation and Performance in New American Schools

Three Years Into Scale-Up

Mark Berends

Sheila Nataraj Kirby

Scott Naftel

Christopher McKelvey

Prepared for New American Schools

RAND
EDUCATION

The research described in this report was supported by New American Schools.

Library of Congress Cataloging-in-Publication Data

Implementation and performance in New American Schools : three years into scale-up / Mark Berends ... [et al.].
    p. cm.
    "MR-1145-EDU."
    Includes bibliographical references.
    ISBN 0-8330-2902-X
    1. New American Schools (Organization) 2. School improvement programs— United States—Longitudinal studies. 3. Educational change—United States— Longitudinal studies. I. Berends, Mark, 1962– II. Rand Corporation.

LB2822.82 .I44 2000
371.2'00973—dc21

                                    00-062770

Published 2001 by RAND
1700 Main Street, P.O. Box 2138, Santa Monica, CA 90407-2138
1200 South Hayes Street, Arlington, VA 22202-5050
RAND URL: http://www.rand.org/
To order RAND documents or to obtain additional information, contact Distribution Services: Telephone: (310) 451-7002;
Fax: (310) 451-6915; Internet: order@rand.org

As a private nonprofit corporation, New American Schools (NAS) began in 1991 to fund the development of designs aimed at transforming entire schools at the elementary and secondary levels. After competition and development phases, NAS currently is scaling up its designs to form a critical mass of schools within partnering districts. During this phase, RAND's research activities include monitoring the progress of a sample of NAS schools in eight partnering jurisdictions through the 1999–2000 school year.

This is a report aimed at those who want to better understand the burgeoning area of whole-school or comprehensive school reform. It describes trends in implementation, school performance, and related factors for the sample of NAS schools and is based on a three-year longitudinal study of these schools.

The RAND evaluation of NAS schools is ongoing; additional reports should provide additional findings from RAND's five-year experience analyzing NAS, the designs, and the implementing schools.

Other RAND reports and articles about New American Schools include:

"Teacher-Reported Effects of New American Schools' Designs: Exploring Relationships to Teacher Background and School Context," by Mark Berends, *Educational Evaluation and Policy Analysis*, 2000, 22(1), pp. 65–82.

"Necessary District Support for Comprehensive School Reform," by Susan J. Bodilly and Mark Berends, in *Hard Work for Good Schools:*

Facts Not Fads in Title I Reform, edited by Gary Orfield and Elizabeth H. DeBray, Boston, MA: Civil Rights Project, Harvard University, 1999, pp. 111–119.

Assessing the Progress of New American Schools: A Status Report, by Mark Berends, RAND, MR-1085-ED, 1999.

Lessons from New American Schools' Scale-up Phase: Prospects for Bringing Designs to Multiple Schools, by Susan J. Bodilly, RAND, MR-942-NAS, 1998.

New American Schools after Six Years, by Thomas K. Glennan, Jr., RAND, MR-945-NASDC, 1998.

Funding Comprehensive School Reform, by Brent R. Keltner, RAND, internal document, 1998.

Reforming America's Schools: Observations on Implementing "Whole School Designs," by Susan J. Bodilly and Thomas K. Glennan, RAND, RB-8016-EDU, 1998.

Lesson's from New American Schools Development Corporation's Demonstration Phase, by Susan J. Bodilly, RAND, MR-729-NASDC, 1996.

Reforming and Conforming: NASDC Principals Discuss School Accountability Systems, by Karen Mitchell, RAND, MR-716-NASDC, 1996.

"Lessons Learned from RAND's Formative Assessment of NASDC's Phase 2 Demonstration Effort," by Susan J. Bodilly, in *Bold Plans for School Restructuring: The New American Schools Designs,* edited by Sam Stringfield, Steven Ross, and Lana Smith, Mahwah, NJ: Lawrence Erlbaum Associates, 1996, pp. 289–324.

Designing New American Schools: Baseline Observations on Nine Design Teams, by Susan J. Bodilly, Susanna Purnell, Kimberly Ramsey, and Christina Smith, RAND, MR-598-NASDC, 1995.

Funding for this research was provided under a contract with NAS and was supported by the Ford Foundation and another donor. This report was written under the aegis of RAND Education.

CONTENTS

Chapter Six

FIGURES

TABLES

Spurred by the piecemeal approach to school reform that had produced little change in the nation's test scores, New American Schools (NAS) launched its efforts for whole-school reform in 1991. As a private nonprofit organization, NAS's mission is to help schools and districts dramatically raise the achievement levels of large numbers of students by using whole-school designs and design team assistance during the implementation process. NAS is currently in the scale-up phase of its effort in which the designs are being widely diffused in partnering jurisdictions across the nation.

The purpose of this report is to provide an overview of the progress in implementation and performance in a longitudinal sample of schools three years into the scale-up phase. These schools adopted one of seven designs:

- Audrey Cohen College [AC] (currently renamed Purpose-Centered Education);

- Authentic Teaching, Learning, and Assessment for All Students [AT];

- Co-NECT Schools [CON];

- Expeditionary Learning Outward Bound [EL];

- Modern Red Schoolhouse [MRSH];

- National Alliance for Restructuring Education [NARE] (currently renamed America's Choice Design Network); and

- Roots & Wings [RW].

The report is based on a variety of data gathered from the schools: principal and teacher surveys conducted during the 1997 and 1998 school years; data provided by districts on test scores; and school demographic characteristics. In addition, the report relies on other RAND studies that included site visits to schools and school districts to gather information about district and school administrators' and teachers' reports of the progress of the NAS initiative (Bodilly, 1998).

This report is not intended to be a "summative" evaluation of NAS and the design teams. This seems premature given the variation in designs among different sites, the support and leadership provided by districts, and the stages of implementation. The intent of this report is to provide an interim progress report that will provide information to NAS, the designs, and the public to improve efforts aimed at whole-school restructuring and comprehensive school reform.

SOME IMPORTANT LIMITATIONS

There are some important limitations of this research that need to be kept in mind.

First, the sample of schools analyzed here consisted of, for most design teams, the first schools to which they had provided assistance with implementing their designs on a fee-for-service basis. There were many changes in both the designs and the assistance provided as the teams and the schools gained experience. Thus, when interpreting the findings in this report, it is important to note the unique features of the population of schools we have studied.

Second, the fact that designs were evolving over time as design teams gained experience and adapted designs to local contexts makes a longitudinal evaluation difficult.

Third, the school-level measures we use to compare performance in NAS schools with that of the district as a whole are also subject to some important limitations. For example, these aggregated measures may fail to capture changes in the tails of the distribution, or they may miss some significant achievement effects that might be more easily measured if student-level data were available and comparable across jurisdictions.

THE ANALYSIS SAMPLE

The target population of schools for this study was all schools beginning implementation of a NAS design during school year 1995–1996 or 1996–1997 in seven jurisdictions that chose to partner with NAS at the beginning of the scale-up phase: Cincinnati, Ohio; Dade, Florida; several districts in Kentucky; Memphis, Tennessee; Philadelphia, Pennsylvania; San Antonio, Texas; and several districts in Washington State.

The analysis sample consisted of 104 schools in which principals reported that they were implementing designs in both 1997 and 1998, and which had complete data (i.e., from teachers and principals) in both years. The teacher sample consisted of 2,100 teachers.

Overall, NAS partnered with jurisdictions that were predominantly urban, high poverty, and high minority (Berends, 1999). In the analysis sample, MRSH and RW tended to be in the poorest schools, while AC and RW tended to be in the schools with the highest percentage of minority students.

STATUS OF IMPLEMENTATION

We find that implementation of designs was higher among schools with greater experience with the design, as one would expect, but this overall pattern masks some important trends. For example, we find that mean implementation levels increased from 1997 to 1998 among schools that had been implementing for one year in 1997, but mean implementation remained essentially unchanged between 1997 and 1998 in schools that had been implementing for two or more years in 1997.

The lack of continued increases in implementation over time needs to be examined further and validated against other designs in other sites. It may point to problems with the level of design-based assistance and support tailing off beyond the second year, with maintaining a stable and supportive school and district environment that would allow implementation to deepen, or with implementing a complex design not well-suited to the school's needs. Alternatively, in schools that are more mature, it may point to an expected leveling off of implementation because the designs have become a more routine part of the school. However, in this latter case, we would have expected declines in the variation of implementation within these schools, which do not show up in our data. In any event, this finding deserves further attention.

FACTORS AFFECTING IMPLEMENTATION

Teachers' Perceptions

Not surprisingly, teachers' perceptions of students and their readiness to learn were all significantly related to the level of implementation. Teachers who reported that lack of basic skills was not a hindrance to their students' academic success, that lack of student discipline and parent support was not a problem, or that students could learn with the resources available also reported higher implementation than those who felt otherwise.

School Characteristics

Reported levels of implementation were higher in elementary than in secondary schools and in small schools relative to large schools. Implementation was not related to the racial-ethnic or socioeconomic status (SES) composition of the schools in our sample.

Principal leadership was strongly correlated with reported levels of implementation: Schools in which teachers reported strong principal leadership also reported much higher levels of implementation. We find that this variable was strongly correlated with teachers' reports of the level of resources—in terms of materials, funds, and time—available to them to implement designs.

Designs and Design Team Assistance

Our results emphasize the importance of design-related factors and design team assistance. High reported levels of implementation were related to clear communication by design teams and higher levels of teacher support for the designs. The level and adequacy of resources also clearly mattered in implementation.

District Support

There were large differences in levels of implementation between jurisdictions. In general, levels of implementation were higher in those districts that were more supportive of the NAS designs and characterized by stability of district leadership (e.g., Memphis).

PERFORMANCE IN NAS SCHOOLS

Our analysis of performance trends focused on whether NAS schools made gains in test scores relative to their respective jurisdictions. Fifty percent or more of the schools in Cincinnati, Dade, Kentucky, and Memphis improved in mathematics, while half or more of the schools in Cincinnati, Philadelphia, San Antonio, and Washington showed improvement in reading. In total, of the 163 schools for which we have data allowing us to compare performance relative to the district or state, 81 schools (50 percent) made gains relative to the district in mathematics and 76 schools (47 percent) made gains in reading.[1]

The results by design team varied across mathematics and reading tests. For example, for the 8 AC schools, 5 made progress relative to the district in mathematics, but only 2 did so in reading. With the exception of AT and EL schools, about half of the other design team schools made progress relative to the district in mathematics; in reading, less than half of AC, CON, and NARE schools made gains relative to the district. RW was the most consistent, with 10 out of 21 schools making progress in both reading and mathematics relative to the district. Of the 11 MRSH schools, 7 made progress in mathematics and 8 in reading.

Because of the wide variation in implementation and environments that occurs within schools and among jurisdictions, it may be too early to expect robust performance results across the NAS sites. In addition, better and longer-term performance data are needed in order to make conclusive judgments about designs and their effects on school performance.

---

[1]These results do not vary if we limit the sample to the 104 schools for which we have data on implementation.

CONCLUSIONS AND POLICY IMPLICATIONS

NAS and the design teams partnered with schools and districts that are characterized by a host of problems related to poverty, achievement, and climate characteristics. To scale up the designs or replicate implementation in these sites is extremely difficult. Implementation and performance vary both within and across schools and sites. Overall, about half the schools made gains relative to the district.

It is important to examine these results from different perspectives. First, NAS's initial aims were to dramatically improve the achievement of large numbers of students with design teams and the assistance they provided to schools. From this perspective, the findings from our analysis indicate that this goal was overly ambitious, especially over a short period of time. Dramatic achievement gains were not made, although some designs fared better than others.

From another perspective, one might view the findings reported here with cautious optimism. The results that indicate some design teams have worked with challenging schools, implemented their designs at relatively higher levels, and experienced achievement gains suggest that some comprehensive school reform models may hold some promise for improving the achievement of students attending high poverty schools in urban areas of this nation. A great deal of work needs to be done, however, to make such experiences a consistent reality on a large scale.

Overall, our analyses strongly underscore the importance of both the district environment and design team assistance in implementation. Without leadership, support, and availability of resources at the district level; without clear communication, provision of materials and staff support; and without efforts on the part of the design teams to build a consensus of teacher support, implementation is likely to fail or at least lag far behind.

Our findings also suggest that comprehensive school reforms face many obstacles during implementation, and because of this, whole-school designs face continuing challenges in dramatically raising the achievement of all students.

ACKNOWLEDGMENTS

A research project such as this is never accomplished without the collaboration and cooperation of many people and organizations. We would like to thank the Ford Foundation and another donor for providing the research funding to New American Schools (NAS) to support RAND's ongoing assessment. We are grateful to our reviewers, Tom Corcoran, Co-Director of the Consortium for Policy Research in Education at the University of Pennsylvania, and Andrew Porter, Director of the Wisconsin Center for Education Research at the University of Wisconsin-Madison. The report benefited greatly, both in substance and clarity, from their comments.

New American Schools, as an advocate for school reform, deserves a special acknowledgment for supporting independent research on its efforts. For as Seymour Sarason (1996: p. vii) has said, "It is very rare in the arena of school reform for the principal investigator courageously to seek and support an independent, systematic, several years' long description and analysis of an intervention effort." While RAND's research has been mostly formative, providing information back to NAS to improve the initiative, some of RAND's findings have been difficult for NAS to accept at times. Yet, unlike most other advocacy groups, NAS and its Board have continued to support and stress the importance of independent research and analysis to inform public policy. Indeed, both NAS and its Board have used the findings and implications from the ongoing RAND evaluation to improve the initiative. For this, NAS deserves a great deal of credit.

We are also grateful to the teachers and principals in the schools who gave of their time to respond to our questions, the staff in districts and states who helped us piece together relevant data, and the design teams who clarified issues along the way. All played a crucial role in providing information to better understand what kinds of schools the NAS designs are working with, and we appreciate their efforts and dedication to improving the capacity of schools, the professional development of teachers, and the well-being of students.

We thank the members of the Research Advisory Panel (funded by the Annenberg Foundation) who provide critical guidance to RAND's research on NAS. Members include Barbara Cervone, Paul Hill, Janice Petrovich, Andrew Porter, Karen Sheingold, and Carol Weiss. We continue to learn from their experience, expertise, and encouragement. In addition, we are grateful to Tom Corcoran, Adam Gamoran, and Fred Newmann, who shared their expertise during the development of our principal and teacher surveys.

For the Tennessee Value-Added Assessment System test score results for the NAS sites in Memphis, we are indebted to Steven Ross of the University of Memphis and William Sanders of the University of Tennessee. They shared their results, answered our questions, and conducted additional tabulations in the data for us in a very timely fashion. We appreciate their help and the extensive research they have done on the Tennessee test scores.

Several colleagues within RAND also contributed to the research underlying this report. Susan Bodilly, Co-Principal Investigator on this project with Mark Berends, has been intimately involved in this research throughout. Thomas Glennan, senior advisor to this project, also provided helpful insights along the way. Joanna Heilbrunn was responsible for managing the principal phone interviews and administration of the teacher surveys that form the foundation of this report. In addition, Garfield Lindo, Jennifer Sloan, and Thomas Sullivan provided valuable help with the research.

Despite the cooperation, support, and guidance of these individuals and agencies, the errors in this report remain our own.

Chapter One

A BRIEF HISTORY OF NEW AMERICAN SCHOOLS AND RAND'S ROLE IN MONITORING THE EFFORT

School reform in this country has a long and checkered history (Tyack and Cuban, 1995). Spurred by the piecemeal approach to school reform that had produced little change in the nation's test scores, New American Schools (NAS) launched its efforts for whole-school reform in 1991. The mission of NAS is to help schools and districts dramatically raise the achievement levels of large numbers of students by using whole-school designs and design team assistance during the implementation process. NAS defines a design team as follows:

> A Design Team is an organization that provides high-quality, focused, ongoing professional development for teachers and administrators organized around a meaningful and compelling vision of what students should know and be able to do. The vision, or design, offers schools a focus for their improvement efforts, along with guidance in identifying what students need to know and be able to do and how to get there. (New American Schools, 1997, p. 6)

Glennan (1998) describes a design further, saying that it "articulates the school's vision, mission, and goals; guides the instructional program of the school; shapes the selection and socialization of the staff; and establishes common expectations for performance, behavior, and accountability among students, teachers, and parents" (p. 11).

The purposes and approaches of NAS and its design teams are similar to those for schoolwide Title I programs[1] and the Comprehensive School Reform Demonstration program (CSRD), also known as Obey-Porter.[2] Each intends to improve student and school performance through schools' adopting a unified, coherent approach rather than adding fragmented programs or investing in personnel dedicated to a small group of students in pull-out programs. Each intends to serve all students, not just subgroups of students. Indeed, such whole-school reforms can be viewed as tools to help schools implement the ambitious goals of standards-based, systemic reforms being encouraged by the federal government. Such aims include raising academic performance expectations for all students, developing challenging state content and performance standards, implementing new assessments to monitor this progress, changing curriculum and instruction to educate students to standards, improving professional development to assist teachers, and encouraging parent and community involvement.

Thus, findings about NAS and its attempts at whole-school change can help inform the need for policy improvement for Title I, the CSRD program, and standards-based reform efforts more generally—

---

[1] "Schoolwide" programs, available for funding since 1988, allow schools to use Title I money with other dollars to improve school performance as opposed to targeting Title I money solely to qualified students. The 1994 Improving America's Schools Act encourages more wide-ranging adoption of schoolwide programs (see Wong and Meyer, 1998a; American Association of School Administrators, 1995; http://www.ed.gov/legislation/ESEA). Currently, schools can use their Title I funding to improve the entire instructional program throughout the school if at least 50 percent of the students within the school are from poor families. (For a discussion of the 1994 Improving America's Schools Act see U.S. Department of Education, 1993, 1999; and Borman et al., 1996).

[2] To further the implementation of comprehensive, whole-school reforms, the CSRD was established in November 1997. These appropriations committed $145 million to be used to help schools develop comprehensive school reform based on reliable research and effective practices. The majority (83 percent in FY98 and 77 percent in FY99) of the funds are committed to Title I schools. Part of the money ($25 million in FY98 and FY99) was available to all public schools, including those ineligible for Title I, as part of the Fund for the Improvement in Education (FIE) program. Approximately 1,800 schools will receive at least $50,000 per year for three years under the CSRD program, beginning in FY98. There was an increase of $75 million for FY00 ($50 million in Title I/Section 1502 funds and $25 million in FIE funds) over the $145 million appropriated for FY98 and FY99, which will allow 1,000 additional schools to undertake comprehensive reform (see Kirby and Berends et al., in review; http://www.ed.gov/offices/OESE/compreform).

all of which are key pieces of the federal policy initiative in education (see Smith and Scoll, 1995).

HISTORY OF NAS AND RAND'S ROLE

Within the context of standards-based reform during the 1990s, with attention toward improving equity and excellence, the New American Schools initiative was founded. Stemming from gatherings such as the 1989 meeting of former President Bush and state governors, national educational goals emerged. These goals evolved into part of Bush's America 2000 effort to support new elementary and secondary school designs. This support of NAS continued during the Clinton administration with Goals 2000, but it is only with the recent CSRD program that the federal government has more directly funded NAS-like designs.

Beginning in 1991 and funded by the private sector, NAS sought to engage the nation's best educators, business people, and researchers in the task of creating, testing, and fostering the implementation of whole-school designs that were not constrained by existing regulations, work rules, and conventions.

The initial goal of NAS was to help a large number of schools change their organization and practices to improve student learning. To make this goal a reality, NAS initially organized its work into several phases (see Figure 1.1):

- a competition phase to solicit proposals and select designs;

- a development phase of one year to develop the ideas in the proposals in concrete ways;

- a demonstration phase of two years to pilot the designs in real school settings; and

- a scale-up phase in which the designs would be widely diffused in partnering jurisdictions across the nation.[3]

---

[3]A more detailed description of the history of the NAS initiative and the design teams appears in Bodilly, 1998; Glennan, 1998; and Stringfield et al., 1996. See also Desimone, 2000; Herman et al., 1999; Ball et al., 1998; Stringfield and Datnow, 1998; Datnow and Stringfield, 1997; and Ross et al., 1997, 1998. For descriptions of NAS and the

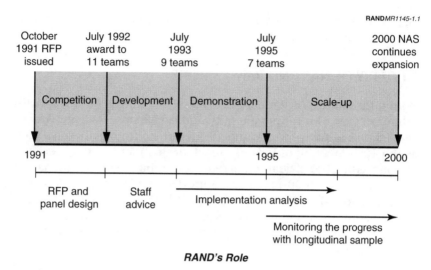

RAND's Role

NOTE: RFP = request for proposal.

Figure 1.1—Phases of New American Schools Initiative and RAND Roles

As NAS entered the scale-up phase, there were seven design teams:[4]

- Audrey Cohen College (AC) (currently renamed Purpose-Centered Education);

- Authentic Teaching, Learning, and Assessment for All Students (AT);

- Co-NECT Schools (CON);

- Expeditionary Learning Outward Bound (EL);

- Modern Red Schoolhouse (MRSH);

---

design teams on the web, see http://www.naschools.org which has links to each design team's website.

[4]Another design—Urban Learning Centers (ULC)—was implementing in the Los Angeles area, but when scale-up began, this design team was not included in the NAS portfolio because the team had not shown the capacity to scale up. Since that time, ULC has shown this capacity and is currently being marketed by NAS as one of its designs.

- National Alliance for Restructuring Education (NARE) (currently renamed America's Choice Design Network);[5] and

- Roots & Wings (RW).

RAND's role in the NAS effort also evolved over time, as Figure 1.1 shows. In the early 1990s, RAND helped NAS design a request for proposals (RFP) and conduct a national competition for design proposals. Subsequently, RAND moved to a more objective evaluative role, monitoring the progress and performance in NAS schools. Throughout, RAND's assessment has been predominantly formative in that RAND has provided information to NAS, the design teams, and the public to improve efforts aimed at whole-school restructuring. For example, previous RAND studies have examined the initial implementation of the designs during the development and demonstration phases, providing feedback to both NAS and the design teams (Bodilly et al., 1995; Bodilly, 1996). RAND's earlier research has emphasized the importance of systemic factors in the success of design implementation (Bodilly et al., 1995; Bodilly, 1996).

NAS's scale-up strategy was based on the belief that school transformation would not occur unless there was strong district support. As such, it sought to partner with a limited number of school jurisdictions, chosen on the basis of demonstrating that these jurisdictions either had operations that would support the implementation of designs or were actively pursuing efforts to create such operations. NAS even provided criteria for identifying a "supportive operating environment" (NAS, 1997). The jurisdictions were to commit themselves to implementing NAS or similar designs in 30 percent of their schools over a five-year period. NAS chose ten partners in the late winter of 1995: Cincinnati, Ohio; Dade, Florida; several districts in Kentucky and Maryland; Memphis, Tennessee; Pittsburgh and Philadelphia, Pennsylvania; San Antonio, Texas; San Diego, California; and several districts in Washington State. In order to formalize these partnerships, NAS sought to develop memoranda of under-

---

[5]NARE's development into America's Choice reflected a major change in the design, from NARE's emphasis on changing the school system (e.g., organization and governance and assessments) to America's Choice additional emphasis on curriculum, instruction, and professional development changes within classrooms and schools. Despite this change, the school principals in the sample analyzed in this report continued to report that they were implementing the principles of the NARE design.

standing (MOUs) detailing NAS's, the jurisdictions', and the design teams' obligations.

At the same time, the design teams themselves were working to finish their designs and prove their viability to gain NAS support for entering the scale-up phase.[6] Thus, as design team scale-up began with marketing efforts in the spring of 1995, the teams were struggling to finish their development, to build their organizations, to specify their fee schedules, and to figure out how to describe themselves to schools and jurisdictions. At the same time, the jurisdictions were trying to understand how to finance and contract with design teams, monitor their work, match schools with designs, and provide support to schools that was needed in areas where design teams did not provide services. RAND and NAS field visits in the summer and fall of 1995 suggested that there was much to be learned on all sides.

All of the jurisdictions insisted that the participating schools meet district or state standards and that students be assessed against district and state mandated tests. Given budget constraints, RAND proposed that data on student outcomes be provided by the partner districts from existing assessment systems and administrative records. In making its proposal, RAND recognized there would be important difficulties. In an internal memo written in August 1995, RAND noted "a few of the problems to be faced":

- The test measures would be unique to each district, making it difficult to compare the performance of NAS schools or the design teams across different jurisdictions.

- The test measures are likely to have varying alignment with the design team objectives. Thus, traditional standardized tests may not reflect the higher-order skills and problem-solving capabilities sought by all design teams.

- Some of the tests might well change over the course of the five-year time period envisioned by NAS's program.

---

[6]Currently, RAND is documenting the changes to the designs from the initial development of their educational ideas in the original RFPs through the demonstration and scale-up phases where these ideas met the economic, sociological, and political realities of implementation in schools.

- A variety of factors affect school outcomes, some of which are subject to change over time. For example, student populations may radically change over the course of the five years. In some districts, there may be regular and substantial turnover in teachers. School and district leadership may change with an inevitable impact upon school performance. These are inevitable occurrences, but they make the interpretation of the effects of the designs on school performance difficult.

In light of these difficulties in conducting an evaluation, during the 1995–1996 school year, RAND, together with several of the design teams, raised the possibility of administering a common, somewhat broader test across all implementing sites, but this was uniformly rejected by the jurisdictions.

At the time of these discussions, all involved in the effort had high expectations. They expected dramatic results, and indeed the original NAS RFPs made it clear that the organization would not be satisfied with marginal improvements. If dramatic improvements in student performance were obtained, even aggregated data at the school level would reflect these improvements. As this report will show (see Chapter Six), these expectations were optimistic, but it should be pointed out that these data lack the power to detect small, yet statistically significant, effects.

RESEARCH QUESTIONS UNDERLYING RAND'S OVERALL EVALUATION

Within such a context, at the beginning of the scale-up phase, RAND began monitoring a set of schools over time. Within its program of studies, RAND aimed to address questions to document the progress of the NAS scale-up phase, including:

- How have the designs and the assistance they provide evolved over time?

- Are the critical components of the NAS designs being implemented across a wide array of schools? Is there increasing cohesiveness and coherence among school staff and the activities implemented?

- What practices and policies of districts, schools, the design teams, and NAS itself promote or inhibit implementation of designs and design-based assistance?

- Do the NAS designs extend beyond changes in school organization and governance and permeate classrooms to change curriculum and instruction?

- Over time, what is the progress of the schools being assisted by NAS design teams in improving student and school performance?

SIGNIFICANT FEATURES OF RAND RESEARCH

The RAND assessment has a number of significant qualities designed to capture the complex nature of the NAS reform. Throughout the assessment, RAND has focused on implementation, using various methods to determine whether designs can be implemented in real schools facing significant challenges and whether the process for helping schools to choose among designs is effective.

The evaluation recognizes that school transformation and performance are the joint product of a number of important factors: the design itself, the assistance provided by the design team, the environment for implementation provided by the school district, the readiness of the school itself, and the quality of the staff. While it is impossible to completely characterize all these factors, the evaluation tries to provide some understanding of the contribution of each.

The research design emphasizes school improvement over time. Rarely have data been gathered on a similar set of schools over time to monitor the progress of implementation and other critical organizational and performance factors. Within RAND's longitudinal sample of NAS sites, schools serve as their own "controls." We attempt to account for the effects of districtwide changes by comparisons with changes in district performance on outcome measures. We chose not to try more complex quasi-experimental evaluation designs because it appeared unlikely that we would be able to maintain an uncontaminated set of control schools over time due to the scale-up strategy.

The evaluation relies heavily on the cooperation of the local districts in which the NAS designs are implemented. They have reviewed the surveys and supported their administration in participating schools. As pointed out earlier, the jurisdictions also provided the data used to track school performance.

PURPOSE OF CURRENT REPORT

This report focuses on the last research question listed above:

What is the progress in implementation and performance in a longitudinal sample of NAS schools?

We examine implementation and performance of early implementing NAS schools three years into NAS's district scale-up strategy. As we pointed out earlier, the early years of scale-up continued to be a time of uncertainty. There was some chaos and a great deal to be learned on the part of NAS, design teams, districts, and schools. Thus, this report documents experiences that may differ from those of schools beginning implementation today.

At this point in RAND's assessment of NAS, we are not attempting a "summative" evaluation, thereby claiming that the NAS designs have been thoroughly developed and implemented so that program effects can be clearly detected. Such an evaluation seems premature, given the variation in implementation among designs between different sites, the support and leadership provided by districts, and the different stages of design implementation and development. Rather, our intent is more "formative": to provide information to NAS, the design teams, researchers, and the public to improve efforts aimed at whole-school restructuring and comprehensive school reform (see Shadish et al., 1995; Rossi and Freeman, 1993; Scriven, 1980).

Yet we also believe that understanding how things are going and providing some explanations for these early trends is informative. And over time, a more summative evaluation will be possible and necessary to fully inform practitioners, researchers, and policymakers about the effectiveness of whole-school reform that relies on external assistance providers.

The analyses that follow focus solely on schools that were part of NAS's strategy to build partnerships with districts to diffuse the designs to a large number of schools (i.e., scale-up). This is not intended as a report on individual design team's efforts. The designs have been implemented in many other schools across the nation than those examined here. While we present some comparisons among designs, we are more interested in understanding the early progress in implementation and performance within the jurisdictions that partnered with NAS at the beginning of the scale-up phase. Understanding how district, design team, school, and teacher factors contribute to implementation and early performance trends provides important lessons for comprehensive school reform efforts across the nation.

ORGANIZATION OF THE REPORT

The next chapter discusses our conceptual framework for the analysis. Chapter Three provides details of the RAND longitudinal sample of NAS schools and presents a brief baseline description of these schools in terms of their demographic and school climate characteristics and their achievement levels during the baseline year. Chapter Four presents an analysis, by jurisdiction and design team, of various implementation indicators. These implementation indicators are then analyzed in Chapter Five using multivariate models to tease out the net effect of various teacher, school, and implementation factors, controlling for other variables. Chapter Six shifts the focus from implementation to student performance and presents trends in student achievement across the seven jurisdictions. We also discuss the limitations of these data and what one can infer from these trends. We use the data on test score trends to classify schools as those that experienced gains in test scores relative to the district or state. Largely because of the limitations of our data, the limited number of years to establish performance trends, and the preponderance of midlevel implementation in the sites analyzed, we are not able to empirically link performance to implementation in a systematic manner. Chapter Seven examines other outcome measures, such as attendance and teacher-reported effects on student achievement.

The analyses in this report offer both useful and provocative insights that will help inform the NAS effort and larger federal efforts to implement comprehensive school reform in at-risk schools. We summarize our results and discuss their implications in Chapter Eight.

Chapter Two

ANALYZING IMPLEMENTATION AND PERFORMANCE IN NAS SCHOOLS: A CONCEPTUAL FRAMEWORK

NAS's mission is to help schools and districts dramatically raise the achievement levels of large numbers of students with design-based assistance (New American Schools, 1999). In fact, improving student and school performance is a critical goal of all comprehensive school reforms. Student or school performance can be measured in a variety of different ways, such as standardized test scores (which may be based on a variety of tasks—e.g., multiple choice, performance-based, open-ended paper and pencil). Student or school performance might also be based on more subjective measures such as teacher-reported effects on student engagement, achievement, and readiness to learn. Other important outcome measures may include attendance rates, graduation rates, and incidence of disciplinary problems.

CORE ELEMENTS OF DESIGNS

To accomplish the goal of improving performance, each design team has a "theory of action" that establishes a link between elements of the design and student performance. The NAS designs range from relatively specific descriptions of how schools should be organized and what materials and professional development should be relied on to less specific visions and processes for school restructuring.

One of the more specific NAS designs is RW, which builds on years of research and implementation experience with the reading and writing program *Success for All*. RW provides an abundance of print materials, assessments, professional development, and specified organizational changes (e.g., homogeneous instructional groups that are reorganized frequently to address students' needs). The design begins implementation with a specific focus on changing curriculum and instruction.

In contrast, some of the other NAS designs are more process oriented. For instance, EL is less structured than RW and is based on design principles that reflect the design's origins in the Outward Bound program. Students' experiences in EL schools consist primarily of engaging in multidisciplinary, project-based learning expeditions that include intellectual, service, and physical dimensions. Teachers play a critical role in developing the expeditions, which involve a great deal of effort and imagination.

Thus, it is important to remember the unique attributes of each design in terms of the components of schooling emphasized, the different strategies for implementation, and the complexity and specificity of the design. Certainly, we cannot capture all of the uniqueness of each design in the current report, but RAND's other studies of NAS have pointed to these characteristics and the importance of looking at changes in the designs over time (Bodilly, forthcoming; Berends, 1999; Glennan, 1998).

While each design is unique, they all tend to emphasize five core components:

- organization and governance;
- professional life of teachers;
- content and performance expectations;
- curriculum and instructional strategies; and
- parent and community involvement.

Organization and governance refers to the authority relationships among the various parties in the school. An example of changing governance arrangements is reorganizing the decisionmaking processes for budgets and staffing to include teachers and other school employees and parents. Giving authority to the school site has received a great deal of attention in the education community. According to Murphy (1992) the central focus on governance restructuring stems from a belief that change must reside with those who are closest to the learners (see also Bryk et al., 1998a; Smith, Scoll, and Link, 1996). NAS and many of the designs strongly share this belief.

The professional life of teachers refers to the roles and relationships in which the teachers participate during the school day. In effect, when referring to restructuring schools, particularly those in poor, urban areas, this involves overhauling the conditions under which teachers work by changing their responsibilities and tasks and by developing a more professional culture in schools (Newmann et al., 1996; Murphy, 1992; Sykes, 1990; Wise, 1989). In contrast to teachers working in isolation without contact with their colleagues (see Louis and Miles, 1990; Lortie, 1970), design teams aim to build a collaborative environment for teachers. Thus, it is important to understand the extent to which teachers collaborate and engage in activities together, such as professional development, common planning time, and critiquing each other's instruction.

Additionally, each of the designs aims to bring all students to high standards, even though each may differ in the process to attain this goal. To monitor whether designs are making progress toward this end, critical indicators might include the degree to which: (a) student assessments are explicitly linked to academic standards, (b) teachers make performance expectations explicit to students, and (c) the curriculum and performance standards are consistent and coherent across grade levels.

Most of the designs are concerned with shaping student experiences within classrooms to further their academic achievement growth. NAS designs embrace alternative instructional strategies that involve different relationships between teachers and students and between students and subject matter. Yet again, each design differs somewhat in the specific nature of these activities. Conventional classrooms are often characterized by teachers' talking at students and filling their heads with knowledge with students' responding with the correct answers at appropriate times (see Gamoran et al., 1995; Sizer, 1984; Powell, Farrar, and Cohen, 1985). In contrast, design teams tend to emphasize alternative instructional practices such as students working in small groups, using manipulatives, engaging in student-led discussions, or working on projects that span a long period of time (e.g., a marking period or semester).

The design teams also address a particular set of instructional strategies revolving around student grouping arrangements. How students are grouped for instruction and the effects of this on student achievement are subjects of heated debate among educators and researchers (see Slavin, 1987, 1990; Gamoran and Berends, 1987; Oakes, Gamoran, and Page, 1992; Hallinan, 1994; Oakes, 1994). Yet most researchers agree that alternatives to inflexible grouping arrangements are worth further exploration. Thus, the NAS designs have experimented with such alternative student groupings. For example, students within an EL or CON design may have the same teacher for a couple of years. RW emphasizes flexible uses of grouping by organizing students according to their achievement levels in reading for part of the day and mixing achievement levels for other subjects. These groupings are assessed every eight weeks or so to see if students would be better served by being placed in a different group. In short, each of the designs is sensitive to the issue of ability grouping and is working with schools to group students in more effective ways.

Conventional wisdom suggests that the parent-child relationship and parent involvement in the child's education are critical components to school success. The NAS designs have embraced this issue as well. Several of the designs aim to have individuals or teams within the schools serve as resources to help provide social services to students and families (e.g., AT and RW). Other designs emphasize students' applying their learning in ways that directly benefit the community (e.g., AC, EL, and NARE). Of course, each design desires that parents and community members be involved in positive ways in the educational program.

The critical assumption underlying the designs is that coherent, focused, and sustained implementation of the key components described above will eventually change school and classroom learning environments and thereby student performance. Implementation consists of the process of putting into practice the elements or set of activities defined by design teams as core components of their design. However, throughout the history of educational reform efforts, another theme that has emerged is that the process of planned educational change is much more complex than we had anticipated

(Fullan, 1991; McLaughlin, 1991). This is largely because of the number of players involved and the number of factors that need to be aligned to support such fundamental change.

FACTORS AFFECTING IMPLEMENTATION

Based on an extensive literature review, Fullan (1991) groups the factors affecting implementation into four main categories: (a) attributes of the change itself, in terms of need and relevance of the change, clarity, complexity, and quality, and practicality of the program; (b) characteristics at the school district level, including support and stability; (c) characteristics of the school, including leadership, peer relationships, and teacher characteristics and orientations; and (d) characteristics external to the local system such as role of outsiders and external assistance. We draw and expand on these factors to highlight the role of each when assessing NAS's whole-school reform initiative (see Figure 2.1).

We need to incorporate the perspectives of a variety of actors throughout the system—district and school administrators and teachers—to understand the relative impact of them in implementing a program such as comprehensive school reform or whole-school designs. No doubt the process of school change to improve student achievement is complex and difficult. It requires the coordination of a variety of actors and factors to make it work. The framework shown in Figure 2.1 portrays some of that complexity, and it continues to develop as researchers continue to investigate the relative contribution of factors related to schoolwide change. Here we examine some of the teacher, school, district, and design team factors that RAND is examining in its ongoing analysis of implementation and performance indicators in NAS. Within the conceptual framework in Figure 2.1, we also discuss other factors related to implementation and fully realize that there may be others that we have not considered.

For many of the results that follow, we rely mostly on teacher reports, for they are the "street level bureaucrats" who are the individuals at the end of the line affecting the implementation of whole-school designs in their classrooms (Weatherly and Lipsky, 1977). Fullan (1991, p. 72) elaborates on the importance of teachers: "Changes in schools must pass the 'practicality ethic' of teachers. . . . Practical changes are those that address salient needs, that fit well with the teachers'

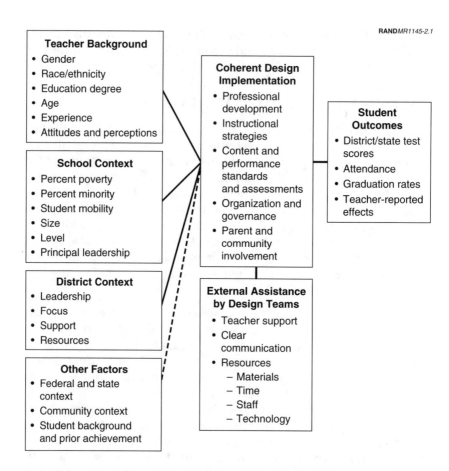

RAND*MR1145-2.1*

Figure 2.1—A Conceptual Framework for Analyzing Progress and
Performance in NAS Schools

situation, that are focused, and that include concrete how-to-do-it
possibilities."

External Assistance by Design Teams

Because NAS believes that most schools have benefited from focused
assistance in implementing the design, it now believes an important
contribution to whole-school reform is the support and development
of design-based assistance organizations (Glennan, 1998). The

unique aspect of design-based assistance is the commitment of the design teams to provide ongoing assistance and a variety of services to further implementation and the transformation of the whole school—its organization, curriculum, instruction, and professional development of staff. NAS believes that guided by a design and assisted by an external agent (the design team), whole-school reform will promote greater cohesiveness and coherence in the program of the school as well as collaboration among its staff. Such an approach will lead to school-based programs that better serve the needs of students and result in improved academic outcomes.

Toward this end, NAS believes teachers and staff in schools need to have a significant amount of choice when adopting design-based assistance, which is consistent with NAS's strategy that educational change cannot be mandated "from above." NAS states its strategy as follows:

> . . . if a school is to engage in an effective transformation process through design-based assistance, its faculty and community must have the opportunity to choose a design, rather than being required to implement one mandated from above (New American Schools, 1997, p. 7).

How schools go about selecting a design has implications for the implementation that follows (Bodilly, 1998; Ross et al., 1997). For example, if a school is forced to adopt a design, it is not surprising that teachers would resist engaging in the activities of the design. Yet some schools are often targets for forced restructuring efforts, particularly those that exhibit chronic poor performance. Often, the alternative such schools face is reconstitution. Thus, a critical aim of the NAS designs before implementation even begins is to obtain the buy-in of teachers for the planned restructuring activities. Most of the designs require between 75–80 percent of the teachers voting in favor of the designs. The rationale is that if the vast majority of the staff vote to adopt the design, they will commit to making the changes necessary during the implementation process.

Clear communication by design teams to schools is critical for not only the selection of the design but implementation of it—something that external assistance providers have found challenging when attempting to help a large number of schools (Bodilly, 1998). Communication to schools both in the selection and implementation process can take several different forms, including design fairs, print materials, use of computer software and the internet, workshops, retreats, school visits, and site-based facilitators. For instance, school visits by design team staff on a regular basis to help teachers address issues related to developing curriculum units or the use of rubrics to assess students are intended to help teachers implement project-based learning and the assessment of that learning within the context of the design. Other types of communication might be effective as well, and the clearer and more consistent the information provided about implementation by design teams to schools, the smoother the implementation process is likely to be.

For implementation of any program, resources are critical (Keltner, 1998; McLaughlin 1990). It is a common finding that when resources decrease or disappear, the implementation is likely to diminish (Glennan, 1998; Montjoy and O'Toole, 1979). If teachers receive the funds, the professional development from design teams for design implementation, the materials to support implementation, and the time to plan and develop the program, it is likely that implementation will deepen over time.

Teacher Background

Without willing and able teachers who embrace reform and provide the necessary leadership, no reform can be enacted, no matter how effective it may be. As mentioned above, teachers are the "street level bureaucrats" at the core of educational change (Weatherly and Lipsky, 1977). As Fullan succinctly states, educational change depends on "what teachers do and think—it's as simple and as complex as that" (Fullan, 1991, p. 117).

Educators must respond to multiple, simultaneous pressures and demands. For many teachers, policy goals and activities are simply part of a broader environment that presses in upon their classrooms. Their ability to cope with these demands and their commitment to change are crucial to coherent and sustained implementation. Thus, teachers matter: Their experience, subject-based expertise, attitudes, and orientations (and characteristics that may affect those attitudes such as age, gender, race/ethnicity) are important in determining the degree and level of implementation.

In short, teachers are central to any organizational changes that might alter student-teacher interactions occurring in classrooms to improve student learning (Gamoran et al., 1995; Oakes, Gamoran, and Page, 1992). Teachers carry with them a great deal of knowledge based on their educational attainment, teaching experience, and other personal characteristics that together are likely to be related to their engagement in whole-school restructuring activities (Louis and Marks, 1998). Thus, it is important to examine the relationships among various teacher background characteristics, design implementation, and reported effects of whole-school designs on teachers and students.

School Characteristics

Clearly, schools matter: their environment, climate, and leadership. Research has consistently shown that the principal strongly influences the likelihood of change (Fullan, 1991; Berman and McLaughlin, 1978). For example, in their study of innovations in the teaching of science in 60 elementary schools, Hall, Hord, and Griffin (1980) conclude that "the single most important hypothesis emanating from these data is that *the degree of implementation of the innovation is different in different schools because of the actions and concerns of principals*" (p. 26, emphasis in original). However, the influence of the principal may be most effective when facilitating the change process. For example, leadership of the principal may translate into the ability to obtain sufficient resources for the school and support teachers in their efforts to implement change.

Characteristics of schools are also likely to influence the adoption of whole-school designs and their effects on student learning. In our work, we examine whether a school's "structural" characteristics, such as the minority and socioeconomic composition of the school, student mobility, school size, and school level (elementary, middle, high school), are related to implementation and performance (Berends, 1999).

Schools that serve high concentrations of poor students face many challenges and are often difficult to change. Yet because federal funding such as Title I is oriented toward disadvantaged students and schools, these resources may help promote school restructuring efforts. In fact, since the 1994 reauthorization of Title I, schools with more than half of their students eligible for free and reduced priced lunch may use Title I funds for schoolwide programs. Thus, there may be a positive relationship between high-poverty schools and whole-school implementations such as NAS designs because of such funding sources.

Other school structural factors (student mobility, size, and level) may inhibit schoolwide implementation of whole-school reforms. For example, highly mobile student populations pose problems for both school implementation and performance. For example, high turnover may also be disruptive to the classroom environment and the implementation of design team activities. Moreover, if testing includes those students who are at the school for only part of the year, then it may be difficult to show overall school improvement.

In addition, larger and secondary schools are more complex organizations and are likely to resist organizational change (Perrow, 1986). Moreover, larger schools may be characterized as more bureaucratic in organization rather than communitarian resulting in a climate where teachers are less likely to collaborate around a common mission and vision as envisioned by whole-school designs (see Lee, Bryk, and Smith, 1993; Lee and Smith, 1995, 1997). For example, Newmann, Rutter, and Smith (1989) have found that teachers were more likely to report a communal atmosphere (e.g., teachers seen as colleagues who share beliefs and values, teachers can count on other staff members to help, and cooperative efforts among staff) in smaller schools than larger ones (see also Bryk and Driscoll, 1988).

District Factors

Research also underscores the importance of the external environment, especially district support and stability of leadership, in the process of change (Bodilly and Berends, 1999; Bodilly, 1998; Glennan, 1998; Fullan, 1991). The district can facilitate and foster change by providing resources for the school and for professional staff development, and showing active support for schools implementing designs.

For example, Bodilly (1998) has found that districts played a strong role in determining the initial and sustained viability of the relationship between the school and the design team. Early on in the scale-up phase, many schools' staff members had complaints about the district's poor planning and providing too little time for making decisions, issues brought up in other assessments of the adoption of schoolwide programs (Wong and Meyer, 1998b).

RAND's prior case studies (see Bodilly, 1998; Bodilly and Berends, 1999) have revealed that higher average levels of implementation were found in districts that had a stable district leadership that placed a high priority on the effort, that lacked a major budget crisis or other crisis, and that had a history of trust between the central office and the schools. School-level respondents directly linked these factors to greater efforts at implementation. When these factors were missing, school respondents reported that their own efforts stalled or were less intense.

Moreover, while crucial, central office political support and attention can be buttressed by significant changes in regulatory and financial practices. Schools attempting comprehensive school reform to address their particular problems can be supported through increased site-level control over their curriculum and instruction, their budgets, their positions and staffing, and most essentially their mission. Comprehensive school reform is not confined to the adoption of a new mandated curriculum or a few new instructional strategies. Instead, it requires the rethinking and adoption at the school-level of new curriculum and instructional approaches and the accompanying professional development. District flexibility in allowing schools to pursue this rethinking is a critical aspect for design-based schools. Development and implementation of such curriculum and instructional strategies at the school level may be significantly hampered without district support through resource allocation for instructional positions, materials, technology, professional development, etc.

In short, district-level politics, policies, and practices may promote or derail the whole-school reform efforts such as the NAS designs. In fact, schools may look to district leadership, climate, and regulations to understand if it was worth their time and effort to invest in transforming. If schools receive the support they need to begin a legitimate effort at implementation, it is worth examining the progress these schools make in terms of both implementation and performance.

Other Factors

Those who have studied implementation of educational programs have pointed to other factors that affect implementation such as the federal and/or state policy environment; the larger community context, including parent support for school change; and student background and prior achievement (e.g., Elmore and Rothman, 1999; Berends et al., 1999; Grissmer and Flanagan, 1998; Fullan, 1991).

The federal and state policy context is likely to play a role in implementing whole-school reform (see Fullan, 1991; Koretz and Barron, 1998). For example, the recent Comprehensive School Reform Demonstration (CSRD) program directly supports design-based reforms such as NAS by providing at least $50,000 annually to schools to pay for the related services. Some states and districts with high-stakes accountability systems may force low-performing schools to adopt designs. They may also facilitate a more effective matching process for schools to select designs based on their local needs (see Bodilly and Berends, 1999; Bodilly, 1998; Smith, Scoll, and Link, 1996).

The larger community and parent support for reform are likely to affect implementation as well (Fullan, 1991). Parent and community demand for reform, their readiness for it, and their ongoing support of it has important ramifications for implementation. One of the main obstacles to implementing a variety of restructuring efforts vis-à-vis the educational bureaucracy may be that much of the public does not see the need for change (Berends and King, 1994). These observations correspond to recent polls that show a large gap between how adults "grade" the nation's public schools versus how they grade the schools in their community. According to a recent Gallup Poll, 24 percent of those polled gave the grade A or B to the nation's public schools. In contrast, 49 percent gave an A or B to the public schools in their community, and 66 percent gave an A or B to the school their oldest child attends (Rose and Gallup, 1999). Without a perceived need for change, efforts to reorganize the nation's schools may be severely hindered (see also Jennings, 1996, 1998).

An additional set of factors that affects implementation of school restructuring efforts and their effects is student background and prior achievement. Within school reform efforts, it is important to understand how changes in schooling activities are related to students' social background characteristics, their home environments, their mobility patterns between schools, and their preexisting levels of academic achievement, attitudes, and engagement in school (Berends et al., 1999; Koretz, 1996; Meyer, 1996). While policymakers focus on manipulating the "lever" at the school level to improve learning opportunities and performance, several studies have shown the importance of student background in the learning process (see Coleman et al., 1966; Jencks et al., 1972; Gamoran, 1987, 1992; Bryk, Lee, and Holland, 1993).

While we understand the importance of these "other" factors, the analyses that follow are of more direct measures of the factors in the boxes in Figure 2.1 with solid lines between them. The information on the "other factors" is much more indirect, so the line between this box and implementation is depicted with a dotted line.

IMPLEMENTATION AND PERFORMANCE

Throughout the history of research on program initiatives, one finding has emerged again and again: Implementation dominates outcomes (see Fullan, 1991; Pressman and Wildavsky, 1973). As McLaughlin (1991, p. 186) states, "the consequences of even the best planned, best supported, and most promising policy initiatives depend finally on what happens as individuals throughout the policy system interpret and act on them" (see also Berman and McLaughlin, 1978). She elaborates on the lessons learned from implementation of a variety of social programs over the past several decades.

> Perhaps the overarching, obvious conclusion running through empirical research on policy implementation is that it is incredibly hard to make something happen, most especially across layers of government and institutions. It's incredibly hard not just because social problems tend to be thorny. It's incredibly hard to make something happen primarily because policymakers can't mandate what matters. We have learned that policy success depends critically on two broad factors: local capacity and will.

RAND's analyses of NAS to date support this conclusion (Bodilly and Berends, 1999; Bodilly, 1998).

Thus, by gathering information about different aspects of the system, from the district to teachers in schools, we hope to shed light on how the NAS initiative is unfolding in terms of implementation and performance in districts across the United States. It is to this understanding that we turn in future chapters. Before we do so however, we discuss the sample of schools we are monitoring over time.

Chapter Three

RAND'S SAMPLE OF NEW AMERICAN SCHOOLS

In this chapter, we present the details of the longitudinal sample of NAS schools that is the focus of this analysis.

A SAMPLE OF NEW AMERICAN SCHOOLS

The original sample of schools consisted of those schools initiating implementation of NAS designs in eight jurisdictions that NAS named as its partners during scale-up in either 1995–96 or 1996–97. These eight jurisdictions include:

- Cincinnati;
- Dade;
- Kentucky;
- Memphis;
- Philadelphia;
- Pittsburgh;
- San Antonio; and
- Washington State.[1]

---

[1]At the time we decided on the longitudinal sample of schools, Maryland and San Diego were not far enough along in their implementation to warrant inclusion in RAND's planned data collection efforts. Since then, several of the design teams report that they are implementing in Maryland and San Diego.

The choice of these jurisdictions reflected RAND's desire to obtain a sample including all the designs that were participating in the scale-up phase and the judgment that the costs of working in the additional jurisdictions would not yield commensurate benefits. While jurisdictions and their support of the NAS reform will no doubt continue to change over time, these jurisdictions reflect a range of support for implementation—from relatively supportive to no support at all (see Bodilly, 1998).

Historical Context of Sample

For most design teams, these were the first schools to which they had provided assistance with implementing their designs on a fee-for-service basis. In addition, most of the design teams reported to RAND that their designs were still unfinished. As a result, the early years of implementation on which we report saw many changes in both the designs and the assistance provided as the teams and the schools gained experience.

The strategy that NAS developed for scale-up (New American Schools, 1997) focused on a small number of jurisdictions that persuaded NAS that they possessed what NAS called supportive operating environments in which the designs could be implemented. In fact, for the most part, these districts did not possess such environments. They had limited understanding of whole-school reform and the sort of design-based assistance that NAS design teams were intending to provide. The districts, NAS, and the design teams collectively and individually invented procedures and policies for design teams and the assistance they provided as the implementation unfolded. For example, districts varied widely in the processes set up for matching schools and designs, the contracts set up with designs, the services to be acquired, and the ways they monitored implementation of the designs (Bodilly and Berends, 1999; Bodilly, 1998).

In short, the early years of scale-up continued to be a time of uncertainty. There was some chaos and a great deal to be learned on the part of NAS, designs, districts, and schools. Thus, this report documents experiences that may differ from those of schools beginning implementation today. NAS and the design teams might have matured due in large part to the lessons learned about the ways in which jurisdictions and schools must work together (Bodilly and Berends, 1999; Bodilly, 1998). Indeed, most implementations today are not part of district-level initiatives of the sort envisioned by NAS's original strategy.

Whether changes in the design teams and the improved knowledge concerning appropriate district roles will lead to more effective implementation of designs and better student outcomes than we describe in this study can only be determined by future research and evaluation. Thus, when interpreting the findings in this report, it is important to keep in mind these features of the population of schools we have studied.

Toward the Final Analysis Sample

Our aim was to collect data on all the NAS schools that were implementing within the partner jurisdictions. NAS believed that as of the early fall of 1996, there were 256 schools implementing NAS designs across these eight jurisdictions. However, based on conversations with design teams, jurisdictions, and the schools, the sample was reduced to 184 schools for several reasons, including:

- There were 51 RW schools in Dade that were low-performing and on the verge of serious sanctions, so the district promised these schools that they would not be burdened with researchers.

- An additional 21 schools declined to participate because they did not want to be burdened with research, were not implementing, or dropped the design.

Thus, for our surveys of teachers and principals, the target sample was 184 schools (see Table 3.1). To some extent, limiting our sample to schools that were implementing and were not on the verge of serious sanctions biases our sample in a positive direction in terms of expected implementation.

Of the 184 schools in our 1997 sample, we completed interviews with 155 principals. Based on our interviews with principals in the spring of 1997, most of these schools reported they were indeed

Table 3.1

1997 Target Sample for RAND's Longitudinal Sample:
Principal Interviews and Teacher Surveys

Jurisdiction	Design Team							Total
	AC	AT	CON	EL	MRSH	NARE	RW	
Cincinnati			5	5			6	16
Dade	5		4	1	3		4	17
Kentucky						51		51
Memphis	5	5	5	5	4		9	33
Philadelphia		12	4		2			18
Pittsburgh						12		12
San Antonio				8	5			13
Washington		8				16		24
Total	10	25	18	19	14	79	19	184

implementing a design.[2] Yet some were not. Figure 3.1 shows that 25 of the 155 schools (about 15 percent) reported that they were in an exploratory year or a planning year with implementation expected in the future. About 85 percent (130/155) of the schools for which we had teacher, principal, and district data reported implementing a NAS design to some extent.[3]

Because our interest was in understanding the specific activities that are occurring within the 130 schools that were implementing a NAS design to some extent (the nonwhite areas of Figure 3.1), we limited our analysis sample to these 130 schools.

In the spring of 1998, all 184 schools were once again surveyed. The completed sample size of implementing schools consisted of 142 schools. However, the overlap between the 1997 and 1998 samples was incomplete. For purposes of this analysis, which is partly

---

[2]The first question we asked principals was about the status of the school's partnership with a NAS design. Principals could respond that they were in an exploratory year (that is, the school had not committed to a design yet); in a planning year (the school had partnered with a design team and was planning for implementation next school year) in initial implementation for part of the school (i.e., a subset of the staff was implementing); continuing implementation for part of the school; in initial implementation for the whole school (i.e., all or most of the staff were working with the design); or continuing implementation for the whole school.

[3]These were schools that had complete principal data, at least five teachers responding to the teacher surveys, and complete district data.

RAND*MR1145-3.1*

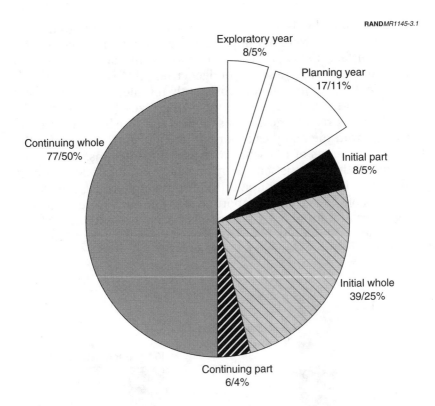

Figure 3.1—Principal Reports of Implementation Status, Spring 1997

longitudinal in nature, we limited the analysis sample to schools that met two criteria:

- Schools were implementing in both 1997 and 1998, and;

- Schools had complete data (i.e., from teachers and principals) in both years.

Of the 130 schools implementing in 1997 for which we had complete data, 7 had either dropped the design or had reverted to planning, and another 17 had missing or incomplete data. Thus, 106 schools met both criteria. Figure 3.2 shows the derivation of the sample.

Of these 106 schools, there were two schools in Pittsburgh that we later discovered were not implementing and had dropped the design. In fact, throughout RAND's monitoring of the schools in Pittsburgh, there were severe budget crises. RAND's site visits and principal phone interviews consistently revealed that NAS implementation in Pittsburgh was not taking place (also see Bodilly, 1998). As a result, these two schools (and Pittsburgh) were excluded from the analyses reported here; our final sample for the analysis consists of 104 schools across 7 jurisdictions. The distribution of the analysis sample by jurisdictions and design teams is shown in Table 3.2. About a third of the sample consists of NARE schools, of which a large proportion is in Kentucky. Four other designs account for about 12–16 percent each, while AC and MRSH have the smallest number of schools in the sample (5 and 7, respectively).

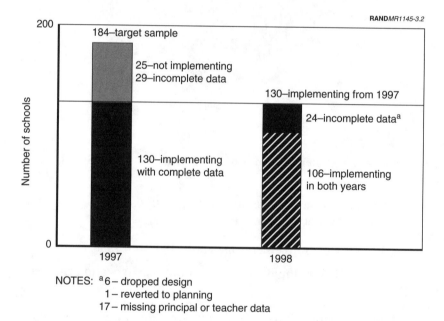

NOTES: [a]6 – dropped design
    1 – reverted to planning
    17 – missing principal or teacher data

Figure 3.2—Derivation of Analysis Sample for the Longitudinal Analysis

Table 3.2

**Analysis Sample: Schools That Were Implementing in Both
1997 and 1998, with Complete Data in Both Years**

Jurisdiction	Design Team							
	AC	AT	CON	EL	MRSH	NARE	RW	Total
Cincinnati			5	5			6	16
Dade	1		2				1	4
Kentucky						20		20
Memphis	4	4	5	5	3		8	29
Philadelphia		6			1			7
San Antonio				6	3			9
Washington		7				12		19
Total	5	17	12	16	7	32	15	104

Table 3.3 presents the distribution of the analysis sample by years of implementation as of spring 1998. Because of the way we defined our analysis sample, all 104 schools had been implementing at least 2 years. Of the 104 schools, about 40 percent of the schools reported 2 years of implementation, 35 percent of the schools reported 3 years of implementation, and 25 percent of the schools reported 4 years or more of implementation. It is worth noting the significant number of NARE schools—more than half—that reported 4 or more years of implementation.

The various criteria we used to define the sample all biased the sample to some extent in a positive direction in terms of expected implementation. RAND's sample of NAS sites was drawn initially from a set of NAS schools that expressed interest in implementing designs in districts that had formed a partnership with NAS. In addition, we chose schools where principals reported they were

Table 3.3

Distribution of Analysis Sample by Years of Implementation, 1998

Number of Years	Design Team							
	AC	AT	CON	EL	MRSH	NARE	RW	Total
2 years	1	15	4	7	6	8	1	42
3 years	4	2	7	8	1	7	6	35
≥4 years	0	0	1	1	0	17	8	27

implementing the designs either partly or wholly for at least two years in 1998. This was done to ensure some degree of comparability across schools in terms of where they were in implementing designs. But omitting schools that reported they were not implementing or had just started implementing in 1998 from the sample made our analysis relatively more likely to find effects of designs on teaching and student achievement, where they exist.

Teacher Sample

The sample of teachers who responded to the survey in 1997 is 2,350; the sample size was slightly lower—2,158—in 1998. Figure 3.3 shows the response rates for the two years by jurisdiction across the 104 schools. Response rates were generally lower in 1998 compared with 1997, markedly so in Philadelphia and Washington State.

Dade schools had by far the lowest response rate—only about a third of the teachers responded to the survey; this was at least partly due to the fact that there was little district support for the survey. Philadelphia sent a letter supporting the survey in 1997 but

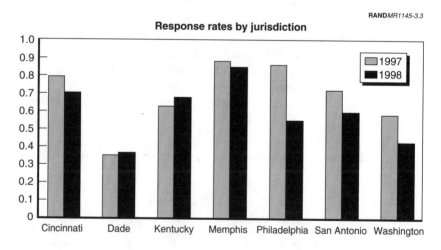

Figure 3.3—Response Rates for the Teacher Survey by Jurisdiction,
1997 and 1998

did not do so in 1998. In Washington State, RAND's key point of contact was on special assignment in 1998 and was unable to send a letter encouraging the schools to participate in our survey. With the exception of Washington in 1998 and Dade in both years, response rates were 55 percent or higher in every jurisdiction for both years.[4]

Response rates by design team are shown in Figure 3.4. Nearly all the design teams had response rates of 60–80 percent and higher in both years. There was a marked decline in the percent of teachers in AT schools responding to the survey in 1998, primarily because AT schools are located both in Philadelphia and Washington State.

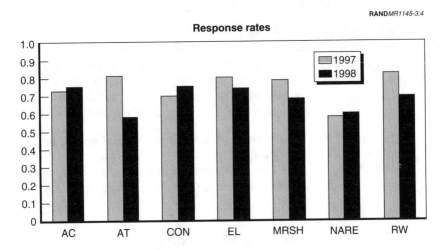

RANDMR1145-3.4

Figure 3.4—Response Rates for the Teacher Survey by Design Team,
1997 and 1998

OVERVIEW OF NAS SCHOOLS IN ANALYSIS SAMPLE

It is helpful to provide a broad overview of the schools in the analysis sample. Overall, NAS partnered with jurisdictions that were

---

[4]There were a small number of schools that had response rates of between 20–30 percent—six in the 1997 sample, nine in the 1998 sample. We retained these in the sample provided that at least five teachers in the school had responded to the survey.

predominantly urban, high poverty, and high minority (Berends, 1999). For example, Table 3.4 shows the poverty and minority compositions of the NAS schools compared with the district averages. Compared with the jurisdictions, most of the NAS designs were assisting schools with disproportionately high percentages of poor and minority students.

The NAS design teams in Cincinnati, Dade, Memphis, and San Antonio were assisting schools that have a vast majority of minority students. By contrast, the NAS schools in the states of Kentucky and Washington were mostly non-Hispanic white schools. If the Kentucky and Washington schools were removed from the sample, over 80 percent of the students in NAS schools would be minority.

When examining implementation and performance of the NAS schools, it is important to consider the particular challenges that NAS design teams face when implementing their design. Table 3.5 shows selected school characteristics by design team. MRSH and RW tended to be in the poorest schools, while AC and RW tended to be in the schools with the highest percentage of minority students.

High student mobility is likely to have an adverse effect on implementation as well as school performance. As is evident from Table 3.5, highly mobile student populations characterized many of the schools that design teams were assisting. For example, nearly one

Table 3.4

Comparison of School Composition: NAS Schools vs. Jurisdiction Schools

	Percent Free/Reduced Lunch		Percent Minority	
	NAS Average	Jurisdiction Average	NAS Average	Jurisdiction Average
Cincinnati	74.9	58.0[a]	71.3	69.0
Dade	83.6	59.3	95.3	87.0
Kentucky	50.4	40.3	23.2	11.1
Memphis	80.2	66.0	89.6	86.0
Philadelphia	68.1	42.0[a]	56.4	80.0
San Antonio	99.2	91.1	95.0	95.0
Washington	8.5	10.3[a]	13.2	16.3

NOTE: [a]Data obtained from Common Core of Data for students on free lunch only.

Table 3.5

Selected School Characteristics by Design Team
(in percent)

	Free/Reduced Lunch	Minority	Mobility	English Language Learners	N
AC	79.6	95.8	7.8	2.8	5
AT	47.2	50.3	14.9	4.4	17
CON	71.9	80.6	19.3	1.2	12
EL	82.9	80.8	17.8	4.9	16
MRSH	88.1	84.3	13.4	3.9	7
NARE	40.3	19.5	10.3	2.0	32
RW	88.2	88.9	20.0	0.1	15
NAS Average	63.9	59.0	14.5	2.6	104

in five students in RW and CON schools was likely to move during the academic school year.[5]

When examining issues related to implementation and performance in these schools, we need to keep in mind the significant challenges posed by the characteristics of these schools.

The average school size was 662, but the standard deviation of 434 was quite large. Eighteen percent of the schools had fewer than 400 students. The distribution of the 104 schools across levels reveals that 64 percent were elementary schools, 14 percent were middle schools, and 14 percent were high schools. Eight percent were mixed levels.

Teachers in our sample were mostly female (84 percent), mostly white (68 percent), and the majority had their master's degree or above (52 percent). Over three-fifths were over 40 years old, mirroring the national teacher profile (U.S. Department of Education, 1996). Teachers also reported that, on average, they had been in their current school for 7 years.

---

[5]Mobility rates are based on the following question in the principal survey: "On average, what percentage of your total student body enrolled at the beginning of the school year are still enrolled at the end of the school year?" Percentages in Table 3.5 are calculated as 100 minus this reported percentage.

Understanding the progress of NAS sites, particularly in terms of their performance on achievement tests, requires an understanding of where the schools were before implementing a design. Berends (1999) has shown that most of the schools receiving design team assistance could be considered socially and academically disadvantaged in terms of poverty, racial-ethnic composition, climate, and student test scores. The NAS sites in our sample were below "average" when comparing a number of school characteristics to national norms.

As we have already noted, the NAS design teams are assisting mostly urban schools facing significant challenges related to school poverty and racial-ethnic isolation.

How do the school climates in the NAS sites compare to the nation? NAS principals reported greater problems with absenteeism and school readiness when compared to the nation's principals (for details see Berends, 1999). Some of the design teams were in schools where the reported problems of readiness were more severe, such as RW and EL. School readiness included principal reports about problems such as students coming to school unprepared to learn, poor nutrition, poor student health, student apathy, and lack of academic challenge. By and large, school safety was not perceived by principals to be a greater problem in the NAS sites when compared to the nation's principals.

This provides a context for our discussion of the progress of implementation and performance in NAS schools that is the focus of the remainder of the report.

Chapter Four

STATUS OF IMPLEMENTATION

This chapter addresses whether schools implemented critical components of the NAS designs. Specifically, we focus on the status of implementation of the NAS designs as of the spring of 1998, although we do track trends between 1997 and 1998. As we showed earlier, by the spring of 1998, all of the schools in our sample claimed they had been implementing for at least two years, and about 40 percent of the sample had been implementing for four or more years. We examine a variety of indicators measuring implementation of key components of the NAS designs, including organization and governance, teacher professional life, performance expectations of students, instructional strategies, and parent and community involvement. The results for these indicators appear in Appendix B.

RESEARCH QUESTIONS

In this chapter, we address the following questions:

1. What is the mean level of implementation of NAS designs across this set of early implementing NAS schools? Has this changed over time? We should expect an increase in the mean level of implementation over time as implementation takes hold, but the change in implementation is likely to vary depending on whether schools are in the relatively early phase of implementation or are more experienced with the designs. For example, if—as seems likely—implementation follows a polynomial function, increasing sharply over the first few years and then leveling off, we would expect sharp increases in mean implementation in the first few

years after adoption, as schools moved to adopt and deploy key components of the designs. After a few years, however, there should be a tailing off of the increases in mean implementation levels, as designs become more schoolwide and more an integral part of the daily work life of principals, teachers, and students.

2. Has implementation deepened over time both within and between schools, as measured by the change in variance of the implementation index within and between schools? As implementation deepens, we should expect a decrease in the variance of the implementation index both between and within schools, as designs become more schoolwide and there is greater consensus, clarity, and coherence in what teachers within a school are doing as well as what teachers in schools adopting a particular design are doing. This latter effect will be tempered by jurisdictional effects because of the varying degrees of support from districts as well as changes in the designs themselves as the design teams seek to adapt to local contexts.

MEASURING IMPLEMENTATION WITHIN AND ACROSS DESIGNS

Measuring progress in implementation broadly across a wide set of schools in several partnering jurisdictions involves a number of challenges.

First, each design is unique. Attempting to develop a common set of indicators that measures implementation *across* designs is difficult, particularly when design teams adapt their programs to the local needs of the schools (Bodilly, forthcoming). However, despite their differences, design teams do aim to change some key conditions of schools in common ways, such as school organization, expectations for student performance, professional development, instructional strategies, and parent involvement.[1] We attempted to draw on these commonalties to guide the construction of an index that could be used to broadly measure "core" implementation across designs, al-

---

[1]With the recent support of the federal CSRD program, schools need to make sure that their plan covers these areas. If one particular design team or CSRD model does not cover these and several other areas of school improvement, then schools need to adopt more than one design or model (Kirby and Berends et al., in review).

though one can certainly argue about whether individual items selected capture the specific focus of each design team. While it is perhaps not accurate to call this "core implementation," we believe that the index and our analysis of it provide information that is useful in understanding the progress of the NAS schools during this phase of scale-up. Moreover, the items included on the survey were based on the description of the design teams at that time and on RAND's work to develop benchmarks for monitoring implementation in our case study work (see Bodilly, 1998).

Second, while the purposes of this study are more broad, even studies that are focused on *one* particular design team confront problems when attempting to measure all the aspects of a given design and its implementation. A recent study of Comer's School Development Program (SDP) is a case in point (Cook et al., 1999). While the authors went to a great deal of effort in developing measures of implementation within a randomized experimental design, they were criticized by the model developer for making "critical errors and omissions in their description of the SDP" (Comer and Haynes, 1999, p. 600).

Third, the difficulties of constructing indices that capture the key components of a design are compounded by the fact that these design components may themselves be evolving (see Bodilly, forthcoming). For example, design teams may change the theory of education inherent in their designs, particularly the design elements, based on their experiences during implementation or attempts to address student needs, or to accommodate extant political power structures. Moreover, design teams may change their implementation strategies because of lessons learned during development and implementation experiences in various sites.

Fourth, even if one developed measures on which there was general agreement that these measures fully captured the key facets of designs, the local context introduces a great deal of variability that must be taken into account (Bodilly, 1998; Bodilly and Berends, 1999). For example, while a design may focus on project-based learning over several weeks of the semester, this may be superseded by district-mandated curricula that take priority over significant portions of each school day. Implementation of key components of designs may be highly variable across jurisdictions because of variation in support and alignment of programs. Thus, examination of implementation across jurisdictions is a complex process, and we attempt to address this issue by incorporating information gathered from district interviews and observations and by analyzing such factors in a multivariate framework.

Fifth, it is important to note that all the results reported here on implementation are based on teachers' responses to surveys. The usefulness of what we can learn and infer from the analyses is heavily dependent on the quality of the data that are obtained from these surveys. In some instances, what we find has been validated by RAND's early case studies and other research (Bodilly, 1998; Ross et al., 1997; Datnow and Stringfield, 1997; Stringfield and Datnow, 1998), but for some indicators, all we have are teacher-reported survey measures. Such self-reports within an evaluation context may be positively biased if the respondents have a stake in the initiative. However, while we cannot conclusively determine the accuracy of teacher reports, any bias should not have much of an influence on the changes between 1997 and 1998 discussed in this report. We would expect any bias to be constant across the two waves of the teacher surveys, and we know of no evidence that suggests such teacher bias is not constant over time (see Garet et al., 1999). Future validity studies should address such data quality issues within the context of comprehensive school reform (for an example of this type of validity study linked to a larger national data collection, see Burstein et al., 1995).

Sixth, in the analysis sample of NAS schools that we examine, small sample sizes for some design teams make traditional tests of statistical significance somewhat more difficult to apply. With larger sample sizes, we would have more power to detect differences and effects. Thus, in the school-level descriptive analyses in this chapter, we focus on what appear to be educationally substantive differences where appropriate.

Despite these challenges, as we said earlier in Chapter One, evaluation remains an important component of any effort to change schools, and it is important to develop and refine sets of indicators that are informative not only for research but for design teams, educators, and policymakers.

IMPLEMENTATION INDICES

In order to address the questions about implementation stated at the beginning of this chapter, we developed two implementation indices:

1. A core implementation index that broadly measures implementation of the *major* shared components of the designs across the sites; and

2. A design team–specific implementation index that measures implementation of both shared and some unique aspects of the designs.

The core implementation index is useful for understanding the progress of the NAS schools during the scale-up phase across jurisdictions and designs. The design team–specific index allows us to measure implementation of each design on components that are unique to and emphasized by the design. The shortcoming of this index is that it is not directly comparable across designs because it varies both in terms of items and number of items included in the index and thus is not strictly comparable across design teams as the core index is.

We should reiterate that this design team–specific index was not designed to measure *all* the unique aspects of the designs. Indeed, we could not construct such a measure with the available data, given that this was a broad study of NAS schools, not a detailed case study of one particular design. As a result, the design team–specific index measures what we consider to be some of the key components of the designs.

Our focus in this chapter is on variation in implementation both among jurisdictions as well as design teams, where appropriate. The small sample size for some designs, the widely differing environments facing designs implementing in different jurisdictions, and the varying degree of support from districts make comparisons of implementation across design teams somewhat problematic.

In what follows, the school is the unit of analysis, although we look at differences both within and between design-based schools over time. For each indicator, we calculate summary statistics such as school-level means, medians, quartiles, and variance, and then examine variations in these statistics for sets of schools grouped by jurisdiction or design team.

Most of the results that follow are portrayed with box-and-whisker diagrams, which show the distribution of the particular indicator being examined. In a box-and-whisker diagram, the line in the box is at the median value—half the values fall above the line and half fall below. Each "box" captures the middle 50 percent of the distribution. The lines, called "whiskers," at each end of the box show the range of scores beyond the upper and lower quartiles. Outliers are indicated by the shaded circles. The box-and-whisker plot thus allows us to compare the centers (median or center of the box), spread (measured by the interquartile range or the height of the box), and tails of the different distributions.

We also conduct multiple comparison tests of differences among means, but small sample sizes mean that finding significant differences is somewhat more difficult in these data.[2] In addition, outliers can make the means less representative than in more well-behaved distributions. These tests remain useful, however, in highlighting differences across jurisdictions and design teams that are both substantively and statistically meaningful. However, our primary emphasis in this chapter is on the patterns that emerge from the analyses taken together rather than on particular differences for any given indicator.

Core Implementation Index

The core implementation index is a summative scale of teacher responses as to the degree to which the following described their

---

[2]Statistically significant here refers to the mean differences being significant at the .05 probability level or less. This is based on the multiple comparison test using the Bonferonni correction. When conducting multiple tests, say n, and setting the critical level to α for each test, the chances of falsely rejecting *at least one* of the hypotheses is $1 - (1 - .05)^n$ if the tests are independent. The Bonferonni correction allows us to control for the fact that we are conducting multiple tests and to ensure that the overall chance of falsely rejecting each hypothesis remains α.

school (on a scale of 1–6, with 1 = does not describe my school, and 6 = clearly describes my school):[3]

- Parents and community members are involved in the educational program;

- Student assessments are explicitly linked to academic standards;

- Teachers develop and monitor student progress with personalized, individualized learning programs;

- Student grouping is fluid, multi-age, or multi-year;

- Teachers are continual learners and team members through professional development, common planning, and collaboration; and

- Performance expectations are made explicit to students so that they can track their progress over time.

There were some other measures that we would have liked to include in this index—such as shared decisionmaking—but, as we mentioned, these data were not available for Dade schools.

We analyze this overall implementation measure for two reasons:

First, the core function of schools is teaching and learning. Therefore, we selected those teacher-reported implementation indicators that were related more directly to influencing what goes on in teachers' lives and inside classrooms. From an organizational perspective, classroom instruction is the core technology of school organizations and the primary mechanism through which learning occurs (Gamoran et al., 1995; Gamoran and Dreeben, 1986; Parsons, 1959). It is this core function of schools that the designs ultimately want to influence and it is this aspect of implementation that our overall implementation index aims to measure.

Second, we want to examine factors related to implementation, and this summary measure allows us to present our results in a parsimonious manner.

---

[3]The alpha reliability of this index was 0.82. The range of correlations for the individual items was 0.27 to 0.60.

We find fairly large differences in the distribution of the core implementation index across the jurisdictions, although not within a jurisdiction. Figures 4.1 and 4.2 show the distribution of this index by jurisdiction and design team. The overall mean for the sample schools was 4.20 (SD = .58). Kentucky and Memphis ranked relatively high on this index with means of 4.56 and 4.49, while Philadelphia and San Antonio ranked the lowest (means of 3.73 and 3.60, respectively). The differences between the highest and lowest jurisdictions were all statistically significant.

Comparisons among design teams reveal that CON, RW, and NARE ranked comparatively high on the core implementation index while MRSH generally ranked the lowest. Figure 4.2 shows that the levels of implementation tended to be higher in the CON, RW, and NARE schools (means of 4.50, 4.41, and 4.31 respectively) while MRSH schools (mean = 3.75) tended to lag behind all other designs.

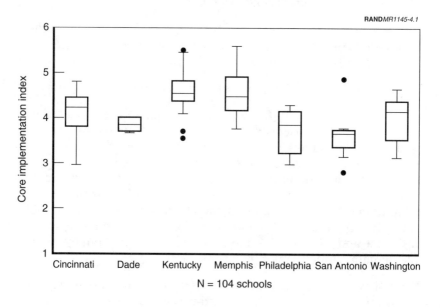

Figure 4.1—Overall Implementation Index by Jurisdiction, Spring 1998

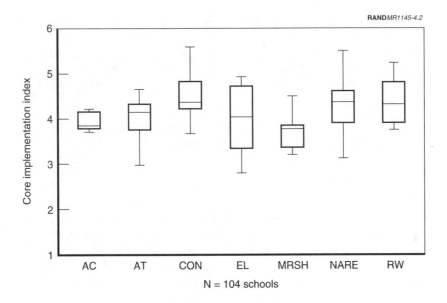

Figure 4.2—Overall Implementation Index by Design Team, Spring 1998

However, in terms of differences in means, none of these differences is statistically significant.

The results for the core implementation index by jurisdictions and design teams are consistent with the results that we find when examining a wider set of indicators separately (see Appendix B). In addition, we also conducted sensitivity analyses of our results by constructing more diverse and more inclusive indices of implementation (see Berends, 2000 for an example of a larger index). The results were quite consistent across these different indices.

Change in Implementation over Time and by Number of Years of Implementation

When we examine changes in implementation over the two years, we find that the overall implementation index was stable over time. The mean was 4.17 (SD = .60) in 1997 across all 104 schools and 4.20 (SD = .58) in 1998. However, because the change in implementation should be a function of number of years that schools have been implementing, it is important to disaggregate the change in the mean level of implementation by number of years that schools have been implementing.

Tables 4.1–4.2 show the means and standard deviations for the core implementation index and its components, for schools grouped by years of implementation in 1997—one year, two years, and three or more years.

For each group of schools, we calculated a mean change in implementation levels between 1997 and 1998. For the first set of schools—those that had been implementing for one year in 1997—this represents a change in implementation levels between year 1 and year 2 of implementation; for the second set of schools, it represents a change between year 2 and year 3 of implementation; and for the third set of schools, the change between year 3 and year 4 of implementation.

Some interesting patterns emerge from the table:

- The core implementation index went up by 0.25 between year 1 and year 2 of implementation for those schools that were in the first year of implementation in 1997. This is a large change amounting to a little over four-tenths of a standard deviation. However, it remained essentially unchanged among schools that reported two or more years of implementing the design as of 1997.

- For schools that reported implementing for one year in 1997, every single indicator increased between 1997 and 1998. Some showed particularly large changes. For example, the indicator "student assessments are explicitly linked to academic standards" showed an increase of 0.50; this is likely linked to standards-based reform being adopted in most states (see Berends and Kirby et al., in review).

- As expected, the mean for every implementation indicator was higher in every case for schools that had been implementing for two or more years compared with schools implementing for one year. This suggests that implementation does deepen with

Table 4.1

Means of the Core Implementation Index and Its Components by Number of Years of Implementation, 1997 and 1998

Components of the Core Implementation Index	Schools That Had Been Implementing for One Year in 1997 (n = 42)			Schools That Had Been Implementing for Two Years in 1997 (n = 35)			Schools That Had Been Implementing for Three or More Years in 1997 (n = 27)		
	Mean 1997	Mean 1998	Change Between 1997 and 1998	Mean 1997	Mean 1998	Change Between 1997 and 1998	Mean 1997	Mean 1998	Change Between 1997 and 1998
Parents and community members are involved in the educational program	3.56	3.68	0.11	3.95	3.77	-0.19	4.21	4.14	-0.07
Student assessments are explicitly linked to academic standards	4.15	4.65	0.50	4.43	4.63	0.20	4.66	4.76	0.11
Teachers develop and monitor student progress with personalized, individualized learning programs	3.79	4.00	0.21	4.23	4.22	-0.01	4.17	4.20	0.03
Student grouping is fluid, multi-age, or multi-year	3.19	3.56	0.37	3.87	3.91	0.04	4.22	4.13	-0.09
Teachers are continual learners and team members through professional development, common planning, and collaboration	4.59	4.72	0.13	4.90	4.83	-0.07	4.86	4.85	-0.02
Performance expectations are made explicit to students so that they can track their progress over time	3.95	4.20	0.25	4.42	4.36	-0.06	4.45	4.38	-0.07
Core Implementation Index	3.87	4.12	0.25	4.30	4.29	-0.01	4.45	4.39	-0.06

Table 4.2

Standard Deviations of the Core Implementation Index and Its Components by Number of Years of Implementation, 1997 and 1998

Components of the Core Implementation Index	Schools That Had Been Implementing for One Year in 1997 (n = 42)			Schools That Had Been Implementing for Two Years in 1997 (n = 35)			Schools That Had Been Implementing for Three or More Years in 1997 (n = 27)		
	SD 1997	SD 1998	Change Between 1997 and 1998	SD 1997	SD 1998	Change Between 1997 and 1998	SD 1997	SD 1998	Change Between 1997 and 1998
Parents and community members are involved in the educational program	0.83	0.87	0.04	0.68	0.91	0.23	0.68	0.77	0.09
Student assessments are explicitly linked to academic standards	0.61	0.57	-0.04	0.68	0.57	-0.11	0.63	0.55	-0.08
Teachers develop and monitor student progress with personalized, individualized learning programs	0.66	0.65	-0.01	0.57	0.62	0.05	0.70	0.66	-0.04
Student grouping is fluid, multi-age, or multi-year	1.23	1.31	0.08	1.18	1.17	-0.01	1.08	1.13	0.05
Teachers are continual learners and team members through professional development, common planning, and collaboration	0.54	0.58	0.04	0.45	0.56	0.11	0.58	0.62	0.04
Performance expectations are made explicit to students so that they can track their progress over time	0.56	0.49	-0.07	0.46	0.50	0.04	0.55	0.60	0.05
Core Implementation Index	0.59	0.56	-0.03	0.52	0.60	0.08	0.54	0.57	0.03

maturity. However, for schools implementing for two or more years in 1997, the changes in indicators between 1997 and 1998 were quite small and negative in some instances, suggesting that implementation appears to have reached a plateau in these schools. This deserves further attention, particularly among schools that had only been implementing for two years in 1997. While we expected a leveling off as schools matured, we hypothesized this might occur at a somewhat later time period than between the second and third year of implementation. It does not appear that these indicators are unchanged because of ceiling effects; on a scale of 1–6, most lie between 3.5–4.5.

- The indicators with the greatest between-school variability were the ones related to student grouping and to parent/community involvement.

- Over time, the variance between schools remained essentially unchanged.

We turn now to the design team–specific implementation index and use it to examine change over time, both between and within schools.

DESIGN TEAM–SPECIFIC IMPLEMENTATION INDEX

As we mentioned above, designs vary in their focus and core components. As a result, we constructed a design team–specific implementation index that included the six core items of the core implementation index and items that were specific to each design team. Table 4.3 lists the specific items included in the specific index constructed for each design team.

Again, the specific measures listed may not have captured all the unique features of the designs. Moreover, the wording of the survey items was fairly general to broadly compare schooling activities across design teams. Nonetheless, the design team–specific indices created here provide additional information about implementation of some of the unique features of the design teams. Such information is helpful for examining changes over time in the teacher-reported implementation, including changes in the means and variance within and between schools.

Table 4.3

Survey Items Included in the Design Team–Specific Implementation Index by Design Team

Survey Items	AC	AT	CON	EL	MRSH	NARE	RW
Core Items							
Parents and community members are involved in the educational program	√	√	√	√	√	√	√
Student assessments are explicitly linked to academic standards	√	√	√	√	√	√	√
Teachers develop and monitor student progress with personalized, individualized learning programs	√	√	√	√	√	√	√
Student grouping is fluid, multi-age, or multi-year	√	√	√	√	√	√	√
Teachers are continual learners and team members through professional development, common planning, and collaboration	√	√	√	√	√	√	√
Performance expectations are made explicit to students so that they can track their progress over time	√	√	√	√	√	√	√
Design-team specific Items							
The scope and sequence of the curriculum is organized into semester- or year-long themes	√						
Students are required on a regular basis to apply their learning in ways that directly benefit the community	√						
Students frequently listen to speakers and go on field trips that specifically relate to the curriculum	√						
This school is part of a K–12 feeder pattern that provides integrated health and social services to improve student learning			√				
Students are required by this school to make formal presentations to exhibit what they have learned before they can progress to the next level			√				

Table 4.3 (continued)

Survey Items	AC	AT	CON	EL	MRSH	NARE	RW
Consistent and coherent curriculum and performance standards have been established across the K–12 feeder patterns		√					
Most teachers in this school meet regularly with teachers in other schools to observe and discuss progress toward design team goals			√				
Technology is an integrated classroom resource			√		√		
Students engage in project-based learning for a significant portion of the school day (i.e., more than 1/3 of the time)			√				
Technology is used in this school to manage curriculum, instruction, and student progress			√		√		
A majority of teachers in this school stay with the same group of students for more than one year				√			
Students frequently revise their work toward an exemplary final product				√			
There are formal arrangements within this school providing opportunities for teachers to discuss and critique their instruction with each other				√			
This school has the authority to make budget, staffing, and program decisions					√		
Curriculum throughout this school emphasizes preparation for and relevance to the world of work						√	
Students are monitored according to annual performance targets established by the school as a whole						√	
Student assessments are used to reassign students to instructional groups on a frequent and regular basis							√

Table 4.3 (continued)

Survey Items	AC	AT	CON	EL	MRSH	NARE	RW
Students are organized into instruct-ional groups using block scheduling for specific curricular purposes							√
This school has specific activities aimed directly at reducing student absenteeism							√
Students who are not progressing according to expectations are pro-vided with extended days and/or tutors							√
This school has a coordinator, facili-tator, or resource specialist assigned on a full- or part-time basis							√
Alpha Reliability Index	0.83	0.80	0.87	0.88	0.90	0.85	0.87

Changes in Implementation Between 1997 and 1998

Table 4.4 presents the means and standard deviations of the design team–specific implementation index across the schools implementing each design. We present both within-school and between-school standard deviations.

Implementation remained the same or increased very slightly for most designs between 1997 and 1998, and the changes are not statistically significant. In general, declines in the variability of reported implementation both within and between these schools were small. As we mentioned, it is possible that jurisdictional effects would be large enough to prevent declines in variance between schools across sites, but on the whole, we would have expected a decline in within-school variance as implementation deepened. Our data show that variance within schools essentially remained unchanged at between 0.80–1.00 for the two years. Of the designs, EL had the greatest between-school variability in reported implementation, and this increased from 1997 to 1998.

We attempted to examine the change in mean implementation for schools grouped by years of implementation in 1997: schools that had been implementing for one year and schools that had been implementing for two years or more. Unfortunately, small sample sizes

Table 4.4

Means and Standard Deviations of the Design Team–Specific Implementation Index by Design Team, 1997 and 1998

Design Team	Sample Size	1997			1998		
		Mean	Within-School SD	Between-School SD	Mean	Within-School SD	Between-School SD
AC	5	4.00	0.94	0.40	4.16	0.91	0.37
AT	17	3.52	0.88	0.42	3.92	0.85	0.43
CON	12	4.55	0.81	0.49	4.59	0.77	0.48
EL	16	4.19	0.86	0.61	4.00	0.84	0.80
MRSH	7	3.64	0.87	0.49	3.85	1.02	0.45
NARE	32	4.23	0.81	0.54	4.34	0.83	0.54
RW	15	4.72	0.77	0.44	4.70	0.80	0.44

made these results less stable for some of the designs. For example, AC had only one school that had been implementing for one year in 1997 as did RW; MRSH and AT had only one and two schools respectively that had been implementing for two or more years in 1997. As a result, we do not show results for this part of the analysis. Among designs for which we had five or more schools that had been implementing for one year in 1997, all the designs showed increases in the mean index of between 0.20 and 0.40 (with the exception of EL, which posted a small decline of about –0.20). Among designs that had five or more schools that had been implementing for two years or more in 1997, the mean implementation level remained essentially unchanged—again with the exception of EL, which showed a small decline of about –0.20.

The lack of increased implementation over time needs to be examined further and validated against other designs in other sites. It may point to problems with the level of design-based assistance and support tailing off beyond the second year, with maintaining a stable and supportive school and district environment that would allow implementation to deepen, or with implementing a complex design not well-suited to the school's needs. Alternatively, in schools that are more mature, it may point to an expected leveling off of implementation because the designs have been more schoolwide and a more routine part of the school. However, in this latter case, we would have expected declines in variability among these schools, which do not show up in our data.

SUMMARY

Differences Across Jurisdictions

We analyzed a great deal of information regarding implementation of various key components of the designs, but the overall patterns are fairly clear (also see Appendix B). Bodilly (1998) has identified several district and institutional factors that contribute to implementation. These are:

- Leadership backing and stability at the district level;

- Centrality of the NAS initiative to the district's agenda;

- Lack of crisis situations;

- History of trust and cooperation;

- Availability of resources for transformation;

- School level authority and/or autonomy;

- Union support; and

- District accountability and assessment systems that were compatible with those of the designs.

Memphis and Kentucky ranked as highly supportive on several of these indicators, so it is not surprising that they ranked high on the majority of the implementation indicators considered here. In our analyses, NAS schools in San Antonio and Philadelphia consistently ranked near the bottom on most indicators. Bodilly (1998) ranked Philadelphia as nonsupportive on most of the factors listed above, so its consistent low ranking is not surprising. However, in direct contrast to our findings, Bodilly found that San Antonio provided high levels of support and at the time of writing had higher levels of implementation.

Because of the differences between the results reported here and those of Bodilly (1998), the San Antonio results require further explanation. One possible reason for the difference is the sampling of schools that were included in the case study analysis of San Antonio in the spring of 1997. Bodilly visited four schools in San Antonio, whereas the results reported here are from nine schools.

A more likely explanation is the variety of reform activities in San Antonio that were being implemented at the same time as the NAS designs.[4] In 1997, when Bodilly conducted site visits to schools, the district office in San Antonio established an Office of Curriculum and Instruction to help establish a coherent academic vision for the district in as efficient a way as possible. Test scores in the district were abysmal, and the district leadership was unsure whether the designs had sufficient curriculum and instruction components to directly affect state test scores (Texas Assessment of Academic Skills, or TAAS). In an effort to raise test scores and assure that all students were learning particular skills and increasing their knowledge base, the central office set out to provide an instructional framework based upon reorganizing and redefining leadership roles. The central office wanted to make sure that across campuses at similar grade levels, comparable instruction could be found taking place. There was indication that in the past, even within the same school at the same grade level, vastly different kinds of activities had been assigned. Much redundancy also was found in the curriculum from one grade to the next. In addition to the NAS designs, the district office soon introduced to all schools research-based instructional programs that targeted the two most basic subjects, reading and mathematics. Thus, by 1997 and 1998, when we administered our surveys, schools were spending a substantial portion of the day on district-mandated curricular programs rather than design team activities. Within this context, it is not surprising that our surveys revealed low levels of implementation of NAS designs in San Antonio, especially in 1998.

Our rankings of districts in terms of implementation were generally consistent across the two years.

Differences Across Design Teams

Bodilly (1998) has identified several design team factors that contribute to implementation. These are:

- A stable team with a capability to serve;

---

[4]We obtained the information reported here as part of a classroom study that RAND is conducting in San Antonio, which compares NAS and non-NAS teachers. Dr. JoAn Chun has played a major role in gathering data for that study.

- Ability to communicate the design well to schools;
- Effective marketing to the district and ability to gain needed resources for implementation;
- Type of design or relative elements emphasized;
- Implementation support to schools.

In Bodilly's case study work, RW ranked high on every factor as did EL, with the exception of strong support to the schools, where EL was ranked average. AT and MRSH ranked weak on every factor, while the others were somewhat in the middle. These findings run somewhat counter to our findings. We find CON, RW, and NARE schools consistently ranked high on most indices while AC, AT, and MRSH ranked at the bottom end of the scale (also see Appendix B).

It is likely that some of these differences can be accounted for by the different samples under study and the timing of the data collection. For example, Bodilly gathered data for her case studies in the spring of 1996 and 1997. AC faced two crises in 1996: The national facilitator retired from the organization, and its founder passed away. AC has always been the smallest of the teams, and Bodilly observed that it did not fully recover from these major organizational crises. By 1998, the second year of our data collection, the AC design team faced real difficulties not found in Bodilly's research.

MRSH also suffered from growing pains during this time period as it tried to acquire and train staff at the same time that it was scaling up. Both AT and MRSH designs are what Bodilly (1998) termed comprehensive and systemic designs attempting to change not only core elements but school and district governance, public involvement, and standards as well. In general, she found that comprehensive designs made less progress in implementation than teams that focused on core elements of schooling. In the analyses reported here, AC ranked in the middle in terms of design-team support to schools, while AT and MRSH again ranked the lowest.

NARE is a somewhat different story. Although Bodilly (1998) ranked NARE low in terms of several factors, the design has undergone substantial maturation and rethinking of its theory of action. While a significant number of the NARE sites analyzed here are located in Kentucky, where state policies were aligned with the NARE design,

Bodilly's case studies examined NARE sites where the jurisdiction was much less supportive (e.g., Pittsburgh, not included in the analyses reported here). The NARE design was very well aligned with the reforms instituted in Kentucky as part of the Kentucky Educational Reform Act (KERA). As a result, the reported level of implementation of NARE designs being high in the results reported here may be due in large part to the large proportion of the NARE sample being in Kentucky. As one of the principals of a NARE school in Kentucky said to us during one of the phone interviews, "It is incredible what we have picked up from them. In fact, the NARE design is a step beyond KERA. For example, NARE content standards were missing from KERA. NARE spelled out basic, national standards in addition to the process standards of KERA."

Although CON ranked in the middle in Bodilly's rankings, it has a number of factors that have worked in its favor. It labeled itself as the "high-tech" design and was consistently listed as the number one or number two choice of most schools. Because it required significant computer and telecommunications technologies in the schools to be successful, it managed to market itself as a demonstration program to districts and so obtained a high degree of support and resources. CON also provided high levels of support for the schools, including "critical friends" visits to perform implementation audits. All of these factors may foster high levels of implementation. In addition, after Bodilly collected her data in the spring of 1997, CON introduced additional assistance to schools, particularly in the amount of technology put in place in CON schools. Thus, Bodilly missed these increases in design assistance and implementation, while the surveys reported here did not.

RW stands out because of its high rankings on all of Bodilly's indicators as well as those reported here. Noteworthy, too, is the lower within-school variance in the RW schools. RW has had the advantage of being relatively more specific than the other NAS designs—evolving out of the *Success for All* program that had been in existence for some time. RW also provided extensive materials to schools to explain and help implement the design. Moreover, RW targeted Title I funds for implementing the design and presented funding options clearly. RW also emphasized the core elements of schooling and provided substantial whole staff training, professional development, and team quality checks. As Bodilly (1998, p. 68) notes, "Districts reported that they knew what they were getting and what they could and could not negotiate."

The one surprise is the average ranking of EL on our indicators despite its emphasis on core elements, its ability to communicate well with schools, and its stable, capable staff. However, in terms of overall design team support, EL ranked in the middle on Bodilly's rankings, and this may partly explain why it ranks in the middle on our indicators.

Differences by Years Implementing

Implementation was higher in schools that had been implementing for more years. It also increased across the NAS schools between the first and second year, but not between the second and subsequent years.

Understanding the factors that are related to high and low levels of implementation is important in a formative evaluation such as this one because it can provide insights to NAS and the design teams to make adjustments to their strategies and services. We analyze factors related to implementation in the next chapter.

Chapter Five

FACTORS AFFECTING IMPLEMENTATION

The conceptual framework outlined in Chapter Two pointed to the possible interrelationships between teacher background characteristics, school characteristics, district support, and assistance provided by design teams and implementation of the key components of designs. The previous chapter described summary measures of implementation: a core implementation index and a design team–specific implementation index. As we noted, there is a great deal of variability in the overall indices across jurisdictions and design teams (also see Appendix B), and it is important to understand the factors that are related to successful implementation. Up to this point, we have used the school as the unit of analysis. However, as the last chapter showed, there is a great deal of variance within schools on these implementation indicators, and it is important to understand what teacher-level and school-level factors are related to implementation. The multivariate analyses presented in this chapter allow us to analyze this variation further by partitioning it into within- and between-school components and relating this variation to a variety of teacher, school, and design team factors.

Unfortunately, the design team–specific implementation index does not lend itself to being modeled because the number and types of items included in the index vary across design teams. Thus, the index is not directly comparable across the design teams. As a result, in the analyses that follow, we use the core implementation index as the dependent variable.[1]

---

[1]Recall that our overall core index is comprised of the following: parents and community members are involved in the educational program; student assessments are ex-

OPERATIONALIZING THE VARIABLES AFFECTING IMPLEMENTATION

The factors listed below are drawn from our conceptual framework. We describe the operationalization of each variable before showing its relationship with implementation in a multivariate framework.

Teacher Background Characteristics

Because the experiences that teachers have accumulated over the years contribute to their teaching practices, it is important to understand whether teacher background is related to support for reform and the effects of that reform on students and teachers.

Here we examine several characteristics of teachers, including gender, race-ethnicity, educational degree, age, and experience within the current school. The operationalization of these measures is straightforward. In our analyses, we included dummy variables for gender (male as reference), race-ethnicity (African American, Latino, other, vs. non-Hispanic white), educational degree (master's vs. bachelor's), and total teaching experience (measured in years) age (30 years or older vs. less than 30). We tried several different specifications for age before settling on a simple dichotomous specification. Because we had a surprising degree of missing data on both experience and gender (10 percent on experience and 20 percent on gender), missing value dummy indicators were also included in the multivariate analysis.

In addition, we also included three measures of teacher perceptions of their students' ability and readiness to learn, including:

---

plicitly linked to academic standards; teachers develop and monitor student progress with personalized, individualized learning programs; student grouping is fluid, multi-age, or multi-year; teachers are continual learners and team members through professional development, common planning, and collaboration; and performance expectations are made explicit to students so that they can track their progress over time. We also examined other teacher-reported indices for performance expectations of students, innovative instructional strategies, and professional development. These indices are described in Appendix B. The results for the multivariate analyses reveal similar patterns to those for the core implementation index (see Appendix C). We comment on similarities and differences in the analyses of these indices, where appropriate.

- *Lack of basic skills is a hindrance to your students' academic success:* Teachers ranked this on a scale on 1–4 with 1 = great hindrance and 4 = not at all.

- *Lack of student discipline and inadequate parent support for students is a hindrance to your students' academic success:* These two separate survey items were summed to create one index. Each was ranked on a scale on 1–4 with 1 = great hindrance and 4 = not at all. We combined the two and obtained an average value.

- *Most of my students can learn with the school resources available to them:* This was measured on a 4-point scale with 1 = strongly disagree and 4 = strongly agree.

School Characteristics

As discussed in Chapter Two, structural characteristics of the schools, school demographic characteristics, and leadership are all important in supporting implementation. We examined the following characteristics in the analyses that follow:

- *Large school:* This is a dummy variable equal to 1 if the school is large (i.e., 400 students or more) (variable equal to 0 otherwise).

- *Secondary school:* This is a dummy variable equal to 1 if the school is secondary (variable equal to 0 otherwise).

- *Percent student mobility:* This is a continuous variable measuring the overall student mobility reported by the principal.

- *School poverty:* This is a continuous variable measuring the percent of students receiving free and/or subsidized lunch.

- *School minority composition:* This is a continuous variable measuring the percent of students who are nonwhite.

- *Principal leadership:* Teachers were asked several questions regarding the degree of support and leadership provided by the principal. These included communicating clearly what is expected of teachers, supportive and encouraging behavior, getting resources for the school, enforcing rules for student conduct, talking with teachers regarding instructional practices, having confidence in the expertise of the teachers, and taking a personal interest in the professional development of teachers. We combined these into a summative index of principal leadership; the alpha reliability for this index was .87, and the correlations ranged from .28 to .65. Unfortunately, these data are not available for Dade schools because we had to administer an attenuated survey in these schools.

Designs and Design Team Assistance

Several researchers have found that design team factors and the assistance they provide are related to implementation (Bodilly, 1998; Datnow and Stringfield, 1997; Stringfield and Datnow, 1998). For example, important implementation factors include clear communication by designs to help implementation, the experience schools have with implementation (i.e., years implementing), whether teachers voted to implement, and availability of resources. These factors are further defined below:

- *Communication by designs to schools* measures the degree to which individual teachers reported that the design team clearly communicated the design so that it could be well implemented. Scores for this variable ranged from 1 = did not communicate clearly at all to 6 = definitely communicated clearly.

- *Attendance at design team workshop* is measured by a dummy variable with 1 indicating attendance.

- *Professional development days devoted to design teams* included those in the last year as reported by the principal. This provided an estimate of the total number of days that the typical teacher in the school received in the past year that were specifically devoted to the NAS design team.

- *Years implementing* is number of years the school has been implementing the design with a range from 2 to 4 or more (from principal interview).

- *Vote* is a dummy variable equal to 1 if there were 60 percent or more of teachers voting to implement design (variable equal to 0 otherwise) (from principal interview).[2]

- *Resources index* is a school measure based on aggregated teacher reports about whether the school had sufficient resources to implement the designs. Teachers could respond to several questions using a 5-point scale ranging from "no resources are available" to "all are available." The resources index is a combination of a number of questions that asked the extent to which the teacher's school had the resources needed to implement the major elements of the design. These questions included:

  - Materials to describe the program;

  - Materials to support instruction;

  - Professional development for teachers;

  - Time for planning, collaboration, and development;

  - Staff or consultant to mentor, advise, and provide ongoing support;

  - Technology; and

  - Funds and funding flexibility.

  The alpha reliability of this scale is .92 (correlations among these items ranged from .50 to .90).

- *Set of dummy variables for designs*: Because there may be unmeasured characteristics of designs that may influence implementation over and above those mentioned above, we also included in some models a set of dummy variables that were equal to 1 if the school had adopted that particular design, 0 otherwise (RW is the reference category).

---

[2]Although conceptually we felt that implementation should be related to this measure, the models we estimated did not include this variable for two reasons. First, it measured support two years ago when the schools were considering the design and we had more direct measures of support. Second, given turnover, this variable may not correctly reflect level of support in the spring of 1998.

District Support

Our earlier research (Bodilly, 1998; Bodilly and Berends, 1999) has highlighted the importance of coherent, sustained, stable district support. We attempted to measure this in two ways:

- *Index of district support*: We ranked jurisdictions along a variety of key dimensions based on Bodilly's earlier work (1998) as well as additional interviews with districts in 1998. As we mentioned earlier, Bodilly (1998) identified several district and institutional factors that contributed to implementation: leadership backing and stability; centrality of effort; lack of crises; history of trust and cooperation; resource support; school autonomy; union support; and aligned assessment. Jurisdictions were ranked on these dimensions; the various rankings were then summed into an overall summative index of district support (alpha reliability of this index was .85, and the interitem correlations ranged from .16 to .77);

- *Set of dummy variables for each jurisdiction*: Because the above index is open to criticism on the grounds of being largely judgmental, we also used the set of separate dummy variables for each jurisdiction, which was used in the earlier chapter, to test in the multilevel analyses (Memphis is the reference category). Another reason for using this set of dummy indicators rather than the index is to capture dimensions of district support that have perhaps not been captured or only partially captured by the district index.

VARIATION IN IMPLEMENTATION: MULTILEVEL ANALYSIS

Because the data are nested—that is, teachers are nested within schools—we relied on multilevel modeling techniques to provide more accurate estimates of the relationships between the dependent and independent measures (see Bryk and Raudenbush, 1992; Bryk, Raudenbush, and Congdon, 1996; Singer, 1998).

First, we partitioned the variance in the dependent variables into their within-school and between-school components. This provided information about whether most of the variance in the dependent variable lies between schools or within schools. Next, we estimated a set of regression coefficients in each school (level 1), and then the constant term in the first equation (level 1) becomes an outcome to be explained by school demographic and implementation factors (level 2).

Specifically, for the implementation index, we estimated the following models:

Individual Teacher Model (Level 1):

$$Y_{ij} = \beta_0 + \beta_1(\text{Female}) + \beta_2(\text{African American}) + \beta_3(\text{Hispanic}) + \beta_4(\text{Other}) + \beta_5(\text{MA Degree}) + \beta_6(\text{Age 30 or more}) + \beta_7$$
(Years of teaching experience) $+ \beta_8$(Lack of basic skills) $+ \beta_9$(Lack of discipline and parent support) $+ \beta_{10}$(Students can learn with school resources)$+ \beta_{11}$(Communication by designs) $+ \beta_{12}$(Support for design) $+ \beta_{13}$(Attended DT workshop) $+ r_{ij},$

where

- Y_{ij} is the dependent variable, the implementation index;

- β_0 is the constant term, and it is the average value of the dependent variable in the school;

- $\beta_{1\text{-}13}$'s are the level-1 coefficients for the listed independent variables; and

- r_{ij} is the level-1 random effect.

School Context Model (Level 2):

$$\beta_0 = \gamma_0 + \gamma_1(\text{School poverty}) + \gamma_2(\text{School minority}) + \gamma_3(\text{Large school}) + \gamma_4(\text{Secondary school}) + \gamma_5(\text{Student mobility})+ \gamma_6(\text{PD Days devoted to DT}) + \gamma_7(\text{Years implementing}) + \gamma_8(\text{Principal leadership index}) + \gamma_9(\text{Resources index}) + u,$$

where

- β_0 in this model is from the teacher-level equation above, and it is the average level of the core implementation index in the school;

- γ_0 is the constant term;
- γ_{1-9} are the level-2 coefficients for the listed independent variables;
- u is a level-2 random effect.

In addition, the school-level model included either:

- a set of jurisdiction dummies, which included Memphis as the reference category because of the greater degree of implementation that has occurred there (Bodilly, 1998; Ross et al., 1999b); or

- a set of dummy variables for the designs, which included RW as the reference category because of the research base from other sources associated with this design team (Herman et al., 1999); and

- an index of district support.

It is important to remember that our sample of NAS schools was not a random sample, but a sample of all those schools in the eight partnering jurisdictions that reported implementation during the spring of 1997 and 1998 and had survey information from teachers and principals. Despite this not being a random sample, we used multi-level modeling techniques to explore the relationships among variables at one point in time—spring 1998. These provided a more accurate *description* of the relationships in these NAS schools for this particular point in time. In previous chapters, we discussed the stability of the implementation indicators between 1997 and 1998. Because of that stability, we focus on the cross-sectional relationships for 1998 in the results that follow.

The Analysis Sample

Table 5.1 provides the means and standard deviations for the variables in the model. The implementation index, which had a mean of 4.22 on a 1–6 scale, was now standardized to a mean of 0 and SD = 1. The analysis sample consisted of 1,842 teachers and 104 schools.

Teacher Characteristics. About 22 percent of the teachers were African American; a small percentage were Hispanic (5 percent).

Table 5.1

Descriptive Statistics of Variables in Multilevel Analysis

Variables	Mean	SD
Dependent Variable		
Implementation index (range 1–6)	4.22	1.06
Implementation index (standardized)	0.00	1.00
Independent Variables for Teachers (n = 1,842) [a]		
Race-ethnicity		
African American	0.22	
Hispanic/Latino	0.05	
Other/missing	0.14	
Educational degree: master's or above	0.52	
Age: ≥ 30 years	0.67	
Years of teaching experience	15.87	11.29
Lack of basic skills a hindrance (1–4, 1 = great hindrance, 4 = not at all)	1.82	0.87
Student discipline and inadequate parent support a hindrance (2–8, 2 = great hindrance, 8 = not at all)	4.58	1.82
Students can learn with available resources (1 – 4, 1 = strongly disagree, 4 = strongly agree)	3.29	0.78
Design-related variables		
Communication by designs to schools (range 1–6)	3.98	1.65
Support for design (1–5)	3.72	1.16
Attended design team workshop in last 12 months	0.69	
Independent Variables for Schools (n = 104) [b]		
Percent poverty	63.27	31.45
Percent minority	59.04	37.58
Large size (> 400)	0.82	
Secondary schools	0.36	
Percent student mobility	14.53	11.45
PD days devoted to design team	6.34	5.80
Years implementing	3.07	1.36
Principal leadership index (range 1–4)	3.23	0.37
Resources index (range 1–5)	3.15	0.51
Jurisdictions:		
Cincinnati	0.15	
Dade	0.04	
Kentucky	0.19	
Philadelphia	0.07	
San Antonio	0.09	
Washington	0.18	
Index of district support (range 9–27)	17.49	2.52
Design teams:		
AC	0.048	
AT	0.163	
CON	0.115	
EL	0.154	
MRSH	0.067	
NARE	0.308	
RW	0.144	

NOTES: [a] Standard deviations are calculated from the teacher sample.

[b] Standard deviations are calculated from the school sample.

About 14 percent of the teachers in our sample were categorized as other or missing (the other group was quite small—a little less than 2 percent). The remaining 60 percent were non-Hispanic white. About half the sample had a master's degree or higher and over two-thirds were 30 years or older (a good proportion are 40 and older). They had been teaching about 16 years on average.

A large proportion of the sample felt that lack of basic skills was a hindrance to their students' academic success. This was reflected in the very low mean of 1.82 for the sample. In terms of lack of student discipline and inadequate parent support, the teachers appeared to be at the midpoint on this measure with a mean of 4.58 on a scale that ranges from 2–8. Teachers were surprisingly positive about their students' ability to learn, given the available resources. The mean was quite high, 3.29 on a scale of 1–4.

When considering whether design teams clearly communicated the design to school staff so that it could be well implemented, we found that the average score for this teacher-level measure was about 4, which was somewhat higher than the midrange on a six-point scale ranging from not all clear (1) to definitely clear (6). There was a great deal of variation around this mean as indicated by the standard deviation (SD) of 1.65. In terms of support for the design, teachers again were in the middle with a mean of 3.71 (SD = 1.16).

About 69 percent of teachers had attended a design team workshop in the past 12 months.

School Characteristics. The mean poverty rate for the sample was 63 percent and the standard deviation was quite large, 31 percent. The schools also had high proportions of minority students: the mean for the sample was around 60 percent. Well-over four-fifths of the sample consisted of large schools (size > 400 students) and over a third were secondary schools. On average, the NAS schools in the analysis sample experienced a student turnover rate of 15 percent, although this varied somewhat across the sample of schools.

Schools reported that typically, teachers devoted about six days in the past year to professional development (PD) activities related to design teams, although the standard deviation (5.80) suggested great variability across the schools. On average, schools were in their third year of implementation. The schools tended to be at the midpoint, when considering the resources available to implement the major elements of the NAS design in their school. On a scale ranging from a low of 1 to a high of 5, the average for the resource availability index was 3.15 (recall this index included aggregated teacher reports about materials; professional development; time for planning, collaboration, and development; consultants to provide ongoing support; technology; and funding).

The mean for the principal leadership index was relatively high: 3.23 on a scale of 1–4, and the standard deviation was 0.37. The schools ranged from 1.9 to 3.8 on this index. Recall that we do not have data on this variable for Dade schools. There is a fairly strong correlation between principal leadership and the resource index (the correlation coefficient is .51).

The set of dummy indicators for jurisdictions showed the proportion of schools in our sample that were in particular jurisdictions. For example, about 15 percent of our schools were in Cincinnati while 4 percent were in Dade. The largest numbers of schools in our sample were in Cincinnati, Kentucky, and Washington.

The set of dummy variables for the design teams showed that AC and MRSH schools were somewhat less well represented in our sample: 5 and 7 percent, respectively, while NARE schools constituted 31 percent of the sample. Other designs—AT, CON, EL, RW—each accounted for between 12–16 percent of the sample.

Variance Components of the Dependent Variable

Before examining the relationship between implementation and teacher and school characteristics, we began by partitioning the variance in the dependent measure into its between- and within-school components. Between 27–28 percent of the total variance in implementation lies *between* schools (depending on whether the sample includes Dade schools or not). This means that most of the variance in implementation lies within schools (i.e., approximately 71–72 percent).

While such findings are not uncommon in analyses of school contextual effects on student and teacher outcomes (see Lee and Bryk, 1989; Gamoran, 1992), this is an important finding for the NAS initiative. When considering school reform and the effects of schools on students, it is critical to understand that most of the differences in critical outcomes—whether in implementation factors or "results"—are likely to occur *within* schools rather than *between* them. Because of such differences within schools, educators, design teams, and policymakers may need to think carefully about how to implement changes throughout the school.

Multivariate Results

We estimated four different models to examine the relationships between the core implementation index and teacher, design team, school, and district factors:

- Model 1: full set of independent variables listed above, plus jurisdiction dummies;

- Model 2: model 1, excluding the principal leadership variable (so as to include the Dade schools);

- Model 3: full set of independent variables listed above, plus design team dummies and an index of district support; and

- Model 4: model 3, excluding the principal leadership variable (so as to include the Dade schools).

In the multilevel regression models, the intercept was modeled as a random parameter. The teacher variables were included as fixed effects. That is, we constrained their between-school variance to zero and centered them around their grand means (i.e., the average values on the teacher variables for all the NAS teachers in this sample). Because of this centering, the intercept may be interpreted as the school mean score on the dependent measure of interest, adjusted for individual teacher characteristics. It was allowed to vary across schools (random effects).

The results from the models are provided in Table 5.2. In these types of regression models, we can examine the relationships between particular teacher characteristics and the outcome measures, controlling for other important teacher and school differences. In the school-level model, the actual dependent measure was the school mean score on the dependent measure of interest adjusted for individual teacher characteristics. To ease interpretation of the results in Table 5.2, all the continuous measures were standardized to have a mean of zero and a standard deviation of one. Thus, the coefficients for the continuous standardized variables represent the increment change in the dependent measure for a standard deviation change in the independent variable.

Teacher-Level Effects

We found some interesting differences in the level of implementation reported by black versus white non-Hispanic teachers. Black teachers tended to report significantly higher levels of implementation than white teachers (about .20 of a standard deviation higher). The other race/ethnic variables were not significant in the model. Somewhat surprisingly, teacher age, experience, and education did not appear to be important factors in implementation, controlling for everything else.

The variables measuring teacher perceptions about students' readiness and ability to learn were highly correlated with implementation. For example, teachers who were one standard deviation higher than the mean with respect to their perceptions of student readiness and ability to learn were between .08–.15 of a standard deviation higher on the implementation index. This reinforces earlier literature on the importance of teachers' sense of efficacy in implementation (Fullan, 1991).

Among design-related variables, clear communication had the largest effect on implementation in the teacher-level model. A 1 standard deviation change in this variable (say from the mean of 4.0 to 5.6) was associated with an increase in implementation of between .24–.26 of a standard deviation. Similarly, an increase of 1 standard deviation in teacher support from 3.7 to 4.8 was associated with an increase in implementation of about .15 of a standard deviation.

Whether or not the teacher had attended a DT workshop in the past year was not related to implementation net of other factors, although it may have had an effect in increasing understanding of or support for the design. Thus, its effect may have been subsumed in one of the other two variables.

Table 5.2

Multilevel Results for the Relationships of Implementation to Teacher, School, and Design-Related Factors

Variables	Model 1		Model 2		Model 3		Model 4	
	Coefficient	Standard Error	Coefficient	Standard Error	Coefficient	Standard Error	Coefficient	Standard Error
Intercept	0.266	0.109	0.341	0.106	0.121	0.145	0.159	0.146
Independent Variables for Teachers								
Race-ethnicity								
African American	0.198[a]	0.050	0.201[a]	0.050	0.206[a]	0.050	0.212[a]	0.050
Hispanic/Latino	0.020	0.120	0.161	0.101	-0.108	0.115	0.051	0.097
Other/Missing	0.006	0.073	0.055	0.071	-0.004	0.073	0.048	0.072
Educational degree: master's or above	-0.058	0.040	-0.044	0.040	-0.036	0.040	-0.021	0.039
Age: ≥30 years	-0.079	0.062	-0.096	0.060	-0.094	0.062	-0.110	0.060
Years of teaching experience	0.003	0.021	0.014	0.021	0.003	0.021	0.014	0.021
Lack of basic skills a hindrance (1–4, 1 = great hindrance, 4 = not at all)	0.074[a]	0.022	0.079[a]	0.022	0.074[a]	0.022	0.080[a]	0.022
Student discipline and inadequate parent support a hindrance (2–8, 2 = great hindrance, 8 = not at all)	0.149[a]	0.024	0.143[a]	0.023	0.153[a]	0.024	0.146[a]	0.023
Students can learn with available resources (1–4, 1 = strongly disagree, 4 = strongly agree)	0.086[a]	0.019	0.086[a]	0.019	0.089[a]	0.019	0.087[a]	0.019
Design-related variables								
Communication by designs to schools (1–6)	0.247[a]	0.023	0.260[a]	0.023	0.243[a]	0.023	0.257[a]	0.023
Support for design (1–5)	0.148[a]	0.021	0.146[a]	0.021	0.142[a]	0.021	0.140[a]	0.021
Attended design team workshop in last 12 mos	0.030	0.044	0.028	0.043	0.029	0.044	0.027	0.043
Independent Variables for Schools								
Poverty	0.006	0.057	0.014	0.056	0.127[b]	0.056	0.141[b]	0.056
Minority	0.053	0.067	0.005	0.064	0.060	0.069	-0.005	0.068
Large size (>400)	-0.220[b]	0.088	-0.237[a]	0.088	-0.202[b]	0.095	-0.234[b]	0.097

Table 5.2 (continued)

Variables	Model 1 Coefficient	Model 1 Standard Error	Model 2 Coefficient	Model 2 Standard Error	Model 3 Coefficient	Model 3 Standard Error	Model 4 Coefficient	Model 4 Standard Error
Secondary schools	-0.124	0.075	-0.161[b]	0.072	-0.068	0.081	-0.137	0.079
Percent student mobility	-0.018	0.036	-0.016	0.035	-0.093[b]	0.039	-0.094[b]	0.041
PD days devoted to design team	0.005	0.039	-0.005	0.038	-0.055	0.044	-0.068	0.044
Years implementing	0.032	0.037	0.025	0.036	0.008	0.044	0.004	0.044
Principal leadership (1–4)	0.094[b]	0.037	—[c]	—[c]	0.122[a]	0.040	—[c]	—[c]
Resources index (1–5)	0.058	0.041	0.098[a]	0.036	0.067	0.051	0.134[a]	0.044
Jurisdictions:								
Cincinnati	-0.170	0.104	-0.232[b]	0.102	—[c]	—[c]	—[c]	—[c]
Dade	—[c]	—[c]	-0.286	0.173	—[c]	—[c]	—[c]	—[c]
Kentucky	0.423[a]	0.139	0.398[a]	0.138	—[c]	—[c]	—[c]	—[c]
Philadelphia	-0.247	0.141	-0.321[b]	0.138	—[c]	—[c]	—[c]	—[c]
San Antonio	-0.562[a]	0.137	-0.626[a]	0.135	—[c]	—[c]	—[c]	—[c]
Washington	-0.236	0.160	-0.311	0.158	—[c]	—[c]	—[c]	—[c]
Index of district support	—[c]	—[c]	—[c]	—[c]	0.094[b]	0.041	0.129[a]	0.041
Design teams:								
AC	—[c]	—[c]	—[c]	—[c]	-0.107	0.207	0.012	0.190
AT	—[c]	—[c]	—[c]	—[c]	0.003	0.146	0.019	0.151
CON	—[c]	—[c]	—[c]	—[c]	0.279	0.144	0.274	0.138
EL	—[c]	—[c]	—[c]	—[c]	-0.146	0.141	-0.123	0.144
MRSH	—[c]	—[c]	—[c]	—[c]	-0.341	0.176	-0.300	0.180
NARE	—[c]	—[c]	—[c]	—[c]	0.317	0.169	0.303	0.173
Sample Size								
Teachers	1,766		1,842		1,766		1,842	
Schools	100		104		100		104	

NOTES: [a]significant at .01 level; [b]significant at .05 level; [c]excluded from the model.

School-Level Effects

Some school demographics were related to implementation, notably size, school level, poverty status, and student mobility, although the effect differed across the models. In the models where we did not control specifically for jurisdiction (models 3 and 4), characteristics of the schools appeared to be more important. Large schools had significantly lower levels of implementation (about one-fifth of a standard deviation lower). Secondary schools also reported lower levels of implementation, although the effect was significant in only one of the models. Surprisingly, high poverty schools tended to implement at a higher level than those with lower levels of poverty (about .13–.14 standard deviation higher). In models 1 and 2, the effect of poverty appeared to be largely captured by the jurisdiction dummies; the coefficient on this variable was considerably smaller in these models and not significant, compared with the results for models 3 and 4. Student mobility had a negative impact on implementation, as one would expect. Schools with higher student mobility reported levels of implementation that were about one-tenth of a standard deviation lower than those with lower student mobility.

The importance of strong principal leadership was amply borne out by the models. Schools in which teachers reported greater principal leadership had higher levels of reported implementation (between .09–.12 standard deviation higher than those that ranked lower on this index). Higher levels of resources were also positively related to implementation, although the size and significance of the effect depended critically on whether we included the principal leadership index in the model. Models with both variables tended to show smaller, nonsignificant effects for the resource index variable. This is largely due to the correlation between the principal leadership and resource availability measures. When we included one or the other, the size of the coefficients on the included variable tended to be much larger and significant. On average, schools that reported more resources for implementation (e.g., materials; professional development; time for planning, collaboration, and development; consultants to provide ongoing support; technology; and funding) had higher levels of implementation. A 1 standard deviation change in the resources index (from say 3.2 to 3.7) was related to a .06–.13 SD increase in implementation.

The school-level model was dominated by the jurisdiction effects. These were all large and mostly significant, even after controlling for school and teacher characteristics.   Compared with Memphis schools, schools in Kentucky reported implementation levels that were about four-tenths of a standard deviation higher while schools in San Antonio were about six-tenths of a standard deviation lower. Cincinnati schools were about two-tenths of a standard deviation lower in implementation than Memphis schools, while Washington schools lagged behind Memphis by about two-tenths to three-tenths of a standard deviation.   The coefficient for Washington was marginally insignificant in the second model ($t = -1.97$). The small sample size of Dade schools made it difficult to find any statistical difference between these schools and Memphis schools in terms of implementation levels, although the coefficient was quite large and negative.

The ranking implicit in the size of the coefficients in terms of implementation levels tracks well with our earlier discussion in Chapter Four where we had shown that Kentucky and Memphis ranked highest on the implementation indicators, while Philadelphia and San Antonio ranked at the bottom.   The models reinforce the importance of district and institutional factors in ensuring the success of comprehensive school reform and point to the need for a careful strategy to involve districts in any reform efforts.

We mentioned earlier that we were interested in seeing whether characteristics of designs other than those measured in our models (clear communication, teacher support, attendance at DT workshop, adequacy of resources) had an independent effect on implementation. We tested explicitly for these effects in models 3 and 4. We found the expected pattern of effects: compared with RW, the reference category, CON and NARE had somewhat higher levels of implementation, while MRSH lagged behind. These coefficients were marginally insignificant, depending on the model.

In models 3 and 4, we also included a measure of district support based on a summary measure from RAND's case study analysis of these districts (Bodilly, 1998). As expected, schools in districts that ranked one standard deviation higher on this index had implementation levels that were about one-tenth of a standard deviation higher than those in less supportive districts, and these effects were statistically significant.

We also estimated two other models that included both the jurisdiction dummies and the design team dummies (one with principal leadership, one without). These models (not shown here) were dominated by the jurisdiction effects and the results were not substantially different from those obtained from models 1 and 2. Introducing the district support variable in models with the jurisdiction dummies essentially diluted the effects of the dummies; none of these variables was significant, suggesting that they measured essentially the same characteristics and the model could not tease apart the net effects of these variables.

Goodness of Fit

The models we estimated explained a significant amount of the between-school variance in these measures. For example, while 27–28 percent of the variance in implementation lay between schools (see Table 5.3), the teacher, school, design team, and district measures considered here explained 74–82 percent of that between-school variance, depending on the model. The models without the jurisdiction dummies did somewhat less well in explaining between-school variance.

Table 5.3

Variance in Implementation Explained by the Model

	Model 1	Model 2	Model 3	Model 4
Sample				
Variance between schools (τ)	0.283	0.270	0.283	0.270
Variance within schools (σ^2)	0.708	0.720	0.708	0.720
Model				
Variance between schools (τ)	0.050	0.050	0.063	0.071
Variance within schools (σ^2)	0.550	0.558	0.551	0.558
Proportion of variance between schools explained by the model	82%	81%	78%	74%
Proportion of variance within schools explained by the model	22%	23%	22%	23%

The models were not as successful in explaining within-school variance, which has traditionally been much harder to explain. The models explained about 22–23 percent of the variance within schools, suggesting that other measures are important for explaining the differences in implementation occurring within schools.

SUMMARY

The analyses shown here further our understanding about the progress NAS schools have made in the first few years of implementation. The overall mean for the sample schools was 4.20 (SD = .58) and essentially unchanged from the 1997 mean of 4.17 (SD = .60), suggesting that schools did not improve in terms of implementation of key components from 1997 to 1998.

Teacher reports about implementation in their school differed much more within schools than between them. That is, about 72 percent of the total variance in reported implementation was *within* schools, and about 27 percent was *between* the NAS schools. We were able to explain between 74 and 82 percent of the between-school variance in our multilevel analysis but only 22–23 percent of the within-school variance.

On average, individual teacher perceptions about students' readiness to learn were positively related to implementation. However, teacher background characteristics (with the exception of black teachers) did not show robust relationships to the dependent measures when other factors were taken into account.

In terms of school characteristics, smaller schools and elementary schools had higher levels of implementation than larger and secondary schools. Higher poverty schools and those with lower student mobility had higher levels of implementation than lower poverty schools or those with higher student mobility.

The models—in terms of the magnitude and importance of the estimated coefficients—strongly underscored the importance of the following in implementation:

- A supportive district environment;
- Clear communication by design teams;

- Teacher support for designs;

- Strong principal leadership; and

- Adequacy of resources (funding for materials, professional development, assistance providers, and time).

Without leadership, support, and availability of resources at the district level; without clear communication, provision of materials and staff support, and efforts on the part of the design teams to build a consensus of teacher support; and without strong principal leadership, implementation is likely to fail or at least lag far behind. These findings are very consistent with RAND's previous case study work (Bodilly, 1998). These are sobering and important lessons for the newly launched federal CSRD program.

Chapter Six

PERFORMANCE TRENDS IN NAS SCHOOLS

As we stated at the outset, the overall mission of NAS is to help schools and districts dramatically raise the achievement levels of large numbers of students by using whole-school designs and design team assistance during the implementation process. Our aim in this report is to provide policymakers and researchers with an understanding of the early implementation and performance progress that NAS has made within the partnering jurisdictions during the scale-up phase.

To repeat, our assessment is formative, not summative. The performance trends portrayed in the pages that follow span only a few years, and several design developers and school reformers emphasize that it takes several years to expect implementation to take hold throughout the school (Sizer, 1992; Hess, 1995; Levin, 1991; Darling-Hammond, 1988, 1995, 1997). In addition, the results presented in Chapters Four and Five clearly show the wide variation in implementation both within schools and among jurisdictions and design teams. Thus, because of this variation in implementation, one should not expect robust performance results across the NAS sites. However, it is important to examine trends in performance to enable improvement.

In this chapter, we focus on one main question relating to performance trends in NAS schools:

Did NAS schools make gains in test scores relative to all schools in their respective jurisdictions?

To answer this question, we present data on trends in mathematics and reading scores for NAS schools and the associated jurisdiction for selected grades in elementary, middle, and high schools, where relevant. Because we are concerned about the variability that particular grade test scores show within a given school, we generally aggregate across NAS schools, using grade enrollment as weights. Thus, the comparisons being made are generally between NAS schools and the district or the state.[1] However, in a couple of cases, the test score information does not lend itself to aggregation. In these cases, we show trends for each NAS school in the sample.

Moreover, it is important to note that some of the designs do not specifically have curriculum and instruction materials, per se, and even some design teams that do may not have been implementing that particular design component. This should be kept in mind when examining the results that follow. However, mathematics and reading are central to improving student learning for large numbers of students. These subject area tests are also central to the accountability systems of the jurisdictions in which NAS schools are located. Thus, we focus on these two subject areas.

The fact that NAS schools began implementing at different times makes clear comparisons of gains over time difficult. Wherever possible, we show data for the baseline and baseline plus two years. For some late implementing schools, we show the baseline and baseline plus one year data. (Appendix D provides more detail on each of the tests used by the various jurisdictions.)

MONITORING ACADEMIC PROGRESS WITH SCHOOL-LEVEL TEST SCORES

As previously stated, because of resource constraints, jurisdictions' hesitancy to have additional testing, and established agreements

---

[1]The comparison we make here between NAS schools and the district averages use absolute gains. In addition, we also calculated and compared percentage gains in test scores for the NAS schools and the jurisdictions. The results were not substantially different from those presented here. Moreover, although not reported here, we compared the gains in test scores of the individual NAS schools to their past performance to see if the schools made *any* gains over time. Again, the results did not differ from those discussed in this chapter.

between NAS and the partner jurisdictions, it was not feasible in RAND's evaluation of NAS to administer a supplemental, common test to the students within the participating schools. Thus, we relied on the tests administered by the districts as part of their accountability system. While not ideal, these were the tests the jurisdictions, NAS, and the design teams expected to influence during the course of the NAS scale-up strategy. In its initial request for proposals, NAS's intent was for "break the mold schools." NAS was not interested in incremental changes that led to modest improvement in student achievement compared to conventional classrooms or schools. Rather, the achievement of students was to be measured against "world class standards" for *all* students, not merely for those most likely to succeed. Moreover, design teams were to "be explicit about the student populations they intend[ed] to serve and about how they propose[d] to raise achievement levels of 'at risk' students to world class standards" (NAS, 1991, p. 21).

If such ambitious effects on student achievement occurred, these large test score changes would be reflected in school level scores. Yet to fully understand the test score trends of NAS schools three years into scale-up, it is important to keep in mind several issues when examining school-level scores.

First, differences in achievement between schools are not nearly as great as the achievement differences within schools. For the past 30 years, a finding on student achievement that has stood the test of time is that about 15–20 percent of the student differences in achievement lie *between* schools; most of the achievement differences (80–85 percent) lie *within* schools (Coleman et al., 1966; Jencks et al., 1972; Lee and Bryk, 1989; Gamoran, 1987, 1992). Understanding the differences between schools remains critically important for making changes that maximize the effects of schools on students. However, it is also important to understand the limits of schools—no matter what the school reform—in explaining the overall differences in student achievement (Jencks et al., 1972).

Second, grade-level scores over time (e.g., 4th grade scores between 1995 and 1998) reflect the performance of different cohorts of students taking the tests. These scores are often unstable because some schools have small numbers of students taking the test in any given year, and these scores are more likely to vary from year to year with different students taking the test. Districts and states use such scores in their accountability systems, and over a longer period of time, they provide some indication of a school's performance trends.

Third, while establishing trends in the NAS schools relative to other schools within the same district is informative, it is important to remember the variety of family, school, district, and design team factors that influence these scores. Research on student achievement has consistently found that individual family background variables dominate the effects of schools and teachers (Coleman et al., 1966; Jencks et al., 1972; Gamoran, 1987, 1992), and such effects are not controlled for when describing school-level test scores. More specific information than districts typically collect or make available is necessary to understand the relative effects of these factors on student achievement.

Fourth, the ways districts report their scores to the public are not always amenable to clear interpretations over time. For example, several districts have changed their tests during the scale-up phase, and the tests in some cases have not been equated, so the test scores are not directly comparable over time. Moreover, in some instances, the form in which test score information is reported (for example, median percentile rank) makes it difficult to detect changes in the tails of the distribution. Wherever possible, we have tried to obtain specific test score information at the school level to clarify the interpretations that can be made.

Fifth, the way that we summarize school performance—comparing whether the NAS schools made gains relative to the jurisdiction—may miss some significant achievement effects that may be captured if student-level data were available and comparable across the jurisdictions. That is, our indicator will only reflect large achievement effects of designs. The data provided by the districts do not support more fine-grained analyses to understand smaller, statistically significant effects on student-level achievement scores, particularly for certain groups of students (e.g., low-income or minority students or students with limited English proficiency).

COMPARING NAS SCHOOLS TO DISTRICT AVERAGES: SETTING EXPECTATIONS

Earlier, we showed that the NAS schools in this sample were predominantly high poverty and high minority, and many faced challenges related to student mobility.[2] It could be argued that comparisons with the district average are unfair to these schools, particularly if they fail to capture smaller albeit significant achievement effects.

However, it must be pointed out that NAS and the design teams agreed to be held accountable to district assessments and to improve student learning for substantial numbers of students. Because of these expectations, NAS requested that RAND examine the progress of these NAS schools relative to the district averages to understand whether the NAS expectations of dramatic improvement were met.

SAMPLE OF NAS SCHOOLS FOR PERFORMANCE TREND ANALYSES

The sample of NAS schools for which we have data on test scores is larger than the sample of 104 schools used for the implementation analysis. Of the 184 schools in the original sample, we have data on 163 schools. Some schools were dropped from the sample because they were not implementing: This was true of the Pittsburgh schools and about 12 schools in Dade. Some of our schools were K–2 schools for which there were no testing data available, and other schools were missing data on test scores.

PERFORMANCE TRENDS IN CINCINNATI

Test scores in Cincinnati illustrate the difficulty involved in establishing performance trends over time. Figure 6.1 depicts implementa-

---

[2]When examining trends in school performance, it is important to consider the state and district accountability system (Berends and Kirby, 2000; Miller et al., 2000; Koretz and Barron, 1998). For example, different exclusion rules for special population students could result in different rates of achievement growth across jurisdictions and bias outcomes for particular groups of schools. However, the comparisons made here are between NAS schools and the jurisdiction average. Therefore, all the schools are supposed to be subject to similar testing provisions and administration.

tion in NAS schools and the change in the testing regime in Cincinnati.

The first cohort of 10 K–8 NAS schools in Cincinnati began implementing designs in the 1995–1996 school year. At that time, Cincinnati relied on the California Achievement Test (CAT) to monitor school performance. The CAT is a conventional test in that it relies on multiple choice responses to measure student performance in particular subject areas. Cincinnati Public Schools had used this version of the CAT for about a decade.

However, a year after most of the NAS schools began implementation, Cincinnati switched tests, from the CAT to the Stanford Achievement Test, Version 9. The Stanford-9, published in 1996, is a commercial test, but it relies on both multiple choice responses as well as open-ended ones so that students can provide answers and explain how they arrived at them.

This switch in tests makes it very difficult to establish trend lines in performance. The district does not equate the CAT and Stanford-9 tests over time. Thus, we are left with examining CAT trends from two years of baseline scores—before the designs began implementation—through the first year of implementation. In the spring of 1997, the tests changed, so from that point we can examine the change on the Stanford-9 between the spring of 1997 and the spring of 1998.

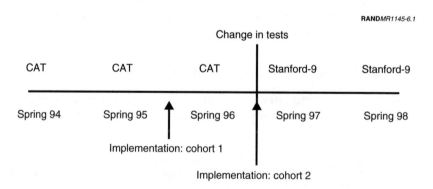

Figure 6.1—Timeline of Implementation and Change in Tests in Cincinnati NAS Schools

The second cohort of 4 NAS schools began implementing in the 1996–1997 school year. For these schools, all we have are two data points using the Stanford-9 but no baseline information. In what follows, we show the CAT scores for this second cohort merely to establish its standing relative to the district.

Grades 3–5 Combined

Figures 6.2 and 6.3 show the CAT mathematics and reading scores for grades 3–5 combined for the two aggregated NAS cohorts of schools and the district between the spring of 1994 through the spring of 1996 and the Stanford-9 scores between spring of 1997 and 1998. Note, that implementation began during the 1995–1996 school year, so for cohort 1, these charts show two years of "baseline" scores (spring 94 and spring 95) to one year after implementation. We do not have baseline data for cohort 2 because of the change in tests.

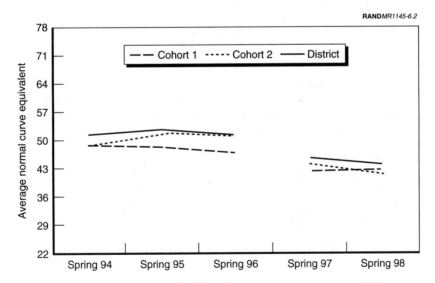

NOTE: Cohort 1 began implementing in 1995–96; cohort 2 in 1996–97.

Figure 6.2—Mean Mathematics Scores in Cincinnati: NAS Schools Compared to District, Grades 3–5 Combined

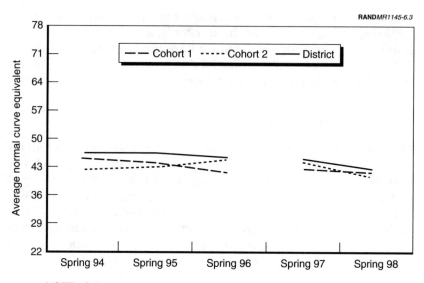

NOTE: Cohort 1 began implementing in 1995–96; cohort 2 in 1996–97.

**Figure 6.3—Mean Reading Scores in Cincinnati: NAS Schools
Compared to District, Grades 3–5 Combined**

The scores are based on aggregating the grade-level scores to the
school level. The test scores are reported as normal curve equivalents (NCEs). Essentially, this means the school test scores can be
compared to the national average of 50 (standard deviation of 21).

Cincinnati schools' scores on the CAT math and reading tests were
essentially flat between the spring of 1994 and the spring of 1996.
The district average on the CAT mathematics test was within 1–3
NCEs of the national average of 50. Note, however, that the CAT had
been used in Cincinnati for about a decade so these schools' CAT
scores may be somewhat inflated due to teaching to the test over this
time period.

Overall, scores for cohort 1 showed a very slight decline in both reading and math from the spring of 1994 to the spring of 1996, while
scores for cohort 2 increased slightly. These changes were about 2
NCEs in magnitude. (This corresponds to about one-tenth of a standard deviation using the student-level standard deviation of 21, or

two-tenths of a standard deviation using the school-level standard deviation of around 10.)

Looking at the Stanford-9 scores (spring 97–spring 98), we find that scores for the two years on the Stanford-9 were flat for cohort 1 and showed very small declines for the district and cohort 2 of about 1–2.5 NCEs.

Grade 7

Figures 6.4 and 6.5 show the test score trends for grade 7. The sample consists of 4 schools in cohort 1. There are no middle schools in cohort 2. Because we are missing data for 2 out of 4 schools for spring 1994, we show trends only from spring 1995 on.

Overall, the NAS schools ranked somewhat lower than the district. For example, in the spring of 1995, the district mean in math was 50 NCEs compared to the mean for the NAS schools of 41 NCEs. In

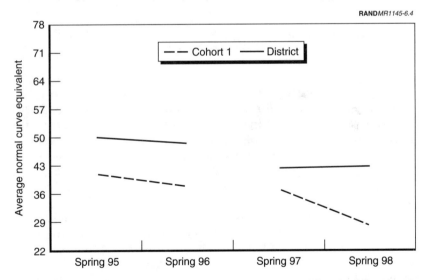

RAND*MR1145-6.4*

NOTE: Cohort 1 began implementing in 1995–96; no middle schools in cohort 2.

Figure 6.4—Mean Mathematics Scores in Cincinnati: NAS Schools Compared to District, Grade 7

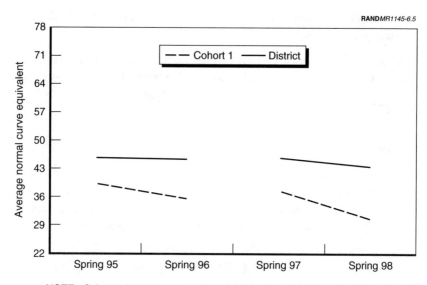

RAND*MR1145-6.5*

NOTE: Cohort 1 began implementing in 1995–96; no middle schools in cohort 2.

**Figure 6.5—Mean Reading Scores in Cincinnati: NAS Schools
Compared to District, Grade 7**

reading in the spring of 1995, the district mean was 46 NCEs compared to the mean for the NAS schools of 39 NCEs. The district experienced a small decline from spring 95 to spring 96; this was mirrored by the NAS schools. However, the NAS schools showed a rather large decline (about 9 NCEs) from the spring of 97 to the spring of 98 on the Stanford-9, while the district remained essentially unchanged.

NAS schools showed a decrease in reading scores across both tests. On the CAT, they experienced a decline of about 4 NCEs while the district scores remained flat. On the Stanford-9, they showed a decline of 7 NCEs while the district experienced a smaller decline of about 2 NCEs.

Summary for Cincinnati

Table 6.1 provides a summary of performance trends of the NAS schools in Cincinnati. It answers the question: Did NAS schools make gains in test scores relative to all schools in the jurisdiction?[3]

For this and all other summary tables shown in this chapter, we do not consider the magnitude of the change or make any judgments about the statistical significance of the change.[4]

Table 6.1

Summary of Performance Trends in NAS Schools in Cincinnati, Spring 97–Spring 98

Stanford-9	Number of Schools	Number Making Gains in Test Scores Relative to the District
Math		
Grades 3–5 combined	14	8
Grade 7	4	1
Combined	18	9
Reading		
Grades 3–5 combined	14	10
Grade 7	4	0
Combined	18	10

---

[3]If both the NAS school and the district experienced a decline in test scores, we compared the relative loss to see whether the NAS school experienced a smaller decline than the district. We also calculated a percentage gain score for the school and compared this to the percentage gain score for the jurisdiction. Because the final outcome was essentially unchanged, we do not show this here.

[4]One of our reviewers suggested using effect sizes to measure the relative performance of the school and to get some measure of the significance of the gain. This is what we had hoped to do in this analysis; unfortunately, the test score data varied across the jurisdictions and did not lend themselves easily to computing effect sizes across the variety of tests and measures. Despite asking jurisdictions for additional assessment information to compute effect sizes, only a few cooperated because of the additional burden. As a result, we were forced to use what is essentially a gross dichotomous measure of success based on whether the school did not make gains relative to the jurisdiction. This measure at least had the virtue of allowing us to compare schools across the sample.

In Table 6.1, because of the change in tests, we use the Stanford-9 and consider changes from spring 97 to spring 98.

The district experienced a small decline from spring 97 to spring 98 (–1.6 NCEs) in math in grades 3–5; over half the NAS schools made gains during that same period. When we look at grade 7, only 1 of the 4 NAS schools made gains relative to the district (which experienced a very small increase of 0.4 NCEs). Across grades in math, one-half of NAS schools made gains relative to the district and one-half made losses.

The district experienced a decline in reading scores (–2.7 NCEs) from spring 97 to spring 98 in grades 3–5. Only 2 of the 14 schools improved their grades 3–5 reading scores, but because of the district decline, 10 of the 14 made "gains" relative to the district (i.e., 8 schools had declines that were smaller than those experienced by the district). None of the NAS schools made gains relative to the district in grade 7 reading (the district made a gain of 2.1 NCEs).

Thus, overall, the picture seems quite mixed. NAS schools in Cincinnati seem to be making modest progress in the earlier grades but not with respect to students in grade 7.

PERFORMANCE TRENDS IN DADE

Dade uses the Stanford Achievement Test, version 8 (SAT-8), an earlier version than the Stanford-9 used by Cincinnati but similar in terms of being a norm- and criterion-referenced achievement test for students in kindergarten through 12th grade. We were unable to get normal curve equivalents from Dade; this would have allowed us to aggregate across NAS schools as we did in Cincinnati schools. All we have are median percentile rank scores reported for each school. This median percentile shows how the school's students at a particular grade level rank relative to a national group of students. For example, if the median percentile of 5th graders in a school on the SAT-8 is 30, then one-half of the students in that school scored at or below the 30th national percentile, and half scored above. In a national sample, we would expect only 30 percent of students to score at or below the 30th percentile. These percentile ranks do not lend themselves to aggregation; as a result, the graphs below show data on individual schools relative to the district.

Most of the NAS schools in Dade began implementing in the 1995–1996 school year, but some began implementing in the following year. We have data from the spring of 94 to the spring of 97; so for most schools, this shows trends from over a year before implementation to a year after implementation.

Grade 5

Figures 6.6 and 6.7 show the median percentiles for the five Dade elementary schools and the district. Overall, Dade schools showed significant progress on the SAT-8 math application test from spring 93 to spring 97; the median percentile rank for all Dade schools increased from 44 to 55, which was better than the national norm. All NAS schools showed large gains as well, in the range of 8–21 percentile points, with three schools showing gains larger than those of the district.

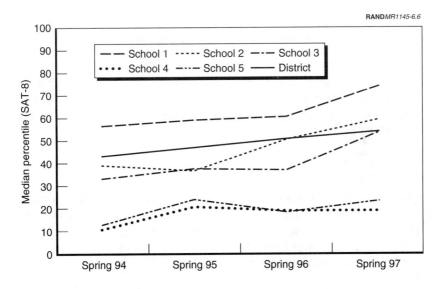

Figure 6.6—Median Percentiles for Math Application in Dade: NAS Schools Compared to the District, Grade 5

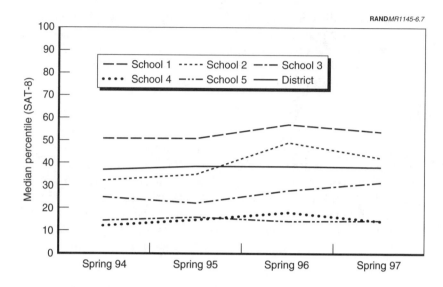

**Figure 6.7—Median Percentiles for Reading in Dade: NAS Schools
Compared to the District, Grade 5**

In terms of reading, the district scores remained essentially flat, at
around the 38th percentile. Unlike the district, four of the five NAS
schools showed some progress, increasing their median percentile
ranking by 2–11 points.

Grade 8

Figures 6.8 and 6.9 show the performance trends for grade 8 in math
application and reading. There were four NAS schools in the sample.
The district made a gain of 7 percentile points in math but showed a
small decline of about 3 percentile points in reading. Two schools of
the four NAS schools made large gains in math and one school made
gains in reading.

Grade 9

There are two NAS high schools in Dade. One of the two opened in
the 1995–1996 school year; as a result, testing data are available only
for the spring of 96 through spring 97 and only for grade 9. Figures

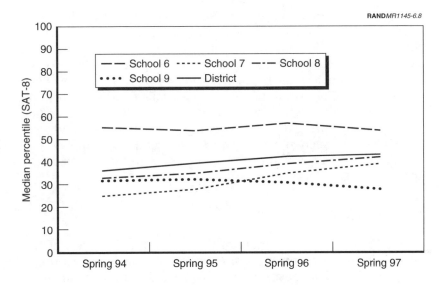

Figure 6.8—Median Percentiles for Math Application in Dade: NAS Schools Compared to District, Grade 8

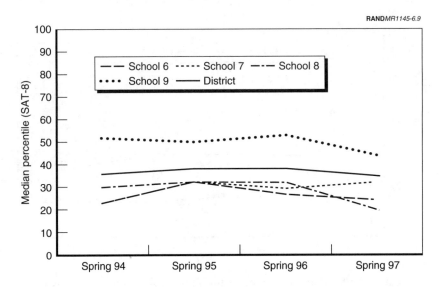

Figure 6.9—Median Percentiles for Reading in Dade: NAS Schools Compared to District, Grade 8

6.10 and 6.11 present the data for the two schools and the district for grade 9 math and reading. The older NAS school ranked below the district in terms of performance on the SAT-8 in both reading and math being at around the 15th–19th median percentile rank, compared to the district, which was at around the 35th–37th median percentile rank. The district remained essentially flat during this time period in both reading and math, although math showed a small decline in the spring of 97. One of the NAS schools showed some variability; the second school showed a decline of 6 median percentile rank points in math and an increase of 2 points in reading in the second year of its existence.

Summary for Dade

Table 6.2 presents a summary of the relative performance of NAS schools in Dade over the most recent two-year time period (spring 95 to spring 97). For most schools, this represents a comparison of baseline to baseline plus two years (for two schools, the comparison is between the baseline and baseline plus one year).

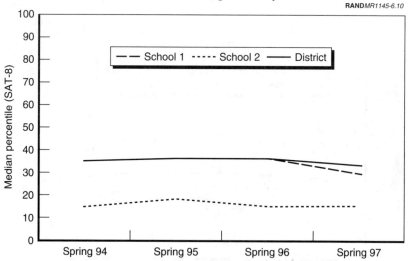

RAND*MR1145-6.10*

Figure 6.10—Median Percentiles for Math Application in Dade: NAS
Schools Compared to District, Grade 9

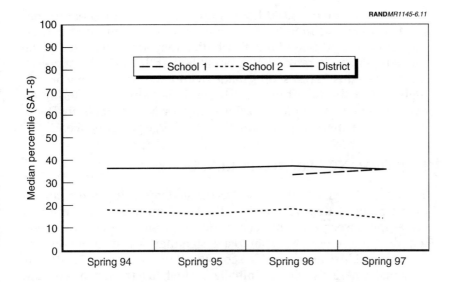

Figure 6.11—Median Percentiles for Reading in Dade: NAS Schools Compared to District, Grade 9

Table 6.2

Summary of Performance Trends in NAS Schools in Dade, Spring 95–Spring 97

SAT-8	Number of Schools	Number Making Gains in Test Scores Relative to the District
Math		
Grade 5	5	3
Grade 8	4	2
Grade 9[a]	2	1
Combined	11	6
Reading		
Grade 5	5	2
Grade 8	4	1
Grade 9[a]	2	1
Combined	11	4

NOTE: [a] For one of the high schools, this represents a one-year change, from spring 96 to spring 97.

Note that the metric used here is not directly comparable to that used to assess schools in Cincinnati. As we mentioned earlier, movements in the tails of the distribution may not be reflected in the median percentile rank, so it is possible that this metric underestimates the gains in test scores made by those at the very low or very high end of the distribution. The table is helpful in offering an overall picture of student performance in NAS schools in Dade, based on the metric used by the district to judge performance.

PERFORMANCE TRENDS IN KENTUCKY

The NARE design was the only NAS design team being implemented in the State of Kentucky during the scale-up phase. During this scale-up phase, NARE changed its design from an educational system design (see Bodilly, 1998) to a design that focused more on curriculum and instruction inside schools. With this change, NARE was renamed America's Choice. Initially, NARE had a team that provided assistance to the NARE schools across the 16 districts in the state. After the 1996–1997 school year, this assistance diminished dramatically because the key staff of the NARE team was promoted within the Kentucky State Department of Education to improve curriculum and instruction throughout the state. Yet even with these changes in the NARE design and the assistance provided in Kentucky, principals continued to report that they were implementing the components of the original NARE design. During our phone interviews, principals emphasized that the NARE design fit well with the KERA reform in Kentucky and provided a useful tool for meeting KERA demands. Thus, RAND continued to monitor the progress of the NARE sites in Kentucky that continued their implementation even without the direct assistance provided by NARE.

Between 1992 and 1998, Kentucky relied on test scores from the Kentucky Instructional Results Information System (KIRIS) for the state's accountability purposes. The KIRIS was administered to multiple grade levels. Kentucky began by administering subject area tests in grades 4, 8, and 12. Depending on the subject area, the KIRIS tests contained several components, including multiple choice items, open-ended paper and pencil items, performance events, and portfolio assessment. Kentucky published scores using the KIRIS cognitive index for each tested subject area. This index ranges from 0 to 140, where "novices" are given a score of 0, "apprentices" a score of 40, "proficient" a score of 100, and "distinguished" a score of 140.

Over time, the KIRIS subject area tests and test administration to student groups have been modified substantially. The multiple choice items were dropped from the assessment in the spring of 1995 and 1996 because of the desire for performance-based assessments. However, the multiple choice component of the KIRIS was restored in the spring of 1997. Second, testing of mathematics, reading, science, and social studies shifted from the 12th to the 11th grade in 1995. Third, the administration of tests also changed across grades in order to reduce testing burden on students. Thus, in 1997, the elementary school and middle school assessments were each split between two grades. Since 1997, reading and science have been assessed in grades 4 and 7, while mathematics and social studies have been assessed in grades 5 and 8. Prior to 1997, all assessments were in grades 4 and 8.

Despite the changes that have occurred to the KIRIS and some of the problems in establishing valid test score trends, Kentucky has awarded tens of millions of dollars to schools based on their test score gains according to the KIRIS indices. When considering the evidence presented here, it is important to keep in mind that this kind of high stakes testing inevitably leads to inflated gains. (For more information on the validity of KIRIS gains, see Koretz and Barron, 1998).

Because the NARE schools in Kentucky began implementing at various times, we grouped them into four cohorts based on their implementation dates. Table 6.3 shows the number of schools in each cohort by school level and the year of implementation.

Grades 4–5

Figures 6.12 and 6.13 show the trends in mean student test scores based on the KIRIS index for math for grades 4–5 and reading for grade 4. Recall that math testing was shifted to grade 5 in 1997; hence the break in the trend line in Figure 6.12. NAS schools are compared to the state for two reasons: the KIRIS is a statewide assessment and the schools span 16 different school districts, many

Table 6.3

Cohorts of NAS Schools in Kentucky

Cohort	Date of Implementation	Number of Schools
Cohort 1	1993–94	13
Elementary Schools		5
Middle Schools		4
High Schools		4
Cohort 2	1994–95	3
Elementary Schools		1
Middle Schools		0
High Schools		2
Cohort 3	1995–96	15
Elementary Schools		6
Middle Schools		6
High Schools		3
Cohort 4	1996–97	20
Elementary Schools		12
Middle Schools		4
High Schools		4

with one or two schools, so small sample sizes in each district were a problem.

Regardless of whether we look at grade 4 or grade 5 math, both NAS schools and the state made substantial gains over time. Because this is a high-stakes test, one needs to be cautious in attributing all these gains to either real increases in student learning or the NAS design (Koretz and Barron, 1998). The state gained almost 17 points on the math KIRIS index from spring 93 to spring 96 in grade 4 and remained flat in terms of grade 5 math scores from spring 97 to spring 98. All the NAS cohorts posted equally impressive gains, ranging from 13–41 points; cohort 3, which was well below the state in the spring of 93, was well above the state average by spring 96. However, the large gains for this cohort occurred between spring 93 and spring 95, the year before implementation. Unlike the state, all the NAS cohorts continued to show gains of between 5–15 points in grade 5 math from spring 97 to spring 98.

The trends are similar in reading. The state showed an impressive gain of 26 points in grade 4 reading over this six-year period, but the NAS cohorts did even better. For 3 of the 4 cohorts, the gains were *larger* than the state average. Indeed, cohort 3 showed an incredible

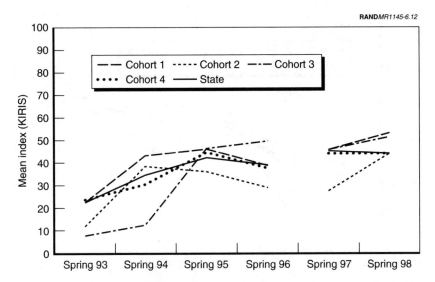

RAND*MR1145-6.12*

NOTE: Cohort 1 implementation: 1993–94; cohort 2 implementation: 1994–95; cohort 3 implementation: 1995–96; cohort 4 implementation: 1996–97.

Figure 6.12—Mean KIRIS Math Scores in Kentucky: NAS Schools Compared to the State, Grades 4–5

gain of 50 points, starting from a low of 14.2 in spring 93 to 64.3 by the spring of 98, but the real gains were experienced the spring prior to implementation.

Grades 7–8

Kentucky made substantial gains in grade 8 math; the state average was about 29 points over the six-year period, as shown in Figure 6.14. The gains made by the NAS schools were equally impressive: 23–36 points on average. Most of the gains were made early in the period: from spring 93 to spring 95.

The change in test administration in reading is reflected in the break in the trend lines in Figure 6.15; testing shifted from grade 8 to grade 7 by the spring of 1997. The gains were considerably smaller when we examined grade 8 scores from spring 93 to spring 96. The state made a gain of about 7 points; all the NAS schools did better, posting

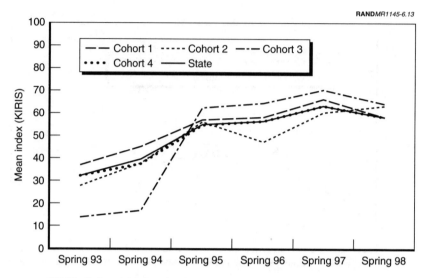

RAND*MR1145-6.13*

NOTE: Cohort 1 implementation: 1993–94; cohort 2 implementation: 1994–95; cohort 3 implementation: 1995–96; cohort 4 implementation: 1996–97.

Figure 6.13—Mean KIRIS Reading Scores in Kentucky: NAS Schools Compared to the State, Grade 4

gains of between 10–12 points. However, the scores for grade 7 math showed small declines for the state of about 2 points and somewhat larger declines for NAS schools.

Grade 11

There were four high schools in cohorts 1 and 4, two in cohort 2 and three in cohort 3. Figures 6.16 and 6.17 depict the trends in test scores for grade 11 in these high schools relative to the state from spring 95 to spring 98. (We omit the earlier years because test administration changed from grade 12 to grade 11 in 1995). Three of the four cohorts were above the state average in spring 95. Math scores remained essentially flat during this time period with some fluctuations both in the state and in NAS schools.

The picture is quite different when we look at trends in reading for grade 11. Here the state as a whole gained almost 18 points over this

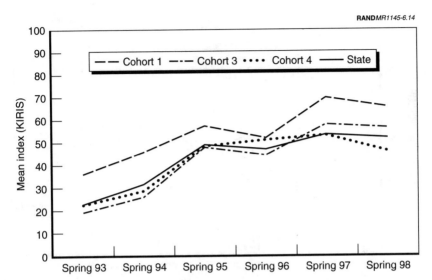

NOTE: Cohort 1 implementation: 1993–94; cohort 2 (no middle schools); cohort 3 implementation: 1995–96; cohort 4 implementation: 1996–97.

Figure 6.14—Mean KIRIS Math Scores in Kentucky: NAS Schools Compared to the State, Grade 8

four-year period; this was matched (and in some cases more than matched) by most NAS schools.

Summary for Kentucky

Summarizing these various trends in a table is complicated for several reasons. First, because of the different times that NAS schools began implementing NAS designs, it would not be "fair" to compare test scores say from 1996 to 1998 for all schools because some had been implementing for several years by this time. We decided that one way of keeping the playing field level would be to compare the relative performance of schools from baseline to baseline plus two years—i.e., examining NAS schools when they each had been implementing for two years. Second, the problem was exacerbated by the change in tests across grades. For example, for cohorts 3 and 4, we had no baseline against which to compare these schools because

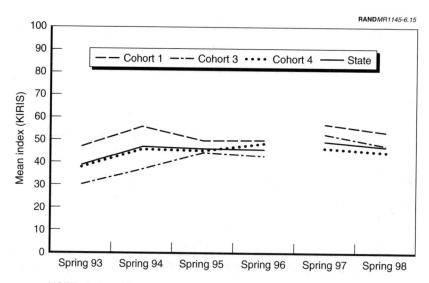

NOTE: Cohort 1 implementation: 1993–94; cohort 2 (no middle schools); cohort 3 implementation: 1995–96; cohort 4 implementation: 1996–97.

Figure 6.15—Mean KIRIS Reading Scores in Kentucky: NAS Schools Compared to the State, Grades 7–8

of the change in tests. For these cohorts, we use the change in scores from spring 97 to spring 98, a one-year rather than a two-year change. Third, because the actual time period over which the schools are being compared in real time is different, the comparisons become somewhat suspect if there are exogenous factors that affect achievement in different school years and they vary across years. Despite this, we believe it is useful to attempt to summarize our findings with respect to performance trends in Kentucky, just to give an overall picture as we did with the other jurisdictions. However, these several cautions need to be kept in mind when looking at Table 6.4.

Summarizing trends in this manner rather than aggregating schools into cohorts shows that the picture is more mixed than one would have thought, based on the cohort analyses. The table shows NAS schools did relatively well in improving math scores. Sixty percent of NAS schools made gains over the two-year time period; of these,

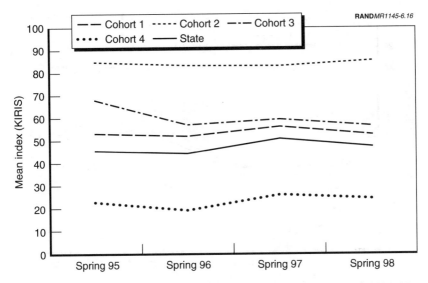

NOTE: Cohort 1 implementation: 1993–94; cohort 2 implementation: 1994–95; cohort 3 implementation: 1995–96; cohort 4 implementation: 1996–97.

Figure 6.16—Mean KIRIS Math Scores in Kentucky: NAS Schools Compared to the State, Grade 11

almost all showed gains larger than or equal to those of the state. In reading, we find that somewhat less than half of the schools experienced gains over time but these 22 schools progressed at a faster pace than the state.

PERFORMANCE TRENDS IN MEMPHIS[5]

Memphis has used the Comprehensive Test of Basic Skills, version 4 (CTBS/4) since 1990. This is a commercial multiple choice test that measures skills in reading, mathematics, and other subject areas. In the spring of 1998, Memphis adopted the CTBS/5 Complete Battery

---

[5]We are indebted to Steven Ross of The University of Memphis and William Sanders of The University of Tennessee for making these data available to us. We thank Steven Ross for many useful discussions and for his patience with our questions regarding the meaning and interpretation of the Tennessee Value-Added Assessment System (TVAAS).

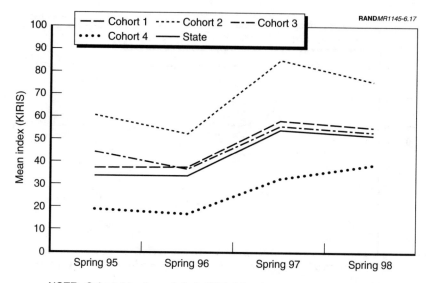

NOTE: Cohort 1 implementation: 1993–94; cohort 2 implementation: 1994–95; cohort 3 implementation: 1995–96; cohort 4 implementation: 1996–97.

Figure 6.17—Mean KIRIS Reading Scores in Kentucky: NAS Schools Compared to the State, Grade 11

Table 6.4

Summary of Performance Trends in NAS Schools in Kentucky, Baseline to Baseline Plus Two Years

KIRIS	Number of Schools	Number Making Gains in Test Scores Relative to the District
Math		
Grades 4–5	24	17
Grade 8	14	5
Grade 11	13	8
Combined	51	30
Reading		
Grade 4	24	10
Grades 7–8	14	4
Grade 11	13	8
Combined	51	22

Plus (Terra Nova). This latter version of the CTBS as tailored to the state of Tennessee is also multiple choice but concentrates on higher order thinking skills to a greater extent than the previous CTBS/4, and scores have been equated across the two tests. Produced by CTB/McGraw-Hill, both forms of the test contain items developed specifically for students in the State of Tennessee.

Tennessee has a sophisticated testing and assessment program called the Tennessee Value-Added Assessment System (TVAAS), which enables tracking of the academic progress of every student in the state in grades 3–8 and beyond (as high school testing is implemented) in science, math, social studies, language arts, and reading (see Sanders and Horn (1994, 1995) for more details on this system and the methodology used to measure student progress). TVAAS reports annually on the gains that students have made in each grade and each subject grouped by achievement levels. These reports have information on the three most recent years as well as the three-year average gains. The state monitors all school systems that are not achieving national norm gains; those systems "achieving two or more standard errors below the national norms must show positive progress or risk intervention by the state. Each school and system is expected to achieve the national norm gains regardless of whether its scale scores are above or below the national norm" (Sanders and Horn, 1994, p. 302).

The raw data for TVAAS are the scaled scores from the CTBS/4 and now CTBS/5, which form a part of the Tennessee Comprehensive Assessment Program (TCAP). All students in grades 2 through 8 are tested yearly; this information is linked to the school and the teacher by subject area and grade. The longitudinal nature of the data allows each student to serve as his or her own "control." TVAAS uses statistical mixed-model methodology to estimate a multivariate, longitudinal model of student achievement and then to aggregate these data to the classroom or the school level. The gain scores of a school's students are estimated and compared to the national norms. Thus, deviations from the national norms can be calculated to see how the school is doing with respect to a national sample of students.

The index of student achievement used in the analyses is the Cumulative Percent of Norm mean (CPN). This measures the percent of national (expected) gain attained by the school in the reported grades (Bratton, Horn, and Wright, 1996). For example, if a school had a CPN equal to 75 percent in fifth grade reading, then the average gain of the fifth grade students in the school was .75 of the expected year-to-year gain based on a national sample.

Grades 3–5

Relying on the TVAAS, earlier reports have provided an analysis of the achievement results in the Memphis restructuring schools, most of which were implementing NAS designs and also non-NAS designs such as Accelerated Schools and Paideia (Ross et al., 1998; Ross et al., 1999b).

Here we show results for two cohorts of NAS schools: cohort 1, which consisted of 20 elementary and 4 secondary schools, began implementing in the 1995–1996 school year; cohort 2 (4 elementary and 2 secondary schools), the following year. Figure 6.18 presents the mean CPN in math for the two cohorts and the district and state for grades 3–5 combined. In 1995, cohort 1 schools were about 8

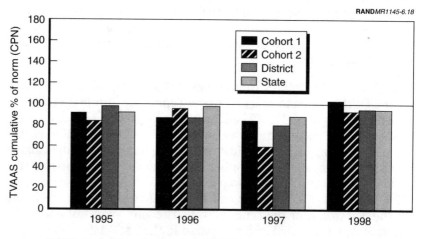

NOTE: Cohort 1 implementation: 1995–96; cohort 2 implementation: 1996–97.

Figure 6.18—Mean Math Cumulative Percent of Norm (CPN) in Memphis: NAS Schools Compared to the District and State, Grades 3–5

CPN points below the district and cohort 2 schools were about 15 CPN points below. The district was close to the national norm. By the spring of 1997, cohort 1 schools were outperforming the district by about 4 CPN points, and there is a large difference in 1998, with NAS schools above the national norm (103.5), while the district was close to 96 percent of the national norm. Cohort 2 lagged behind in 1997 (CPN equal to 60.7), but by 1998 it was close to the district CPN.

In terms of reading, NAS schools outperformed the district and state in 1995, but all NAS schools posted declines in 1996 (see Figure 6.19). By 1998, both cohorts of NAS schools had a CPN of 97–98, higher than the district mean CPN of 88.7 and a little lower than the state mean of 101.8.

Grades 7–8

The small sizes of the secondary school cohorts make these data somewhat more variable than the aggregations across elementary grades. Figures 6.20 and 6.21 show the results for secondary schools for grades 7–8 combined for the two subject areas. In 1995, cohort 1

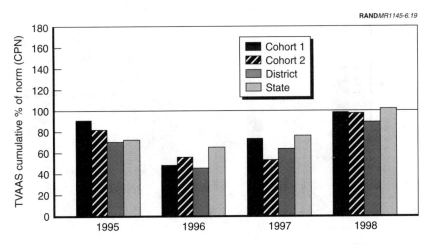

RAND*MR1145-6.19*

NOTE: Cohort 1 implementation: 1995–96; cohort 2 implementation: 1996–97.

Figure 6.19—Mean Reading Cumulative Percent of Norm (CPN) in Memphis: NAS Schools Compared to the District and State, Grades 3–5

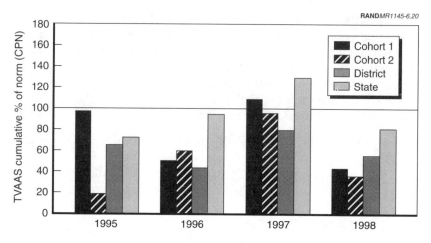

NOTE: Cohort 1 implementation: 1995–96; cohort 2 implementation: 1996–97.

Figure 6.20—Mean Math Cumulative Percent of Norm in Memphis: NAS Schools Compared to the District and State, Grades 7–8

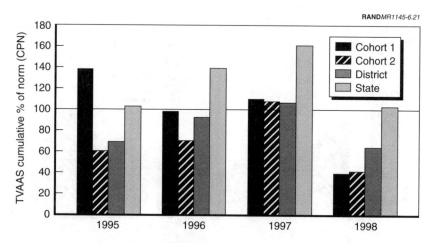

NOTE: Cohort 1 implementation: 1995–96; cohort 2 implementation: 1996–97.

Figure 6.21—Mean Reading Cumulative Percent of Norm in Memphis: NAS Schools Compared to the District and State, Grades 7–8

schools did considerably better than the district in math (CPN equal to 97.5 and 67.1, respectively) while the two schools of cohort 2 posted gains equal to only 20 percent of the national norm. By 1997, all groups had improved and the NAS schools showed gains that were 29 CPN points above the district average of 81. Cohort 2 also showed a gain of 16.8 CPN points above the district. The state posted gains well above the national norm with a CPN equal to 130.5. The 1998 scores were surprising: all schools—NAS, district, and state—showed a marked decline with CPNs equal to 45.2, 37.6, 56.5, and 82.7, respectively.

The results for reading are equally variable. Cohort 1 schools experienced considerably higher gains than the district in 1995 (CPN of 138.4 and 69.4, respectively) while cohort 2 schools were a little lower than the district (CPN equal to 61.7). By the spring of 1997, the district was above the national norm as were NAS schools. Both cohorts were slightly higher than the district mean CPN of 107.6. The state as a whole posted extraordinarily high gains in both 1996 and 1997. By 1998, the data showed the same large decline in reading achievement as we had seen in math. NAS schools were well below the district with a CPN average of 41.2, compared to the district CPN of 64.6.

Summary for Memphis

Table 6.5 provides a summary of two-year changes in performance for the NAS schools relative to the district. For cohort 1, we used relative changes between the schools and the district between spring 95 to spring 97; for cohort 2, we used relative changes between spring 96 to spring 98. For each, we compared these changes to the change in the district over the relevant time period. Among the 30 NAS schools, a little over half made gains in math relative to the district over the two-year time period; 11 of the 30 schools made gains in reading.

Ross et al.(1998, 1999b) provide a careful examination of the relative performance of restructuring elementary schools in Memphis from 1995 to 1998. They compare gains in the restructuring schools on the TCAP to nonrestructuring (NR) elementary schools and the state. Their results show that cohort 1 schools significantly outperformed other elementary schools across all subjects averaged in the second year of implementation; indeed, the difference was 10.9 CPN points.

Table 6.5

Summary of Performance Trends in NAS Schools in
Memphis, Baseline to Baseline Plus Two Years

TVAAS	Number of Schools	Number Making Gains in Test Scores Relative to the District
Math		
Grades 3–5	24	13
Grades 7–8	6	3
Combined	30	16
Reading		
Grades 3–5	24	8
Grades 7–8	6	3
Combined	30	11

Cohort 2 did not show the same advantage in the second year of implementation. By 1998, both cohort 1 (in year 3 of implementation) and cohort 2 schools (in year 2 of implementation) demonstrated "small, nonsignificant advantages over the NR schools." (Ross et al., 1999b, p. 3). An additional important finding is that higher poverty schools appeared to derive the greatest benefits from these reforms. The authors' overall conclusion is that although the effects have varied by year and by cohort, restructuring has been successful in raising achievement in elementary schools in Memphis.

The data we show here for math and reading for elementary schools are somewhat different from Ross et al. (1998, 1999b) for several reasons. First, we compare the NAS schools to the district, and they compare the NAS school designs to "nonrestructured" schools between 1995 and 1998. Second, Ross et al. also include some non-NAS schools in their analyses. Third, to be consistent with what we have done for other jurisdictions, we compare Memphis NAS schools to the district using base year of implementation to two years after implementation. Had we used the 1998 results for cohort 1, our results would have looked more similar to Ross et al. Fourth, we also examine secondary schools, where the picture seems somewhat more mixed: It varies by year, and the most recent year is the least encouraging, with NAS schools well below the district average.

PERFORMANCE TRENDS IN PHILADELPHIA

Since the spring of 1996, Philadelphia has relied on the Stanford Achievement Test, version 9 (Stanford-9), which is also used in Cincinnati. Nineteen NAS schools also began implementation in Philadelphia in the 1995–1996 school year. The results here are presented as changes in normal curve equivalents (NCEs) between the spring of 1996 and 1997. Recall that NCE scores can be compared to the national average of 50 (standard deviation of 21 at the student level and around 8–10 at the school level).

Grade 4

In both reading and math, the district and NAS schools made small gains over the two-year time period for which we have data: spring 96 to spring 98.

In 1996, the district mean on the math Stanford-9 was about 35 NCEs, which was 15 NCEs below the national average (see Figure 6.22). By 1998, the district had gained about 4 NCEs. NAS schools started out slightly above the district mean at 37 NCEs, and by 1998 they had gained 1.5 NCEs.

In reading, both the district mean and the mean for NAS schools were 40 NCEs in 1996 (see Figure 6.23). By 1998, the district gained 4.5 NCEs and the NAS schools gained 5 NCEs.

Grade 8

Figures 6.24 and 6.25 show the results for grade 8. Essentially, there was little change over this time period. In math, NAS schools were above the district by 3.7 NCEs in the spring of 1996; by the spring of 1998, the district made a small gain of about 2 NCEs while NAS schools showed a very slight decline of 1.4 points. In reading, both the district and NAS schools had a mean of 44 NCEs in the spring of 1996. NAS schools posted a small gain of 2 points while the district increased its mean by 1 NCE.

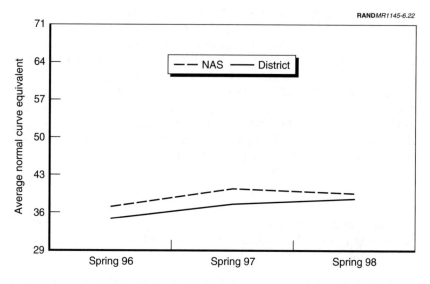

Figure 6.22—Mean Mathematics Scores in Philadelphia: NAS Schools Compared to the District, Grade 4

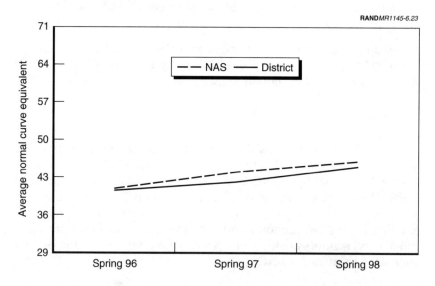

Figure 6.23—Mean Reading Scores in Philadelphia: NAS Schools Compared to the District, Grade 4

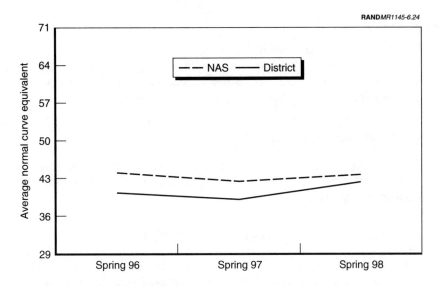

Figure 6.24—Mean Mathematics Scores in Philadelphia: NAS Schools Compared to the District, Grade 8

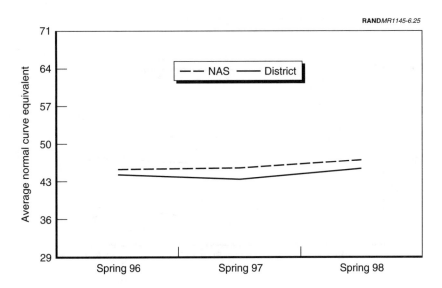

Figure 6.25—Mean Reading Scores in Philadelphia: NAS Schools Compared to the District, Grade 8

Grade 11

The one NAS high school in Philadelphia was well below the district mean (by about 10 NCEs in math and 8 NCEs in reading), as shown in Figures 6.26 and 6.27. In both subjects, student performance remained flat.

Summary for Philadelphia

Table 6.6 provides a summary of performance trends in NAS schools in Philadelphia. Seven out of 19 NAS schools did better than the district in math and 11 in reading.

PERFORMANCE TRENDS IN SAN ANTONIO

All Texas schools use the Texas Assessment of Academic Skills (TAAS), a norm- and criterion-referenced achievement assessment for students in the 3rd–8th grade or exiting high school. The TAAS reports the "percent passing" in each subject. To pass the TAAS,

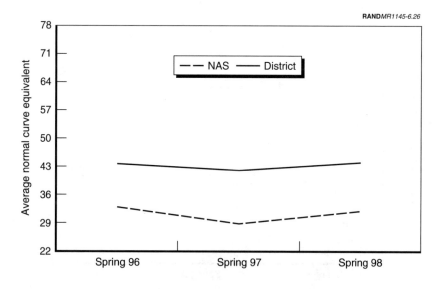

Figure 6.26—Mean Mathematics Scores in Philadelphia: NAS Schools Compared to the District, Grade 11

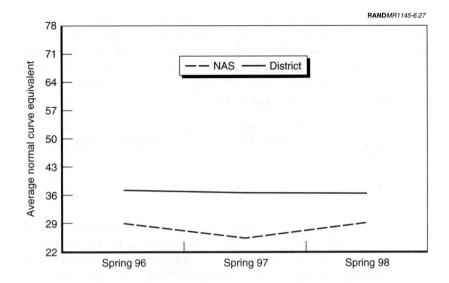

RAND*MR1145-6.27*

**Figure 6.27—Mean Reading Scores in Philadelphia: NAS Schools
Compared to the District, Grade 11**

Table 6.6

**Summary of Performance Trends in NAS Schools
in Philadelphia, Spring 96 to Spring 98**

Stanford-9	Number of Schools	Number Making Gains in Test Scores Relative to the District
Math		
Grade 4	12	4
Grade 8	6	3
Grade 11	1	0
Combined	19	7
Reading		
Grade 4	12	7
Grade 8	6	3
Grade 11	1	1
Combined	19	11

students generally have to get at least 70 percent of the items correct. The "percent passing" standard represents the minimum acceptable passing standard as established by the state. While the items differ from year to year, the state equates the scores across the years, and they continue to require that students get 70 percent of the items on the test correct to obtain a passing mark.

There are eight elementary schools, two middle schools, and two high schools in San Antonio that began implementing NAS designs by the 1996–1997 school year.

Grades 4–5

We show results for grades 4 and 5 combined from spring 1995 to spring 1998—i.e., two years before to two years after implementation. As Figures 6.28 and 6.29 show, NAS schools were at the district standard in the spring of 1995 in both math and reading but well below the state average. San Antonio schools, including NAS schools, made remarkable gains over the four-year time period. NAS schools posted gains of about 25 percentage points in math from spring 1995

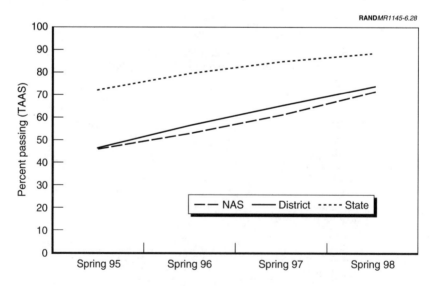

Figure 6.28—Mean Mathematics Scores in San Antonio: NAS Schools
Compared to the District and State, Grades 4–5

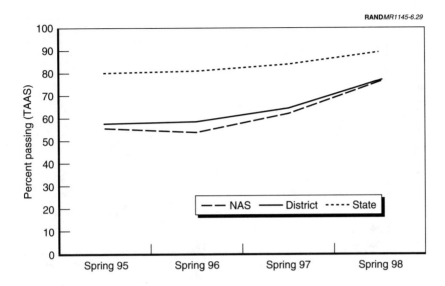

**Figure 6.29—Mean Reading Scores in San Antonio: NAS Schools
Compared to the District and State, Grades 4–5**

to spring 1998 as did the district; in reading, the gains were somewhat smaller but equally impressive, about 20 points. Both the NAS
schools and the district substantially narrowed the gap with the state
in both subjects. For example, in the spring of 1995, San Antonio
schools were 25 percentage points below the state in math; by spring
1998, the gap had narrowed to roughly 15 percentage points.

Grade 8

Compared to the state average of about 60 percent passing in 1995,
both the NAS schools and the district lagged well behind in grade 8
math with passing rates of only 17 percent and 28 percent, respectively (see Figure 6.30). By 1998, NAS schools had gained 30
percentage points, while the district gained 33 percentage points,
somewhat higher than the average gain in the state of 27 percentage
points. In reading, there was a substantial gap between San Antonio
schools and the state of about 20 percentage points in 1995 (see
Figure 6.31). NAS schools were even farther behind the state with a

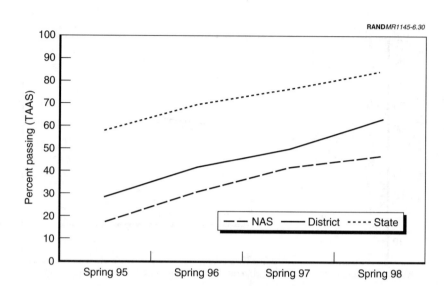

Figure 6.30—Mean Mathematics Scores in San Antonio: NAS Schools
Compared to the District and State, Grade 8

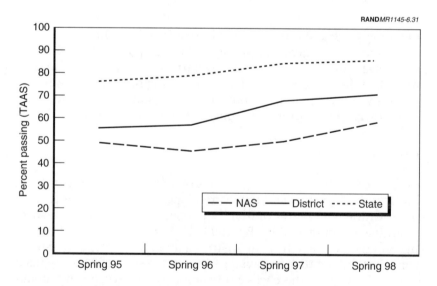

Figure 6.31—Mean Reading Scores in San Antonio: NAS Schools
Compared to the District and State, Grade 8

gap of 33 percentage points. The gains in reading were smaller than those in math; the district made gains relative to the state (15 versus 10 percentage points), while NAS schools gained around 9 points.

Grade 10

Figures 6.32 and 6.33 show similar lags between San Antonio and Texas schools in performance on grade 10 tests in spring 1995. NAS schools had a passing rate of 24 percent in math compared to the state average of 60 percent; district schools were somewhat better than NAS schools at 35 percent (see Figure 6.32). NAS schools showed the greatest gain of 30 percentage points by spring 1998, compared to a district gain of 24 points and a state gain of 18 points.

Schools were generally performing better in reading than in math with around 55–60 percent of San Antonio students passing the TAAS in the spring of 1995 (see Figure 6.33). The state average was considerably higher, 76 percent. NAS and the San Antonio district schools had made substantial progress by spring 1998; about 70 percent of 10th graders in NAS schools and 78 percent in the district passed the

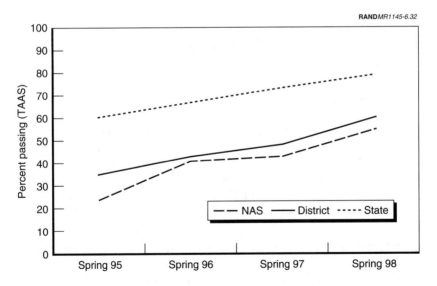

RAND*MR1145-6.32*

Figure 6.32—Mean Mathematics Scores in San Antonio: NAS Schools Compared to the District and State, Grade 10

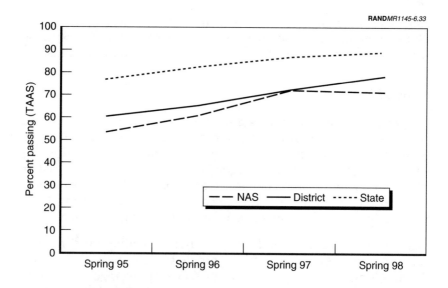

**Figure 6.33—Mean Reading Scores in San Antonio: NAS Schools
Compared to the District and State, Grade 10**

TAAS. This amounted to a gain of 18 percentage points over the
four-year time period. The state made a smaller gain of 12 percentage points.

Summary for San Antonio

Table 6.7 provides a summary of these trends, using data from the
most recent two-year period to assess progress in NAS schools. Although almost all of the NAS schools made gains over time, the district made substantial progress as well. Compared with the district, 4
NAS schools (out of a total of 12) made greater gains in math and 7
made such gains in reading.

PERFORMANCE TRENDS IN WASHINGTON

The Washington State Assessment Program collects information
about student achievement in grades 4, 8, and 11. Students in grades
4 and 8 were tested in the fall of 1991–1997 using the Comprehensive

Table 6.7

**Summary of Performance Trends in NAS Schools
in San Antonio, Spring 96 to Spring 98**

TAAS	Number of Schools	Number Making Gains in Test Scores Relative to the District
Math		
Grade 4	8	4
Grade 8	2	0
Grade 10	2	0
Combined	12	4
Reading		
Grade 4	8	6
Grade 8	2	1
Grade 10	2	0
Combined	12	7

Tests of Basic Skills, 4th edition (CTBS/4) and students in grade 11 were tested with the Curriculum Frameworks Assessment System (CFAS). The CTBS/4 and CFAS require students to read and apply their knowledge critically and to solve problems with multiple steps.

In 1998, new basic skills achievement tests were selected for use in grades 3, 8, and 11: Iowa Tests of Basic Skills, Form M (ITBS) and Iowa Tests of Educational Development, Form M (ITED). These were administered for the first time in the spring of 1999. Although Washington State will continue to publish both the ITBS/ITED and the CTBS/CFAS results for the next few years, they warn that adding the ITBS/ITED results to the CTBS/CFAS trend line would be inappropriate and misleading because of the differences between the tests and the norming populations.

For each school and district, a mean percentile score (percentile equivalent of the mean NCE) is reported. This measures the percentage of students in the national (grades 4 and 8) or Washington State (grade 11) norm group whose scores are lower than the average score for the school or the district. The score of the average student in both the national and Washington State norm groups is always 50 for all subtests. Unfortunately, as we said earlier, these mean percentile scores do not lend themselves to aggregation across schools. As such, in what follows, we report trends for each individual school from fall 1995 to fall 1997, the latest year for which the CTBS/CFAS data are available.

There were 24 schools that were implementing NAS designs in the 1996–1997 school year, spread across three districts in the Seattle area. Because we compared each school to its own district, this added up to a large number of graphs (two subjects, three grade levels, four districts); as a result, we show the mathematics results in the main body of the report and present the reading results in Appendix E.

Grade 4

Figures 6.34–6.36 present the median percentile scores for grade 4 for each of the NAS schools in the three districts in the Seattle area: Everett, Northshore, and Shoreline. In Everett, the district gained about 7 percentile points from the fall of 1994 to the fall of 1997. Three of the NAS schools were below the district average in 1995. The schools displayed year-to-year variability; over the four-year time period, these schools either remained flat or made small gains

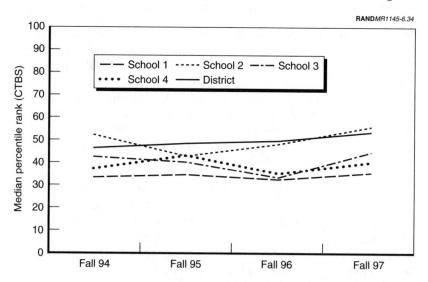

Figure 6.34—Mean Percentile Mathematics Scores in Everett: NAS Schools Compared to the District, Grade 4

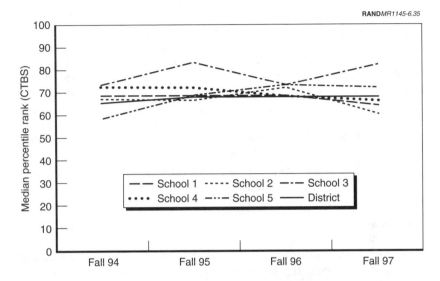

Figure 6.35—Mean Percentile Mathematics Scores in Northshore: NAS Schools Compared to the District, Grade 4

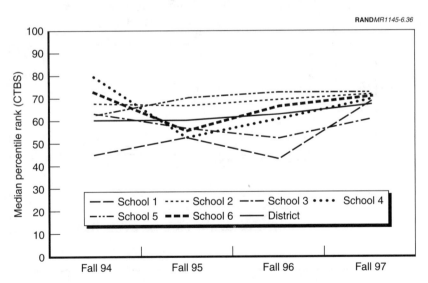

Figure 6.36—Mean Percentile Mathematics Scores in Shoreline: NAS Schools Compared to the District, Grade 4

of 2–3 percentile points. The Northshore schools were at or above the district average in 1994. Between 1994 and 1997, the district gained 11 percentile points; three schools showed gains over this time period, with gains of between 1 and 19 percentile points. The Shoreline district made gains of 7 percentile points from 1994 to 1997; three of the six schools made gains of between 4 and 22 percentile points over this time period.

Figures E.1 through E.3 in the appendix present the corresponding results for reading. Scores tended to be more flat in reading than in math in the districts over the four-year time period; the schools also were largely flat, with a great deal of year to year variation.

Grade 8

The 8th grade mathematics scores are presented in Figures 6.37 through 6.39. Everett and Northshore made gains of 7–8 percentile points between 1994 and 1997 while Shoreline showed a decline of 4 points. Several of the NAS schools made small gains of between 3 and 7 percentile points over the same time period. In reading

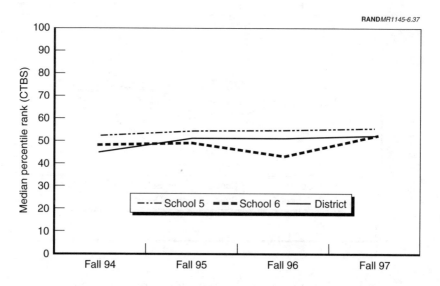

Figure 6.37—Mean Percentile Mathematics Scores in Everett: NAS
Schools Compared to the District, Grade 8

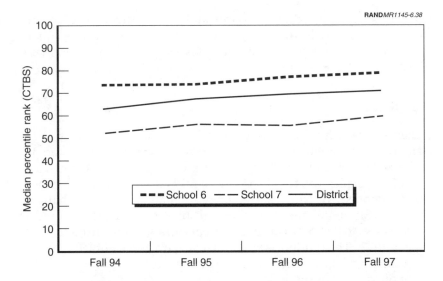

Figure 6.38—Mean Percentile Mathematics Scores in Northshore: NAS
Schools Compared to the District, Grade 8

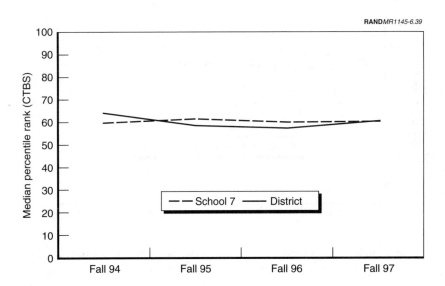

Figure 6.39—Mean Percentile Mathematics Scores in Shoreline: NAS
Schools Compared to the District, Grade 8

(Figures E.4 through E.6 in the appendix), the district scores remained essentially unchanged while the NAS schools were equally divided between those making small losses (–2 to –7) and somewhat larger gains (+3 to +12).

Grade 11

There are four high schools in the NAS sample: two in Northshore and two in Shoreline (these are the only two high schools in the district, so comparisons with the district are not possible). Figures 6.40 and 6.41 display the trends on the CFAS mathematics test for these high schools. In Northshore, scores remained fairly unchanged, while in Shoreline, the two schools displayed a downward trend in test scores, losing between 12 and 16 percentile points from fall 1994 to fall 1997. The results for English language arts resembled the math trends (Figures F.7 and F.8), although the decline in the Shoreline schools was not as marked.

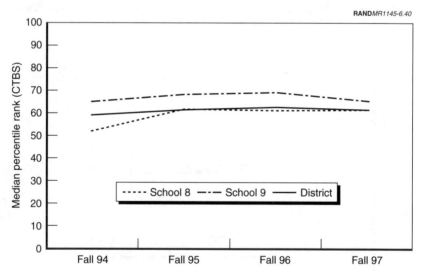

Figure 6.40—Mean Percentile Mathematics Scores in Northshore: NAS Schools Compared to the District, Grade 11

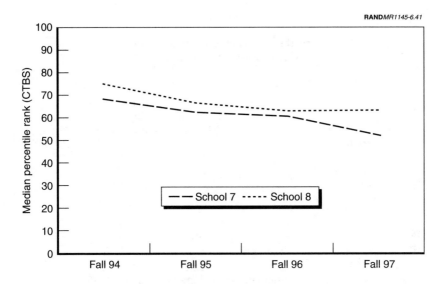

Figure 6.41—Mean Percentile Mathematics Scores in Shoreline: NAS
Schools, Grade 11

Summary for Washington

Table 6.8 summarizes performance trends in the Washington NAS
schools. This is based on a two-year change in test scores, from the
fall of 1995 to the fall of 1997 (baseline to baseline plus one year). Of
the 22 NAS schools, 9 made gains equal to or greater than the district
gains. In reading, 11 schools made gains relative to the district or, in
some cases, had declines smaller than those experienced by the district.

THE LINK BETWEEN IMPLEMENTATION AND
PERFORMANCE

One of the goals of the RAND analysis plan is to monitor progress in
implementation and performance in NAS schools and to understand
the factors that relate to higher implementation and higher performance. Such findings will not only inform New American Schools

Table 6.8

**Summary of Performance Trends in NAS Schools
in Washington, Fall 95 to Fall 97**

CTBS/CFAS	Number of Schools	Number Making Gains in Test Scores Relative to the District
Math		
Grade 4	15	6
Grade 8	5	3
Grade 11	2[a]	0
Combined	22	9
Reading		
Grade 4	15	7
Grade 8	5	3
Grade 11	2	1
Combined	22	11

NOTE: [a]The two Shoreline schools are not included in this table.

but the Comprehensive School Reform Demonstration Program now under way.

However, as this chapter has made abundantly clear, we do not have good, sustained, and coherent measures of student performance that are comparable across jurisdictions and across design teams. The summary tables we showed earlier compared gains in NAS schools to changes in the district test scores, but as we detailed in each section, sometimes the comparisons were across one year, sometimes across two years, and they often covered different time periods, where cohorts of schools were involved.

Our data do not show any clear linkage between implementation and performance in NAS schools. This was disappointing and runs counter to conventional wisdom. If the theory of action underlying comprehensive school reform is correct and if these models are implemented in a sustained coherent fashion, then higher implementation should be related to improved outcomes. As Stringfield, Milsap, and Herman (1997, p. 43) conclude in *Special Strategies for Educating Disadvantaged Children*, "We know that some programs, well implemented, can make dramatic differences in students' academic achievement." Yet, the authors go on to point out the critical challenge in educational reform that has existed in this country for decades:

> . . . after a third of a century of research on school change, we still have not provided adequate human and fiscal resources, appropriately targeted, to make large-scale program improvements a reliably consistent reality in schools serving students placed at risk (p. 43).

We offer some hypotheses for the failure to find a link between implementation and performance. First, despite schools reporting implementation of designs, it remains relatively early for expecting deep implementation that would dramatically affect performance gains. As Sizer (1984, p. 224) points out, "Schools are complicated and traditional institutions, and they easily resist all sorts of well-intentioned efforts at reform." As several design developers and school reformers have pointed out, schoolwide change can take more than five years for a school to accomplish meaningful change (Sizer, 1992; Hess, 1995; Levin, 1991; Darling-Hammond, 1988, 1995, 1997).

Some of the design teams emphasize that it takes several years to expect implementation to take hold throughout the school (Bodilly, 1998; Smith et al., 1998). Only with coherent implementation would one expect school test scores to consistently increase throughout the school. However, our analysis shows a large number of NAS schools near the midlevel implementation points on scales for the wide array of indicators considered here. In addition, there is a great deal of variation among teachers within the NAS sites as measured by within-school variance. While there is a range in implementation levels observed in our analysis, it is probable that implementation is not deep enough throughout the school at this point to raise student scores across grade levels. Over time with more specific test score information and additional measures of implementation, the empirical link might be observed. This remains an open question.

Second, the nature of our dependent variable—a simple 0/1 variable—does not allow for any gradations in student performance. Had we been able to calculate effect sizes, perhaps we would have seen a link between implementation and performance.

Third, the analysis sample may have failed to find evidence of the link between implementation and student performance because of measurement error in our indicators. Although our implementation indicators appear to be credibly constructed and to track well with Bodilly's findings, they may fail to capture important aspects of implementation that are linked to school performance.

Additional research and longitudinal data are needed to address the relationship of implementation and performance in NAS schools. More detailed case studies, using matched pairs of schools, will help us further understand this relationship as well as the other factors that affect both implementation and performance. RAND has conducted such case studies in the spring 2000 and will be reporting on them in the future .

SUMMARY

Overall, the results are mixed (see Table 6.9). Of the 163 schools for which we had data, 81 schools (50 percent) made gains relative to the district in mathematics and 76 schools (47 percent) made gains in reading.

Differences in School Performance by Jurisdiction

Table 6.9 shows the number of schools that made gains relative to the district by jurisdiction. Fifty percent or more of the schools in Cincinnati, Dade, Kentucky, and Memphis improved in mathematics, while half or more of the schools in Cincinnati, Philadelphia, San Antonio, and Washington showed improvements in reading.

Differences in School Performance by Design Team

Examining school performance results by jurisdiction inevitably brings up the question: Which design teams appear to be the most successful in improving student test scores? In many ways, this is an unfair question. School performance and implementation vary importantly across jurisdictions. Given:

- the importance of district environments and support in implementation of the designs;

Table 6.9

NAS Schools Making Gains Relative to Jurisdiction, by Jurisdiction and Design Team

	Number of Schools	Number Making Gains in Test Scores Relative to the District
Jurisdiction		
Math		
Cincinnati	18	9
Dade	11	6
Kentucky	51	30
Memphis	30	16
Philadelphia	19	7
San Antonio	12	4
Washington	22	9
Reading		
Cincinnati	18	10
Dade	11	5
Kentucky	51	22
Memphis	30	11
Philadelphia	19	11
San Antonio	12	7
Washington	22	11
Design Team		
Math		
AC	8	5
AT	24	9
CON	17	10
EL	16	4
MRSH	11	7
NARE	66	36
RW	21	10
Reading		
AC	8	2
AT	24	15
CON	18	6
EL	15	8
MRSH	11	8
NARE	66	27
RW	21	10
Overall		
Math	163	81
Reading	163	76

- the uneven implementation of designs across the jurisdictions;
- the uneven distribution of designs across jurisdictions and small sample sizes for some designs;
- the variation in testing regimes; and,
- the possible lack of alignment between assessments and design team curriculum, instruction, and goals,

it is difficult to compare "success" rates of various designs in a meaningful and fair fashion. Nonetheless, NAS and the design teams agreed to be held accountable to district standards, and NAS expected dramatic achievement gains across design teams. Thus, we present the performance summary results by design to help set expectations for those implementing comprehensive school reforms (see Table 6.9). The results vary across the two subject areas. For example, for the 8 AC schools, 5 made progress relative to the district in mathematics, but only 2 did so in reading. With the exception of AT and EL schools, about half of the other design team schools made progress relative to the district in mathematics; in reading, fewer than half of AC, CON, and NARE schools made gains relative to the district. RW was the most consistent, with 10 out of 21 schools making progress in both reading and mathematics relative to the district. Of the 11 MRSH schools, 7 made progress in mathematics and 8 in reading.

Once again, we warn that these results need to be interpreted in the context of district environments. Because of the wide variation in implementation and environments that occurs within schools and among jurisdictions, one should not expect robust performance results across the NAS sites after only a couple of years at most. In addition, better and longer-term performance data at the student level are needed in order to make conclusive judgments about designs and their effects on student achievement, controlling for important factors (Berends and Kirby, 2000).

Chapter Seven

QUALITATIVE OUTCOME INDICATORS

We mentioned in an earlier chapter that there are different indicators of school outcomes that can be examined to see what effect whole school change has on improving these outcomes. Many design teams explicitly incorporate improvements in attendance and drop-out rates into their designs. We have few high schools, so drop-out rates (alternately, graduation from high school) are not a relevant indicator for most of our schools. Moreover, we found variability in how jurisdictions define and calculate drop-out rates, so comparison over time and across jurisdictions is difficult. Given that most of our schools are elementary schools, class promotion rates are also not very useful; nearly all students in elementary schools are promoted, so there is little variation in this variable nor much room for improvement.

A promising indicator of school outcome is attendance.[1] We examined the attendance rate as reported by principals in 1998 and found that this did not vary a great deal over time or across schools. The median attendance rate for our sample of 104 schools was 94.5 percent, the first and third quartiles—that bound the middle 50 percent of the distribution—were 93 and 95.6 percent, respectively; 90 percent of all schools had attendance rates of 90 percent and over.

We therefore turned to some more proximal indicators of effects of designs on teaching, instruction, and student performance as re-

---

[1]Data on attendance and on the other indicators discussed in this chapter were collected on the principal and teacher surveys. As a result, the analysis sample consists of the 104 schools for which we have complete survey data.

ported by teachers. There are some obvious shortcomings of such teacher-reported data. First, such reports may not translate well into performance on standardized tests. Second, teachers may tend to more positively regard effects of designs on teaching and student achievement than may be warranted. It is useful to examine these indicators because they provide additional information and paint a somewhat broader picture of the effects of designs on teachers, teaching, and students than is provided by our analysis of limited school performance data.

TEACHER-REPORTED EFFECTS ON PROFESSIONAL DEVELOPMENT, TEACHING, AND STUDENT ACHIEVEMENT

We had earlier stressed the importance of professional development activities for teachers in helping them change their instructional strategies in fundamental ways. Teachers were asked about the effect that professional development activities (in the last year) had on their teaching techniques. This was ranked on a scale of 1–4, with 1 = none or did not attend, and 4 = substantial effect. Figure 7.1 shows the distribution of teacher responses on this question, disaggregated by design team. While there was substantial variation within design teams, both AC schools and RW schools ranked high on this indicator compared with other designs, with means of 2.76 (SD = .34) and 2.89 (SD = .35) respectively. Indeed, almost 70 percent of teachers in AC and RW schools reported that professional development had indeed had a positive effect on their teaching techniques. The MRSH and NARE teachers were the least positive, and this was reflected in their relatively low mean scores (mean = 2.31, SD = .63 for MRSH schools; mean = 2.21, SD = .31 for NARE schools). The difference in means between RW and AT and MRSH schools was statistically significant at the .05 level.

When asked about the quality of professional development activities, well over 60 percent of teachers (in all but AC schools) agreed that professional development activities had been sustained and coherently focused; in AT, NARE, and RW schools, this percentage was well over 70 percent.

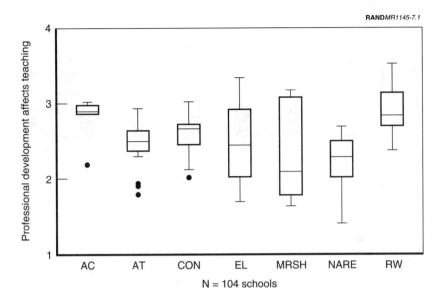

RAND*MR1145-7.1*

Figure 7.1—Effect of Professional Development Activities in the Past Year
on Teaching Techniques by Design Team, 1998

However, these are not direct measures of the effects of designs and
design team activities on teaching and student learning because
professional development activities are provided by schools and districts along with design teams. Instead, we now turn to another
question that is a more direct teacher-reported measure. Teachers
were asked about the effects of *designs* on their teaching, professional growth, students' achievement, and students' engagement in
learning. Teacher responses to this question were recoded on a scale
of –3 to +3, where –3 = great deal of negative effect, 0 = no effect, 3 =
great deal of positive effect. Figure 7.2 shows the distribution of
teacher responses regarding effects of designs on teaching, by design
team. The mean scores for every design team on this measure improved between 1997 and 1998 or remained stable (RW). Three design teams—AT, CON, and RW—had a mean score of about 1.0 in
1998, indicating that teachers were somewhat positive about the

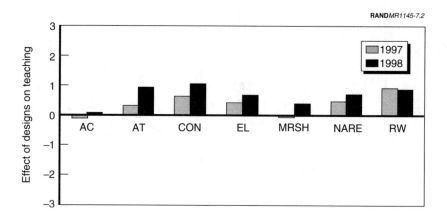

Figure 7.2—Mean Teacher-Reported Score on Effect of Designs on Their Teaching by Design Team, 1997 and 1998

effects on teaching by design teams.[2] Most of this improvement was among teachers in schools that were relatively early in the implementation phase (had been implementing for one year in 1997).

Between 1997 and 1998, there was also improvement in the perception of teachers regarding the effects of designs on their students' achievement (see Figure 7.3). CON and RW had mean scores of close to 1.0 by 1998.[3] Similar results were found with respect to teacher-reported effects on students' engagement in learning (not shown here). While these indicators need to be viewed with caution, they are somewhat positive. Teachers seemed to feel relatively hopeful about the positive effects of designs, especially some designs, on their teaching and on student learning.

---

[2]The mean difference between AT, CON, and RW schools and AC schools on this measure was statistically significant. In addition, the change between 1997 and 1998 within the AT, CON, and NARE schools was significant.

[3]The mean difference between AT, CON, NARE, and RW schools and AC schools on this measure was statistically significant. Moreover, the change between 1997 and 1998 within the AT, CON, MRSH, and NARE schools was significant.

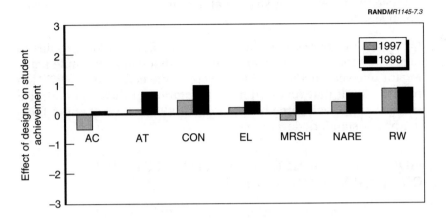

Figure 7.3—Mean Teacher-Reported Effects of Designs on Their Students'
Achievement by Design Team, 1997 and 1998

It is interesting to note that while overall the implementation measures remained stable between 1997 and 1998, the teacher-reported
effects of design teams on their teaching and student achievement
increased modestly. One explanation may be the focal point of the
questions underlying these measures. For example, when asked
about implementation, teachers were asked about the degree to
which the sets of activities described *their school*. However, when
asked about teacher-reported effects, a teacher was reporting the
degree to which the design team had positive or negative effects on
his/her students' achievement this past year or his/her teaching this
past year.

Thus, the questions queried different phenomena—one about the
school as a whole and the other about an individual teacher's judgments about the design team effects—and this may help explain why
implementation remained stable and teacher-reported effects increased between 1997 and 1998.

It is also important to note that mean implementation levels in 1997
and 1998 were just above the midpoint on a six-point scale; the increase in teacher-reported effects of design teams on student

achievement were from slightly above no effect (~.3) to modestly positive (~.6).

Moreover, the increase in teacher-reported effects was largely due to increases reported by teachers in schools that had been implementing for one year in 1997 and thus were in the early implementation phase. Recall that reported implementation in these schools also showed a relatively large increase from 1997 to 1998 of about four-tenths of a standard deviation.

MODELING TEACHER-REPORTED EFFECTS OF DESIGNS ON STUDENT ACHIEVEMENT

We modeled teacher-reported effects on students' achievement as a function of teacher and school characteristics, including level of implementation. The means and standard deviations for this sample were presented earlier in Table 5.1, and because these were largely unchanged, we do not show them here. The mean for the dependent variable was .61 (SD = 1.24), which is somewhat higher than the mid-point of the scale. Table 7.1 presents the results for the multilevel model. Because it does not make theoretical sense to expect the dependent variable to differ by jurisdiction, the model does not include the jurisdiction dummies.

Teacher Level Effects

Hispanic teachers reported greater positive effects of designs on their students' achievement compared with non-Hispanic white teachers—on average, these reports were about three-tenths of a standard deviation higher. There was little difference by age, education, or experience, none of which is significant in the model.

Teacher perceptions of students' readiness to learn (basic skills and discipline and parent support for the students) were positively related to teacher-reported effects of designs on student achievement. These effects are small but significant. Teachers who were one standard deviation higher on their perceptions of students' readiness to learn were also approximately .07 of a standard deviation higher on their reports of positive effects of designs on students' achievement.

Table 7.1

**Multilevel Results for the Relationships of Teacher-Reported Effects
on Students' Achievement to Teacher, School, and
Design-Related Factors**

Variables	Coefficient	Standard Error
Intercept	−0.132	0.103
Independent Variables for Teachers (n = 1,796)		
Race-ethnicity		
African American	0.077	0.050
Hispanic/Latino	0.301[a]	0.092
Other/missing	0.028	0.073
Educational degree: Master's or above	0.001	0.039
Age: ≥ 30 years	−0.088	0.060
Years of teaching experience	−0.011	0.021
Lack of basic skills a hindrance (1–4, 1 = great hindrance, 4 = not at all)	0.073[a]	0.022
Student discipline and inadequate parent support a hindrance (2–8, 2 = great hindrance, 8 = not at all)	0.066[a]	0.023
Students can learn with available resources (1–4 , 1 = strongly disagree, 4 = strongly agree)	0.009	0.019
Design-related variables		
Communication by designs to schools (1–6)	0.061[a]	0.023
Support for design (1–5)	0.481[a]	0.021
Attended design team workshop in last 12 months	0.072	0.043
Core implementation index (range 1–6)	0.139[a]	0.022
Independent Variables for Schools (n = 104)		
Percent poverty	0.074	0.039
Percent minority	−0.020	0.046
Large size (> 400)	0.104	0.070
Secondary schools	−0.032	0.055
Percent student mobility	0.001	0.028
PD days devoted to design team	−0.038	0.029
Years implementing	0.014	0.030
Resources index (range 1–5)	0.022	0.032
Level of district support (range 1–7)	−0.043	0.029
Design team:		
AC	−0.036	0.126
AT	0.163	0.103
CON	0.093	0.094
EL	−0.089	0.100
MRSH	0.040	0.124
NARE	0.119	0.121

NOTES: [a]significant at .01 level.

The importance of implementation is highlighted by our results. While we failed to find a link between higher implementation and our measure of school performance based on an array of standardized tests, the model clearly shows the relationship between higher reported teacher implementation and teacher perceptions of positive effects on students' achievement. A teacher who was one standard deviation higher on the core implementation index was about 0.14 of a standard deviation higher on our measure of reported effects on student achievement. However, it is important to note that both the measure of implementation and the measure of perceived effects are based on teachers' judgments. As such, this relationship may be more tautological than causal.

Design-Related Variables

Clearly the most important variable among the teacher-level variables was the extent of support for design teams. Teachers who supported the designs to a greater degree were much more likely to believe that they were having a positive effect on student achievement. The effect of this variable was close to half a standard deviation; none of the other variables in the model matched this variable in terms of effect size.

Clear communication was also significant in the model, although it had a much more modest effect.

School-Level Variables

Given that we are examining teacher-reported effects, it is not surprising that the school characteristics were not significant in the model. We also included variables to control for the level of resources and district support, but neither of these variables appeared to influence teacher perceptions of effects of designs on students' achievement.

The model also included dummies to test whether designs differed significantly on this measure, controlling for other variables. None of the design team dummies was significant, net of other teacher- and design-related measures.

Goodness of Fit

Table 7.2 decomposes the variance within and between schools with respect to the dependent variable and displays the proportion of the variance explained by the model. The model explained 87 percent of the between-school variance in our dependent variable and a little over one-third of within school variance.

Table 7.2

Variance in Teacher-Reported Effects on Students' Achievement Explained by the Model

	Effects on Students' Achievement
Sample	
Variance between schools (τ)	0.117
Variance within schools (σ^2)	0.882
Model	
Variance between schools (τ)	0.015
Variance within schools (σ^2)	0.563
Proportion of variance between schools explained by the model	87%
Proportion of variance within schools explained by the model	36%

SUMMARY

The qualitative outcome indicators discussed here warrant optimism. Nearly all design teams improved between 1997 and 1998 in terms of teacher-reported effects of the designs and professional development activities on their teaching and students' achievement. Some designs, notably RW, CON, and AT, ranked high on these indicators.

Our multivariate analysis of teacher-reported effects on students' achievement underscores what we found earlier with respect to the implementation index. Our model highlights the relationship between teacher perceptions of improved student performance and:

• Clear communication by design teams;

• Teacher support for designs; and

• High levels of implementation of core elements of designs.

Chapter Eight

CONCLUSIONS AND POLICY IMPLICATIONS

NAS's mission is to help schools and districts dramatically raise the achievement of large numbers of students with design-based assistance. To accomplish the goal of improving performance, each design team has a different approach to improving the professional lives of teachers and the educational opportunities of students. While each design is unique, each aims to restructure the entire school emphasizing changes in organization and governance, the professional lives of teachers, content and performance expectations, curriculum and instructional strategies, and parent and community involvement.

When NAS was launched in 1991, hopes were high for "break the mold" schools that would dramatically improve the academic achievement of the nation's students. The initial RFP for the NAS designs stated that "NASDC is not interested in incremental changes that promise, at best, modest improvement in student achievement compared to conventional classrooms or schools. The achievement of students in the New Generation of American Schools will be measured against world class standards" (New American Schools Development Corporation, 1991, p. 20). The results reported here reveal that a great deal of work lies ahead to accomplish this ambitious goal.

IMPLEMENTATION OF NAS DESIGNS VARIES FOR SEVERAL REASONS

To attain this goal, the designs need to be fully and coherently implemented and sustained over time. As our conceptual framework shows, implementation is affected by a myriad of social, economic, and political factors. The process of changing entire schools to improve student learning opportunities is complex and difficult because so many actors are involved and so many factors have to be aligned to support change. In this report, we have examined several teacher, school, design team, and district factors to better understand the relative contribution of each to implementation and school performance. Our findings will help inform NAS, design teams, and others involved in comprehensive whole-school reform.

Teachers' Perceptions Matter

In the implementation of any educational programs, teachers are the "street level bureaucrats" (Weatherly and Lipsky, 1977). They are the ones who are at the end of the line affecting implementation.

In our multivariate analyses of implementation, we found that teachers' attitudes and perceptions about students' readiness and ability to learn were critical for implementation. Teachers who reported fewer problems with students' lack of basic skills, lack of discipline, and inadequate support of parents also reported higher levels of implementation.

Individual characteristics of teachers (e.g., educational degree, age, and experience) were not associated with implementation once other factors had been taken into account. There was one exception, however. African American teachers tended to report higher levels of implementation when compared with non-Hispanic white teachers.

School Characteristics: Importance of Size, Level, and Leadership

In terms of school characteristics, we found that school size and level were related to implementation. Teacher-reported implementation levels were higher in smaller schools and elementary schools when compared with larger or secondary schools. These findings are consistent with RAND's prior case studies on NAS schools (Bodilly, 1998), as well as other research on school organizations. Larger, secondary schools are more complex organizations and are likely to resist organizational change (Perrow, 1986). Moreover, they may be more bureaucratic rather than communitarian resulting in a climate where teachers are less likely to collaborate around a common mission and vision as envisioned by the NAS designs (see Lee, Bryk, and Smith, 1993; Lee and Smith, 1995, 1997; Bryk and Driscoll, 1988).

Schools with strong principal leaders also had higher levels of implementation than those schools without strong principals. Principal leadership in our analysis was measured by aggregated teacher reports about principals who clearly communicated what was expected of teachers, were supportive and encouraging of staff, obtained resources for the school, enforced rules for student conduct, talked with teachers regarding instructional practices, had confidence in the expertise of the teachers, and took a personal interest in the professional development of teachers. The importance of principal leadership for establishing effective schools has been emphasized by researchers for decades (Edmonds, 1979; Purkey and Smith, 1983; Rosenholtz, 1985), so it is not surprising that such leadership is important for the implementation of NAS designs. While not surprising, the importance of principal leadership should not be overlooked when adopting and implementing whole-school reforms.

Design Teams: Importance of Clear Communication and Teacher Support

While our surveys could not efficiently capture the specific details of the range of assistance activities that NAS design teams provide, some proxies for this support revealed important relationships with implementation. For example, our analyses revealed that clear communication by design teams to schools was positively related to implementation and teachers' judgments about the effects of the designs on student achievement.

In addition, the NAS initiative and its design partners (and other comprehensive schoolwide assistance providers) have received a great deal of support from the recent Obey-Porter legislation and CSRD program. Two to three thousand schools could receive grants of at least $50,000 per year renewable for two years. While this federal funding will provide critical support for the NAS and other designs, it raises concerns about the capacity of designs to provide the necessary clear communication (and other assistance) to schools. For the first time since the scale-up phase—when NAS attempted to work with partnering jurisdictions to widely diffuse the designs to a large number of schools—the designs may be faced with a situation where demand for services exceeds the capacity to supply services. Within such a context, the participating districts, the schools, and the design teams face many challenges to ensure that there is clear communication to support the implementation of the designs. In recognition of this challenge, NAS's program emphasizes the need for clear communication (NAS, 1999).

In addition to the importance of communication, we found that greater teacher support for the design in their school was positively related to implementation. Even after accounting for other factors, the greater the teacher support, the higher the reported level of implementation.

Getting teachers within schools to support, substantively engage in, and sustain the implementation of whole-school designs is critical to the success of the NAS initiative and federal initiatives such as the CSRD program. As policymakers consider reauthorizing Title I in the coming year, and as they consider alternatives to previous shortcomings of Title I spending, it is important to understand the factors related to implementing whole-school restructuring efforts and early indications of their effects. However, implementing designs oriented toward changing the organization of schools, the professional lives of teachers, and curriculum, instruction, and assessments is no easy task for teachers. It is arduous work, which necessitates a great deal of support (Bodilly, 1998; Datnow and Stringfield, 1997; Stringfield and Datnow, 1998; Purnell and Hill, 1992).

District Support Is Critical

In 1995, NAS pursued a strategy that attempted to adapt existing district policies to support scale-up of the designs to large numbers of schools in order to raise student achievement. At that time, NAS partnered with ten jurisdictions. RAND began monitoring schools in eight of these ten jurisdictions.

In our analyses, we observed a great deal of variation in implementation across districts. Kentucky and Memphis tended to rank higher on all of our implementation indicators. San Antonio and Philadelphia consistently ranked near the bottom on most of our indicators. Pittsburgh, we found, was not implementing at all by the spring of 1998, so these schools were dropped from the analyses reported here. During the scale-up phase, Kentucky was implementing the NARE design, which closely fit the demands of KERA reform in the state.

A great deal of attention has been paid to Memphis City Schools because of the strides made there in implementation and performance (Ross et al., 1998, 1999b; Nunnery, 1998; Ross, Alberg, and Nunnery, 1999a). Key aspects of Memphis support for scaling up NAS and NAS-like designs included the stability of the district leadership, the centrality of the NAS effort there amidst other possible reforms, lack of severe crisis (e.g., budgetary or union strikes), and district focus on professional development and performance results (for more information see Bodilly, 1998).

San Antonio, while experiencing dramatic test score increases over the past few years, ranked low on our NAS implementation indicators. During the scale-up phase, not only was San Antonio scaling up NAS designs, but the district was also implementing other district-mandated curricular and instructional programs. For example, in 1997 the district put in place districtwide mathematics and literacy programs. By 1998, this meant that teachers were spending up to 90 minutes a day on the math program and an additional 90 minutes a day on the reading program. Such a schedule, and the rigidity of it as mandated by the district, conflicted with NAS design team activities, some of which emphasized working on long-term interdisciplinary projects over the course of the semester.

Overall, the authority of district offices and the pressures they face have posed frustrating challenges to NAS in its pursuit of establishing solid, effective partnerships with districts. Particularly in low-performing districts in high-stakes accountability systems, the centrality of the NAS initiative vis-à-vis other programs is dependent on district leadership and is often fragile.

Our findings suggest that reforms of a similar nature, such as the CSRD program and other schoolwide Title I programs, can be implemented and come to fruition *only* with significant changes in district-level policy and support. The federal government will need to take an active role in encouraging new district-level practices to support federal initiatives promoting implementation of schoolwide programs.

Appropriate Allocation of Critical Resources

The results of this report suggest that resources are important for the implementation process. Teachers who reported greater resource availability—e.g., materials to support instruction, professional development, time for planning and collaboration, consultants to advise and provide support, and funding—also reported higher levels of implementation. Other RAND work on this issue has also pointed to the importance of resources for implementation of the designs (Keltner, 1998; Bodilly, 1998; Berends and Bodilly, forthcoming).

The findings here about the importance of resources for implementation do not imply throwing more money at the school system. Rather, other RAND research suggests that resource availability is more an issue of resource allocation. Keltner (1998) has found that of the cost to implement a design during the 1996–1997 school year, nearly 40 percent of the resource burden was met through reallocation of budgets for personnel, substitute teachers, and materials. The remaining 60 percent came from resources external to the school—e.g., Title I, district, or grants. Thus the issue is for schools and districts to rethink existing funding streams to support whole-school reform (Bodilly and Berends, 1999; King, 1999, 1994). Yet, as Odden notes in his analysis of NAS design costs, reallocation of funds is not always a straightforward exercise "because it usually involves 'trading in' or redefining the positions of current educational specialist staff for the needed NAS ingredients; however in terms of actively promoting and sustaining real reform, it is the most powerful and effective approach" (Odden, 1997, p. 11).

Attention to resources—whether funding for materials, professional development, assistance providers, or time—will continue to be an issue even with the support of the federal CSRD program. While the funds provided will no doubt further the demand for NAS designs and other design-based assistance organizations, many funding issues remain. For instance, districts and schools control many resources that can supplement the federal funds, and some reallocation will be necessary (Keltner, 1998; Berends and Bodilly, forthcoming).

"SCHOOLWIDE" REFORM?

NAS and the design teams partnered with schools and districts that are characterized by a host of problems related to poverty, achievement, and climate characteristics. Scaling up the designs, even replicating implementation, in these sites is extremely difficult. Our analyses show that implementation varies, with some of these schools implementing at higher levels than others and also showing some early performance gains compared to the district. In this report, we have argued that the variation in implementation can be largely ascribed to a variety of district, school, teacher, and design team factors. An issue that we could not address with our survey data was whether the variation in implementation was due to certain inherent characteristics of the design itself that made it more difficult to implement. This is an important issue that needs to be examined in future studies, particularly given the federal support for comprehensive school reform.

Other findings suggest that comprehensive reforms face many obstacles during implementation, and because of this, whole-school designs face continuing challenges in dramatically raising the achievement of all students. For example, some of the schools at this point in the NAS scale-up phase are at middle or lower levels on our implementation indicators, and some schools remain low-performing relative to the district. Implementation varied widely *within* schools as well as between schools. Moreover, implementation varied across districts and design teams.

We need to know more about how the implementation of a design becomes a *schoolwide reform* effort. Such understanding has implications for education reforms that attempt implementation of schoolwide programs as tools to further standards-based reforms and raise the academic performance of the nation's students. We expected that as the designs continue to provide assistance and as teachers continue to become more familiar with the design team activities in their schools, there will be continued increases in implementation levels and agreement among teachers within schools. However, our data between 1997 and 1998 reveal that the mean levels of our implementation indicators did not increase much in schools that had been implementing for two or more years in 1997, and the variation within schools did not decrease.

Thus, the question remains, how can the designs become school-wide? A danger in educational reform initiatives—especially those within urban settings with many complex economic, political, and social challenges—is that the whole-school designs may be another "program" that is turned on and off at selected times during the school day, week, and/or year. As time goes on, the designs may be at risk of being turned off altogether, especially if districts and schools lose their focus on schoolwide programs such as NAS and turn to some other reform effort.

EARLY PERFORMANCE TRENDS

We have examined whether NAS schools made gains in test scores relative to the average scores in their respective jurisdictions to better understand where the NAS schools started and where they stand a couple years into the scale-up phase. Of the 163 schools for which we have data allowing us to compare school performance relative to the district or state, 81 schools (50 percent) made gains relative to the district in mathematics and 76 schools (47 percent) made gains in reading. In terms of jurisdictions, Cincinnati, Dade, Kentucky, and Memphis schools did relatively better in mathematics, while schools in Cincinnati, Philadelphia, San Antonio, and Washington did better in reading.

The results by design team varied across mathematics and reading tests. For example, for the 8 AC schools, 5 made progress relative to the district in mathematics, but only 2 did so in reading. With the exception of AT and EL schools, about half of the other design team schools made progress relative to the district in mathematics; in reading, fewer than half of AC, CON, and NARE schools made gains relative to the district. RW was the most consistent, with 10 out of 21 schools making progress in both reading and mathematics relative to the district. Of the 11 MRSH schools, 7 made progress in mathematics and 8 in reading.

Once again, we warn that when examining these results, it is important to remember the importance of district environments and support in implementation of the designs; the uneven implementation of designs across the jurisdictions; the uneven distribution of designs across jurisdictions and small sample sizes for some designs; the variation in testing regimes; and the possible lack of alignment between assessments and design team curriculum, instruction, and goals. For these reasons, one should not expect robust school-level performance results across the NAS sites for the time period examined. The test score trends portrayed in this report, while illustrative, are relatively early in the implementation of NAS designs during scale-up. Better and longer-term performance data at the student level are needed in order to make conclusive judgments about designs and their effects on student achievement, controlling for important factors (Berends and Kirby, 2000).

In addition to these patterns of performance trends, we examined teacher-reported effects of the designs on their students' achievement. In these analyses, higher levels of implementation were related to greater teacher-reported effects of the designs on students, but both implementation and teacher-reported effects varied much more within than between schools.

SETTING EXPECTATIONS FOR COMPREHENSIVE SCHOOL REFORM

At this point in comprehensive school reform, there is only limited evidence about the effectiveness of design-based models from studies that rely on rigorous comparative evaluation designs. For example, Herman et al. (1999) find only three models were able to provide convincing results in terms of raising student achievement levels. In addition, in evaluations of the Comer's School Development Program, Cook and his colleagues at Northwestern University (see Cook et al., 1999; Cook, Hunt, and Murphy, 1998) have found no effect of the model on student achievement in Prince George's County, Maryland, but they have found small positive effects on students (less than one-tenth of a standard deviation) in Chicago schools. These Cook et al. studies were based on randomized experimental longitudinal designs, and both point to the importance of further longitudinal studies that carefully examine the approaches of design-based assistance providers and the likely variation in implementation and performance that is likely to occur. Cook et al. (1998) also points to the importance of district-level support and expectations for improving instruction and achievement. Other studies have shown that raising achievement levels in dramatic fashion within urban school districts is a formidable challenge (Bryk et al., 1998b; Orr, 1998; Fullan, 1991).

Whether large numbers of schools can implement whole-school designs in a fashion that can improve student achievement across grade levels remains an open question. The evidence reported here regarding the variation in implementation both within and between schools and the stability of the implementation indicators over time suggests that design teams, districts, schools, and teachers have a great deal of work to do to fully implement designs on a broad scale. Our analyses also point out many difficulties in relating implementation to performance in large samples of schools that span several jurisdictions with different testing regimes and support for comprehensive school reform. Only with additional longitudinal data and analysis will educators, policymakers, and researchers be able to assess the effectiveness of comprehensive school designs.

It is important to place our results in context from different perspectives. NAS's initial aims were to dramatically improve the achievement of large numbers of students with design teams and the assistance they provide to schools. From this perspective, the findings from our analysis indicate that this goal is overly ambitious, especially over a relatively short period of time.

From another perspective, one might view the findings reported here with cautious optimism. The results that suggest some design teams have worked with challenging schools, implemented their designs at relatively higher levels, and experienced achievement gains imply that some NAS designs hold promise for improving the achievement of students attending high poverty schools in urban areas of this nation. A great deal of work needs to be done, however, to make such experiences a reality on a large scale.

Continued research is critical for understanding what it takes to sustain a reform effort such as NAS. If teachers, designs, and districts can sustain some semblance of focus on the NAS designs' coherent visions to structure the educational opportunities of students and teachers, it is likely that the designs will become more widespread in schools. However, accomplishing that goal may take a great deal of perseverance on the part of teachers and a great deal of support from the NAS, the design teams, and perhaps most importantly, the districts.

KEY STUDIES IN RAND'S EVALUATION OF NAS SCHOOL REFORM

A number of reports and articles have addressed various aspects of progress in NAS schools. These, as well as other RAND reports and articles about New American Schools, include:

"Teacher-Reported Effects of New American Schools' Designs: Exploring Relationships to Teacher Background and School Context," in *Educational Evaluation and Policy Analysis* by Mark Berends, 2000, 22(1), 65–82.

"Necessary District Support for Comprehensive School Reform" by Susan J. Bodilly and Mark Berends, in Gary Orfield and Elizabeth H. Debray, eds., *Hard Work for Good Schools: Facts Not Fads in Title I Reform*. Boston, MA: Civil Rights Project, Harvard University, 1999, pp. 111–119.

Assessing the Progress of New American Schools: A Status Report, by Mark Berends, RAND, 1999, MR-1085-ED.

Lessons from New American Schools' Scale-up Phase: Prospects for Bringing Designs to Multiple Schools, by Susan J. Bodilly, RAND, 1998, MR-942-NAS.

New American Schools after Six Years, by Thomas K. Glennan, Jr., RAND, 1998, MR-945-NASDC.

Funding Comprehensive School Reform, by Brent R. Keltner, RAND, 1998, internal document.

Reforming America's Schools: Observations on Implementing "Whole School Designs," by Susan J. Bodilly and Thomas K. Glennan, 1998, (RB-8016-EDU).

Lessons from New American Schools Development Corporation's Demonstration Phase, by Susan J. Bodilly, RAND, 1996, MR-729-NASDC.

Reforming and Conforming: NASDC Principals Discuss School Accountability Systems, by Karen Mitchell, RAND, 1996, MR-716-NASDC.

"Lessons Learned from RAND's Formative Assessment of NASDC's Phase 2 Demonstration Effort," by Susan J. Bodilly, in Sam Stringfield, Steven Ross, and Lana Smith, eds., *Bold Plans for School Restructuring: The New American Schools Designs.* Mahwah, NJ: Lawrence Erlbaum Associates, 1996, pp. 289–324.

Designing New American Schools: Baseline Observations on Nine Design Teams, by Susan J. Bodilly, Susanna Purnell, Kimberly Ramsey, and Christina Smith, RAND, 1995, MR-598-NASDC.

In addition to this report, there are a number of studies underway that will further inform our efforts to monitor the progress and performance in the NAS schools. We summarize the RAND program of studies on NAS in Figure A.1 and provide a brief description below:

ANALYSIS OF SCHOOL IMPROVEMENT

The data and analysis of school improvement is summarized in the main body of this report and provides information from RAND's longitudinal sample of schools with a wide array of data collected from teachers, principals, and districts.

In what follows, we describe additional studies that are currently under way.

ANALYSIS OF CLASSROOM CHANGE AND STUDENT ACHIEVEMENT

A principal hypothesis of the NAS initiative is that whole school reform will be successful with designs being implemented in schools

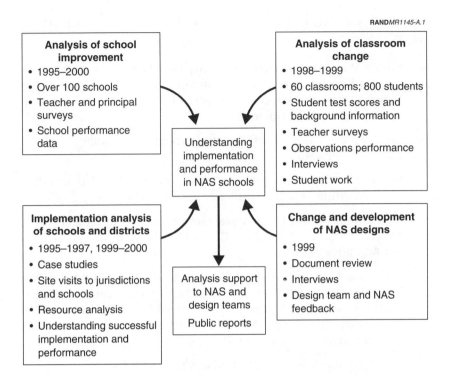

RAND*MR1145-A.1*

Analysis of school improvement
- 1995–2000
- Over 100 schools
- Teacher and principal surveys
- School performance data

Analysis of classroom change
- 1998–1999
- 60 classrooms; 800 students
- Student test scores and background information
- Teacher surveys
- Observations performance
- Interviews
- Student work

Understanding implementation and performance in NAS schools

Implementation analysis of schools and districts
- 1995–1997, 1999–2000
- Case studies
- Site visits to jurisdictions and schools
- Resource analysis
- Understanding successful implementation and performance

Analysis support to NAS and design teams

Public reports

Change and development of NAS designs
- 1999
- Document review
- Interviews
- Design team and NAS feedback

Figure A.1—RAND's Program of Studies to Understand Implementation and Performance in NAS Schools to Provide Feedback to a Variety of Audiences

with the assistance provided by design teams. A critical aim of this whole school reform is to improve classroom instruction and thereby student achievement and engagement.

To examine this hypothesis, RAND is monitoring changes in classroom practices in a supplementary study that examines the following questions: *Do the NAS designs extend beyond changes in school organization and governance and permeate classrooms to change curriculum and instruction and thereby student achievement? What do classroom practices look like in NAS's classrooms? How do they affect student outcomes?* In both the 1997–1998 and 1998–1999 school years, RAND collected qualitative and quantitative data in selected NAS and non-NAS schools in San Antonio. For about 60 elementary classrooms, RAND gathered a wide variety of data over two school years, including:

- Survey data from teachers on instructional practices, implementation of the designs, professional development, parent involvement, judgments about the effects of the design and support, and background characteristics;

- Student-level data for all the students in the elementary classrooms in our study;

- Student background (gender, race-ethnicity, age, at-risk status, poverty, limited English proficient, and prior test scores);

- Test data from the Texas Assessment of Academic Skills (TAAS), which provides significant indicators for the state and district accountability systems;

- Test data from the Stanford Achievement Open Ended Reading Test, Version 9 (Stanford-9)—a supplementary commercial test that asks students to read a passage and answer open-ended questions. The Stanford-9 assessment is aimed to ask students not only to answer questions but explain their answers; and

- Principal phone interviews for the participating schools.

For a subsample of about 15 teachers from the 60 classrooms, RAND collected additional, more specific data on instructional practices, such as:

- Observations of each teacher several times over the course of the school year;

- Illustrative samples of students' work; and

- Teacher interviews and logs about assignments, homework, projects, quizzes and tests, and papers or reports over the course of the year.

The classroom artifacts, observational data, and teacher surveys address the question: Do NAS teachers and students interact with each other and subject materials in ways that reflect the curricular and instructional theories of change of the design teams?

The surveys and achievement data will help address a second question: What is the impact of the NAS designs and design-based assistance on student achievement?

Our analyses and reporting of these data will include descriptive results about whether instructional practices promoted by designs are occurring in NAS classrooms and examine whether these practices are linked to student achievement. There are a number of problems in attempting to identify a "design team" effect independent of other curricular and instructional programs being implemented in San Antonio. Nonetheless, the combined analyses will provide important insights into levels of implementation, extent of assistance as reported by teachers, professional development, and the usefulness of the designs and design-based assistance for creating positive classroom environments that improve student learning.

Examining the determinants of student achievement pertains directly to another key question: what is the impact of the NAS designs and design-based assistance on student achievement? We will examine the relationships between student achievement and a variety of individual and social factors, including: (1) student characteristics (gender, race-ethnicity, at-risk status, age, English as a Second Language); (2) students' prior achievement (i.e., 3rd grade TAAS scores); (3) classroom instruction; (4) design team activities; and (5) teacher background characteristics (education level, experience, age, gender, and race-ethnicity).

As part of this study, we will track the test scores of the 4th grade *cohort* participating in our study this year. For the 4th graders in our spring 1998 sample, we will be able to obtain their scores from the 3rd grade (1997) and 5th grade (1999), so over the course of this study we will be able to track scores for this year's cohort from grade 3 through grade 5. We will compare the trends of these NAS students to their non-NAS counterparts.

CONTINUED CHANGE AND DEVELOPMENT OF THE DESIGNS

Since 1992, the designs and their teams have changed for many different reasons. RAND will report on the evolution of the designs addressing the question: *What changes have been made to the designs and why?* It is a simple analysis based on document review and interviews over several years. Yet it will provide critical information on the designs, the variation in foci among them, and critical changes that were made over time as they faced implementation realities in schools facing significant challenges in terms of accountability systems, low test scores, poverty, diverse student populations, and difficult school climates.

COMPARATIVE CASE STUDIES OF IMPLEMENTATION AND PERFORMANCE IN NAS SCHOOLS

Our previous work indicates that school-level differences contribute significantly to the observed variation in implementation. In the spring 2000, we explored this issue further by conducting site visits to schools that reported implementing the designs. Based on previous analyses of the longitudinal school sample described above and input from the NAS design teams, we classified implementing schools as having produced low performance outcomes or high outcomes. Differences among these two groups will be explored to answer the research question: *Why do performance differences exist in implementing NAS schools?*

FINAL REPORTING

RAND plans to bring together the results of the various analyses and data collection efforts in an executive summary to be published in the coming year.

DESCRIPTION OF ADDITIONAL IMPLEMENTATION INDICATORS OF THE DESIGNS, BY JURISDICTION AND DESIGN TEAM, 1997 AND 1998

In this appendix, we compare additional indicators across jurisdictions and design teams as well as over time between 1997 and 1998. Specifically, we describe indicators of components that each design team could be expected to address—including organization and governance, teacher professional life, performance expectations, instructional strategies and grouping arrangements, and involvement of parents and community. Under the guidance for the federal Comprehensive School Demonstration program (CSRD), externally developed models are to address these and other aspects of schools and schooling activities (see http://www.ed.gov/offices/OESE/compreform).

These survey items were developed to allow us to portray NAS schools according to some common reformlike activities. Clearly, some design teams emphasize specific activities more than others. For example, the use of technology for instructional purposes is much more likely in CON schools than others. As such, CON schools would rank more highly on this indicator. Moreover, in a short survey across multiple designs, it is difficult to capture the unique aspects of each design. However, the indicators are still suggestive about the kinds of schooling activities promoted in this sample of NAS schools and the degree to which teachers reported implementing broad components of the designs.

In the results that follow, we find a great deal of variation in the indicators across jurisdictions and designs (see Table 3.2 for sample sizes). But there is a substantial amount of stability in the indicators between 1997 and 1998, which is somewhat surprising, given that the schools have had one more year of implementation.

ORGANIZATION AND GOVERNANCE

A central focus in design team efforts is that decisions about changes should reside with those who are closest to students (see Murphy, 1992). This component of designs was captured by two indicators: (a) the extent to which schools had the authority to make budget, staffing, and program decisions, and (b) whether teachers shared in school decisionmaking. Teachers answered these items on a scale from 1 ("this does not describe my school") to 6 ("this clearly describes my school").

In our sample in 1998, teachers tended to report that their schools had some authority to make decisions about budget, staffing, and programs. The mean across the 104 implementing NAS schools for this question was 4.44, with a standard deviation of .83. There was little change in this measure across the two years. In 1997, the mean was 4.39 with a SD = .81.

Figures B.1 and B.2 show the distribution of the 104 schools for this indicator by jurisdiction and design team, respectively. There is substantial variation both across the jurisdictions and within a jurisdiction. Kentucky, Dade, and Memphis ranked considerably higher on this scale than the average, while Philadelphia and San Antonio ranked considerably lower (with means of 3.6 and 3.7, respectively). There is, however, substantial variation within the schools in a jurisdiction as shown by the whiskers on the box plots; for example, some schools in Cincinnati and San Antonio had means of 5.5 on this scale. The differences between Kentucky and Memphis with respect to most of the other jurisdictions (although not with respect to each other) were statistically significant.[1]

---

[1]Dade had a small sample size of four schools; this explains why the differences between Dade and other jurisdictions were not significant. Failure to reject the null hypothesis in such comparisons implies only that—given the sample size—the difference between the population means is not large enough to be detected. A related point is that multiple comparisons often result in nontransitive results: Given means for three samples, A, B, C, where $mean_A > mean_B > mean_C$, the difference between

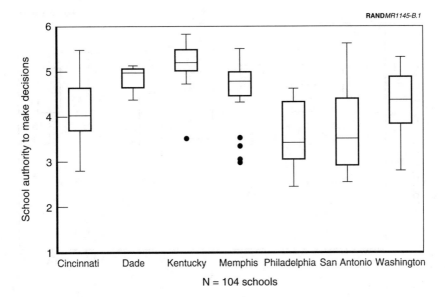

Figure B.1—School Authority to Make Decisions about Budget, Staffing, and Programs by Jurisdiction, Spring 1998

All the designs in their original plans had called for important governance changes in the schools including increased school autonomy, but over time, most of the designs adopted a more pragmatic, progressive approach to school autonomy working with the district to support an "appropriate" level of autonomy. For most of the designs, with the exception of MRSH (mean = 3.47), a large proportion of the schools fall between a 4 and 5 on the 6-point scale for this item (see Figure B.2). One possible explanation for MRSH's poor showing may be lack of support from jurisdictions such as San Antonio and Philadelphia where MRSH schools were located, both of which ranked low on this indicator. Another possible explanation may be that the MRSH design calls for more autonomy, and teachers in our sample recognize that they do not have the autonomy necessary to implement the design. The mean differences between both NARE and CON and MRSH were statistically significant.

---

mean of A and C may be statistically significant while neither is significantly different from the mean of B.

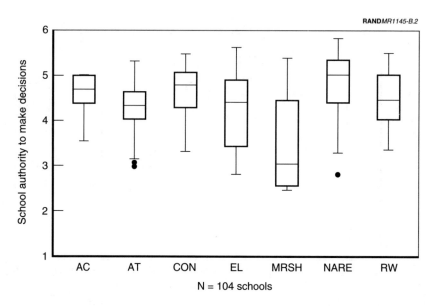

Figure B.2—School Authority to Make Decisions about Budget, Staffing, and Programs by Design Team, Spring 1998

When considering the extent to which teachers report that shared decisionmaking characterizes their school (see Figure B.3), the average level reported was about 4.46 (SD = .83).[2] Again, there was not much change from 1997, when the mean was 4.39 (SD =.70). Figures B.3 and B.4 show the distribution of this indicator by jurisdiction and design team. Washington, Kentucky, and Cincinnati schools scored high on this with means of 4.9, 4.8, and 4.7, respectively while Philadelphia and San Antonio had the lowest means of 3.6 and 3.5, respectively. The differences between the high-scoring and low-scoring groups were significant (although not between the jurisdictions within each group).

There were differences among design teams (for example, NARE and CON reported higher levels of shared authority compared with AC and MRSH) largely because the designs emphasize participatory

_____

[2]The number of schools for this indicator is 100 because Dade County Public Schools refused to allow RAND to ask several items on our teacher survey, so a modified survey was administered.

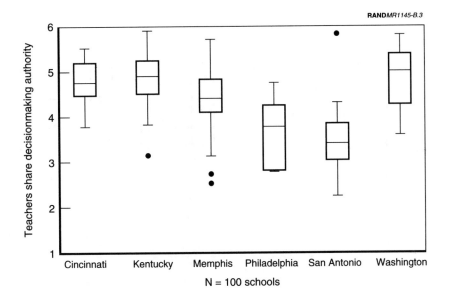

Figure B.3—Teacher Reports About Shared Decisionmaking in Their
School by Jurisdiction, Spring 1998

decisionmaking to a greater or lesser degree. While RW does not
explicitly promote shared decision-making, teachers within the
context of the design need to make frequent decisions (e.g., every six
to eight weeks) about how to group students for instruction based on
frequent assessments. Thus, RW teachers may have reported shared
decisionmaking as a result of this particular decisionmaking process.
It may also be that the organizational changes imposed by some of
the designs may be easier to implement than others.

TEACHER PROFESSIONAL LIFE

As we said earlier, teacher professional life is at the center of reform
efforts. Collegiality, mutual support, continual learning, and peer
relationships are all important in fostering an environment in which
change is not only possible but actively desired. A key part of this is
learning new ways of teaching through staff development that is

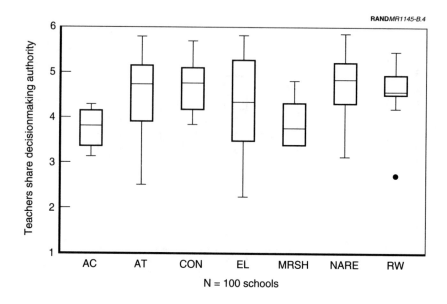

Figure B.4—Teacher Reports About Shared Decisionmaking in Their School by NAS Design, Spring 1998

focused, sustained, and innovative. We measured the quality of teacher professional life in NAS schools by three indicators, two that measure collaborative environments and one, a summative scale that measures the quality of teacher professional development and its effects. These are described below.

Collaborative Environments

Teachers were asked how well the following statements described their school on a 1–6 scale:

- Teachers are continual learners and team members through professional development, common planning, and collaboration.

- There are formal arrangements within this school providing opportunities for teachers to discuss and critique their instruction with each other.

Figures B.5 through B.8 show the distribution of the two indicators by jurisdiction and design team for 1998, three years into the scale-up phase.

Teacher responses about the extent to which their schools could be characterized as collaborative environments varied, depending on how specific the measure of collaboration was. The more general the notion of collaboration, the more teachers tended to say their school was collaborative (as measured by the first indicator above). For example, the mean across the 104 schools on the first indicator was 4.78 (SD = .59), which on a scale ranging from 1 to 6 is quite high. (It was just as high in the previous year, with a mean of 4.76 and SD = .54.) These higher levels were consistent across all jurisdictions and across all design teams (Figures B.5 and B.6). In fact, with one exception,[3] none of the differences in means was statistically significant.

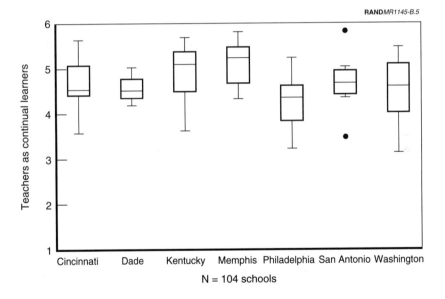

Figure B.5—Teachers as Continual Learners and Team Members by Jurisdiction, Spring 1998

---

[3] The difference in means between Memphis (mean = 5.1) and Washington (mean = 4.6) was statistically significant.

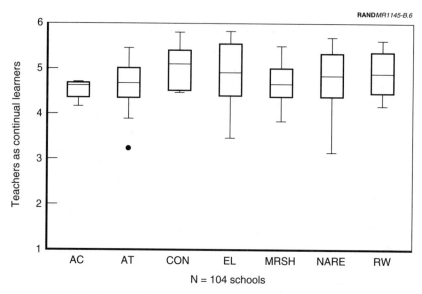

Figure B.6—Teachers as Continual Learners and Team Members by Design Team, Spring 1998

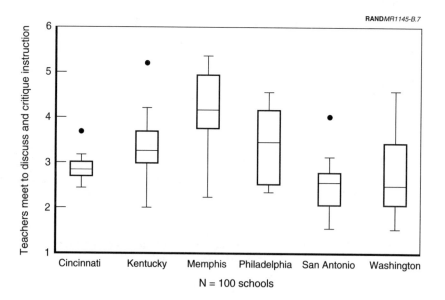

Figure B.7—Teachers Meet to Discuss and Critique Instruction by Jurisdiction, Spring 1998

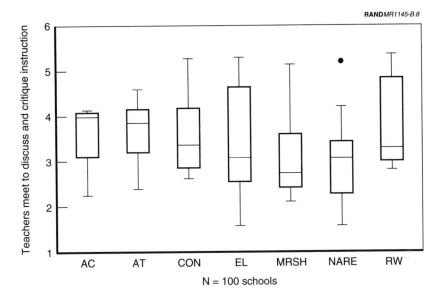

Figure B.8—Teachers Meet to Discuss and Critique Instruction by NAS Design, Spring 1998

However, far fewer teachers in these implementing schools reported meeting together to discuss or critique instruction (Figures B.7 and B.8); there is considerable variation across jurisdictions but not across design teams.[4] There is great variation among schools within a design team (see the box plot for EL and MRSH, for instance). The mean for this indicator was 3.33 (SD = .95), again unchanged from 1997. The means in some jurisdictions (Cincinnati, San Antonio, and Washington) were significantly lower, between 2.6 and 2.9, compared with Memphis, which had a mean of 4.2. Although the differences by design teams were not significant, it is worth noting that RW had the highest score of all design teams (mean = 3.7) while NARE had the lowest (mean = 2.9).

---

[4]Again, Dade County Public Schools did not allow RAND to ask about certain issues including teachers meeting together to discuss and critique instruction.

PROFESSIONAL DEVELOPMENT INDEX[5]

Research has shown the importance of providing support and in-service training during the early implementation period (McLaughlin and Marsh, 1978; Fullan, 1982, 1991). Indeed, "sustained interaction and staff development are crucial regardless of what the change is concerned with" (Fullan, 1982, p. 67). We created an index that measured both the perceived quality of the professional development (PD) activities and the effects of these activities on classroom practice.

Teachers were asked the extent to which they agreed (on a scale of 1–4, where 1 = strongly disagree and 4 = strongly agree) that the professional development activities sponsored by the design teams, the school, or the district during the past 12 months:

- Deepened their understanding of the subject matter taught;

- Led them to make changes in their teaching;

- Deepened their understanding of how students learn the subject matter taught.

In addition, a number of questions asked to what degree specific PD activities—such as content standards, single-subject area teaching, and teaching techniques such as cooperative learning or constructivist classrooms—affected classroom practice. These responses were recoded on a scale of 1–4, where 1 = none and 4 = a substantial amount. A simple summative scale was constructed using the teacher responses on these variables to create an aggregated score for each school that represented an average across all respondents in that school.[6]

The distribution of this index is shown in Figures B.9 and B.10 by jurisdiction and design team, respectively. There is little variation across jurisdictions and design teams. Moreover, most of the schools fall at the midpoint, which is 2.5 on this scale, as indicated by the

---

[5]The questions that form the basis of the professional development (PD) index were added in 1998, so we cannot compare trends across years.

[6]The alpha reliability for this index was .81. The range of correlations for the individual items was 0.30 to 0.70.

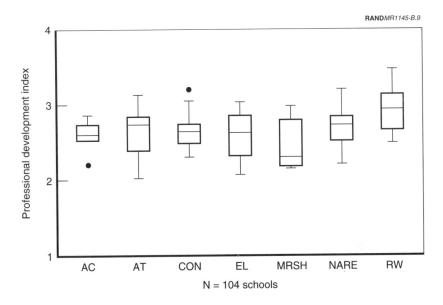

Figure B.9—Professional Development Index by Jurisdiction, Spring 1998

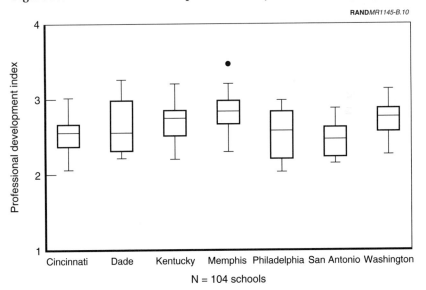

Figure B.10—Professional Development Index by Design Team,
Spring 1998

overall mean of 2.67 (SD = .29). The only differences that are statistically significant are those between Memphis (mean = 2.82) and San Antonio (mean = 2.45) and Memphis and Cincinnati (mean = 2.54). Among design teams, the only statistical differences are between RW (mean = 2.92) and EL (mean = 2.59) and between RW and MRSH (mean = 2.43).

Both the lack of variation and level for this PD index suggest that districts and design teams have a way to go in making their professional development activities coherent enough to influence teacher judgments about effects on their practice. We can offer some reasons for this finding. First, for the most part, the NAS districts failed to provide the number of professional development days or amount of planning time envisioned by the teams (Keltner, 1998; Bodily, 1998). Second, schools did not have full autonomy over hiring and staff development, or promotion. Thus, "the designs had to rethink what professional development might mean given the real constraints faced by schools" (Bodily, forthcoming, p. 39).

PERFORMANCE EXPECTATIONS INDEX

Setting expectations for performance is a critical component of the designs, even though each may differ in the process to attain this goal. Teachers reported whether their schools were explicitly linking student assessments to academic standards, making expectations explicit to students, establishing consistent and coherent curriculum and performance standards, and monitoring students according to annual performance targets.[7] The average across the designs for this index was 4.15 (SD = .55) on a scale that ranged from a low of 1 to a high of 6. This mean was essentially unchanged from the previous year when the overall mean reported across the sample was 4.08 (SD = .66).

Most schools had made considerable progress in setting challenging performance expectations for their students by spring 1998, although some jurisdictions (such as San Antonio) had room for improvement (see Figure B.11). Memphis and Kentucky ranked the highest among

---

[7]The alpha reliability for this index was .77. The range of correlations for the individual items was 0.40 to 0.55.

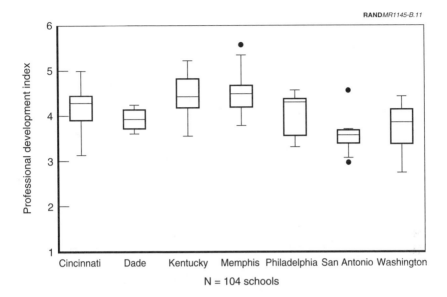

RAND*MR1145-B.11*

Figure B.11—Performance Expectations Index by NAS Design, Spring 1998

all the jurisdictions with means of 4.48 and 4.43, respectively. Washington and San Antonio ranked the lowest with means of 3.74 and 3.55, respectively. The differences between the high and low scoring groups were all significant.

There was little variation in the performance expectations (PE) index across designs. This is not surprising because all the designs accommodated to district insistence that they meet district or state standards and that the student performance be judged against district- or state-mandated tests. RW and CON schools ranked higher on the performance expectations measure, while MRSH ranked the lowest. However, the absolute differences in means were not large, and none of the differences was statistically significant.

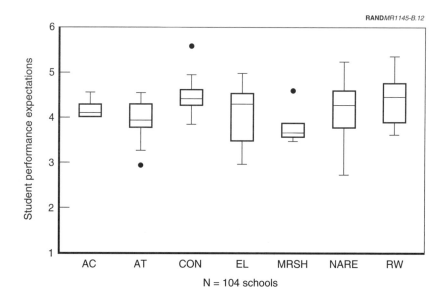

RAND*MR1145-B.12*

Figure B.12—Performance Expectations Index by NAS Design, Spring 1998

INSTRUCTIONAL STRATEGIES INDEX

The interactions between teachers and students are at the heart of the schooling process. The NAS designs provide different visions, yet each embraces instructional strategies that involve different relationships among teachers, students, and subject matter.

Here we examine a simple summative index that combines several different instructional strategies. This set of strategies is by no means exhaustive. While several of them are considered to be reformlike, these indicators do not fully capture the unique instructional activities of each design. Indeed, it would be difficult to do so because design team–specific instructional strategies continue to evolve and adapt to local circumstances (Bodilly, forthcoming) and instruction is difficult to measure (Gamoran et al., 1995; Berends, Kirby, and Sloan, 2000).

The instructional strategies index[8] was comprised of aggregated teacher responses describing the extent (a low of 1 to a high of 6) that the statement describes their school, including:

- Students are required to make formal presentations to exhibit what they have learned before they can progress to the next level;

- Teachers develop and monitor student progress with personalized, individualized learning programs;

- Students frequently revise their work toward an exemplary final product;

- Scope and sequence of the curriculum is organized into semester-long themes;

- Students engage in project-based learning for a significant portion of the school day (i.e., greater than one-third);

- Students frequently listen to speakers and go on field trips that specifically relate to the curriculum; and

- Curriculum throughout this school emphasizes preparation for and relevance to the world of work.

Most of the 104 NAS schools were implementing within the midrange on the 6-point scale for the instructional strategies index (see Figures B.13 and B.14). The 1998 overall mean for the sample of schools was 3.80 (SD = .62), unchanged from 1997, when the mean was 3.83 (SD = .65).

Memphis and Kentucky ranked high on this index, while Philadelphia, San Antonio, and Washington ranked the lowest. The differences between the high-scoring jurisdictions and the three who scored lowest were all statistically significant.

In their original proposals, design teams differed markedly from each other in terms of curriculum and instructional approaches. Some designs (notably AC, MRSH, and RW) developed prescriptive curriculum structures for teachers to use; others relied more on teachers to develop large parts of the curriculum. For the most part, the

---

[8]The alpha reliability for this index was .83. The range of correlations for the individual items was 0.36 to 0.61.

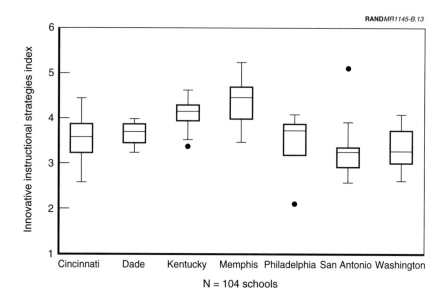

Figure B.13—Instructional Strategies Index by Jurisdiction, Spring 1998

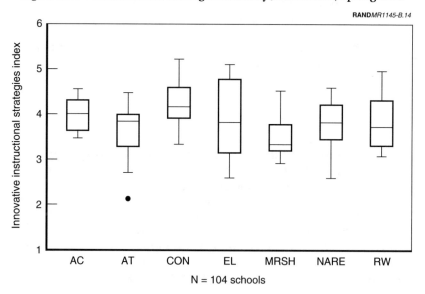

Figure B.14—Instructional Strategies Index by NAS Design, Spring 1998

curriculum tended to be interdisciplinary, project-based, and organized in semesterlong themes. There have been substantial changes over time as the designs faced the realities of working with high-poverty, low-achieving schools. The districts emphasized basic-skills acquisition, which may have narrowed the instructional strategies toward basic-skills strategies rather than the instructional strategies encouraged by the designs. As a result, we do not see much variation in the instructional strategies index among the design teams (see Figure B.14). CON schools ranked the highest (mean = 4.20) and MRSH the lowest (mean = 3.51). However, differences among design teams were not statistically significant.

INSTRUCTIONAL GROUPING ARRANGEMENTS

At some point in their development, most of the NAS designs have explored alternative ways to group students for instructional purposes, including multi-age grouping, having teachers follow a cohort of students across years (i.e., "looping" or multi-year grouping), or experimenting with block scheduling. Over the three years of scale-up, the groupings originally advocated by the designs changed somewhat, with several (such as detracking, multi-age looping, smaller class sizes) largely being dropped or transformed into principles to work toward rather than being implemented up front.

Here we explore the extent of teacher-reported implementation of these different grouping arrangements within the 104 implementing NAS schools (Figures B.15 and B.16).

There is substantial variability across both jurisdictions and design teams as well within jurisdictions (see for example, the box plot for Cincinnati) and design teams (for instance, EL). On average, four jurisdictions clearly supported such instructional grouping arrangements (with means of over 4.0), while Philadelphia, San Antonio, and Washington did not (means of 2.76–2.93). The differences between Memphis and Kentucky and these latter jurisdictions were statistically significant.

Similarly, some design teams stood out. Both CON and RW had means over 4.50 on this indicator, while AT and MRSH had means of

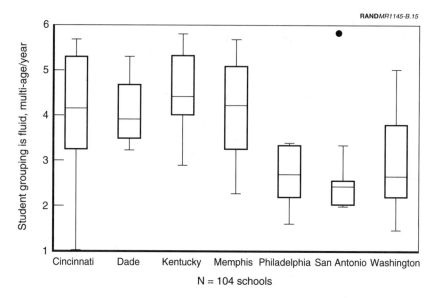

Figure B.15—Alternative Student Grouping Arrangements by Jurisdiction, Spring 1998

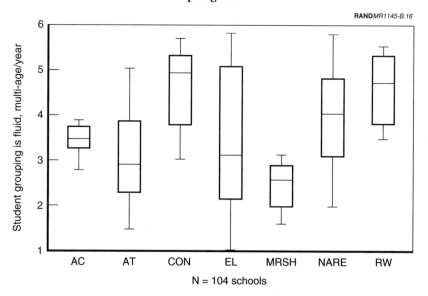

Figure B.16—Alternative Student Grouping Arrangements by Design Team, Spring 1998

less than 3.00, compared to the sample mean of 3.74 (SD = 1.23).[9] These differences (across all four comparisons) were statistically significant.

The overall mean for schools regarding the use of block scheduling for specific curricular purposes was 3.65 (SD = 1.07), essentially unchanged since 1997 (mean = 3.71, SD = 1.08). Figures B.17 and B.18 highlight differences across jurisdictions and design teams. Dade and Memphis were far above the sample average, while Philadelphia and Washington ranked the lowest. The only statistically significant difference in B.17 was between Memphis and Washington, where the difference was 1.14 points.

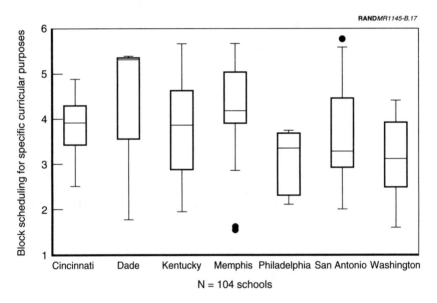

Figure B.17—Block Scheduling for Specific Curricular Purposes by Jurisdiction, Spring 1998

---

[9]As with other variables, we did not see a change in the overall mean from 1997 to 1998. The mean for 1997 was 4.69 (SD = 1.24).

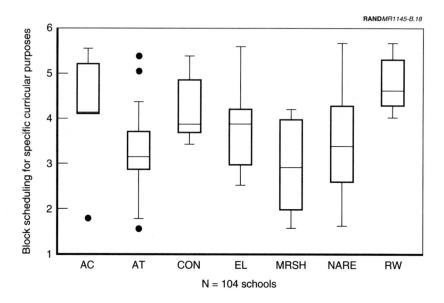

Figure B.18—Block Scheduling for Jurisdiction by NAS Design, Spring 1998

RW schools tended to report the highest levels for the block-scheduling indicator (mean = 4.63) when compared to the other designs. This is not surprising given that RW specifies block scheduling for its three curriculum components, as opposed to other designs that recommend a flexible schedule. The school mean differences between RW and AT, NARE, and MRSH were statistically significant.

INVOLVEMENT OF PARENTS AND COMMUNITY

Involving parents and community in schools has received a great deal of attention by policymakers, educational reformers, and researchers in recent years (Epstein, 1985, 1992). To a certain extent, each of the designs encourages parent involvement in schools to benefit the educational opportunities of students. Originally, five of the designs (AT, EL, MRSH, NARE, and RW) envisioned the school as the center for the provision of social services for students and their families. However, reality forced these designs to largely abandon the concept of social services provision and accept a much more limited role for the school.

In addition to parent and community involvement actions, several of the designs encourage students to think about how their learning applies to the world outside of school.[10] On our teacher surveys, we included items to indicate the extent to which: (1) schools encouraged students to apply their learning in ways that directly benefited the community, and (2) parents and community members were involved in the educational program within the school.

Figures B.19 through B.22 show the distribution of the two indicators by jurisdiction and design team. There is the familiar pattern among jurisdictions with Memphis and Kentucky (means of 4.11 and 3.98, respectively) ranking high and Philadelphia, San Antonio, and Washington (means of between 3.18 and 3.47) ranking low on this scale. The differences in means between Memphis and the three lowest

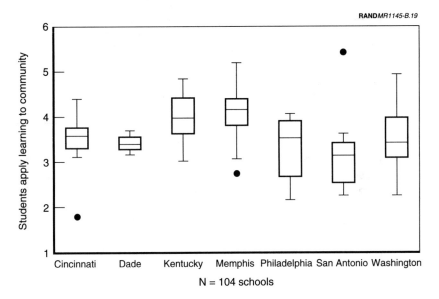

Figure B.19—Students Apply Learning in Ways that Directly Benefit the Community by Jurisdiction, Spring 1998

[10]Application of student learning to the community has received quite a bit of recent attention in restructuring efforts independent of NAS (see Newmann and Wehlage, 1995; Newmann et al., 1996).

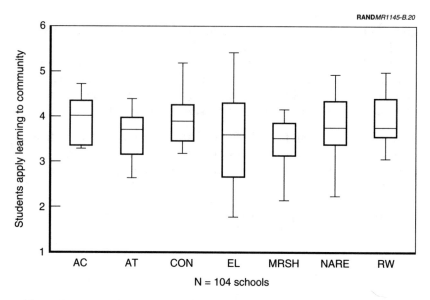

Figure B.20—Students Apply Learning in Ways that Directly Benefit the
Community by NAS Design, Spring 1998

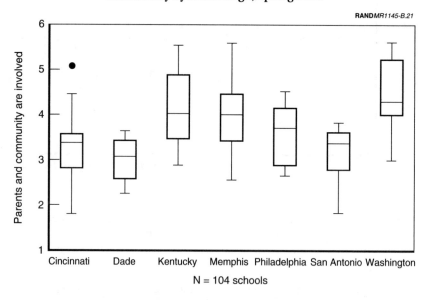

Figure B.21—Parent and Community Involvement by Jurisdiction,
Spring 1998

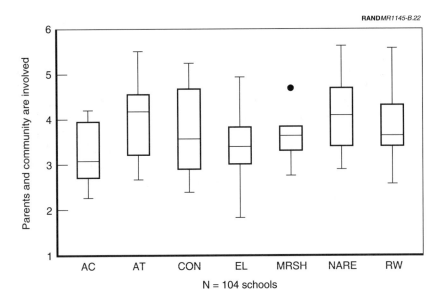

**Figure B.22—Parent and Community Involvement by NAS Design,
Spring 1998**

jurisdictions were all significant, as was the difference between Kentucky and San Antonio. The overall mean for the sample was 3.71, SD = .69.[11] The distribution for schools by design teams showed no significant differences, although AC ranked highest on this indicator. AC requires its students to serve as ambassadors to the larger community and each semester "culminates in a constructive action that has been determined by the students and is directed toward improving the world outside the classroom" (Bodilly, 1998, p. 122).

The overall mean for the sample on the parent and community involvement indicator was 3.82 (SD = .87), and there was no change from 1997 (mean = 3.86, SD = .79). Across jurisdictions, Memphis and Kentucky scored higher on this indicator than San Antonio and Dade; an interesting reversal here was that Washington ranked highest on parent and community involvement of all jurisdictions with a

_____
[11]The 1997 mean was 3.66, SD = .66.

mean of 4.38. Differences between Washington and Dade, Cincinnati, and San Antonio were all statistically significant.

NARE ranked the highest on this indicator because of its emphasis on getting the school staff to reach out to families to support student learning, and helping the school build safety nets, create community partners, and appoint community outreach coordinators. This result about NARE may reflect more of a Kentucky phenomenon than a NARE one; a large proportion of the NARE schools in our sample are in Kentucky, which has implemented family support centers funded by the state. The differences among the design teams were not statistically significant.

MODELS OF PERFORMANCE EXPECTATIONS, INSTRUCTIONAL STRATEGIES, AND PROFESSIONAL DEVELOPMENT AND IMPLEMENTATION INDICES

Table C.1

Multilevel Results for the Relationships of Implementation to Teacher-, School-, and Design-Related Factors

Variables	Performance Expectations Index		Instructional Strategies Index		Professional Development Index		Core Implementation Index	
	Coefficient	Standard Error	Coefficient	Standard Error	Coefficient	Standard Error	Coefficient	Standard Error
Intercept	0.224	0.091	0.519	0.152	0.003	0.093	0.341	0.106
Independent Variables for Teachers								
Race-ethnicity								
African American	0.120*	0.054	0.301**	0.051	0.192**	0.056	0.201**	0.050
Hispanic/Latino	0.079	0.108	0.305**	0.102	0.176	0.114	0.161	0.101
Other/missing	−0.094	0.078	0.154*	0.073	−0.013	0.081	0.055	0.071
Educational degree: Master's or above	−0.011	0.043	−0.052	0.040	−0.071	0.045	−0.044	0.040
Age: ≥30 years	−0.010	0.065	−0.150*	0.061	−0.076	0.068	−0.096	0.060
Years of teaching experience	0.027	0.023	0.031	0.021	−0.005	0.024	0.014	0.021
Lack of basic skills a hindrance (1–4, 1 = great hindrance, 4 = not at all)	0.074**	0.023	0.053*	0.022	−0.011	0.024	0.079**	0.022
Student discipline and inadequate parent support a hindrance (2–8, 2 = great hindrance, 8 = not at all)	0.087**	0.025	0.130**	0.024	0.053*	0.026	0.143**	0.023
Students can learn with available resources (1–4, 1 = strongly disagree, 4 = strongly agree)	0.087**	0.020	0.084**	0.019	0.046*	0.021	0.086**	0.019
Design-related variables								
Communication by designs to schools (1–6)	0.292**	0.024	0.270**	0.023	0.184**	0.025	0.260**	0.023
Support for design (1–5)	0.125**	0.022	0.138**	0.021	0.369**	0.024	0.146**	0.021
Attended design team workshop in last 12 months	0.082	0.047	0.076	0.044	0.220**	0.050	0.028	0.043

Table C.1 (continued)

Variables	Performance Expectations Index Coefficient	Standard Error	Instructional Strategies Index Coefficient	Standard Error	Professional Development Index Coefficient	Standard Error	Core Implementation Index Coefficient	Standard Error
Independent Variables for Schools								
Poverty	0.097*	0.048	-0.042	0.056	0.140**	0.049	0.014	0.056
Minority	0.001	0.054	-0.064	0.064	-0.018	0.055	0.005	0.064
Large size (> 400)	-0.144	0.077	-0.254**	0.088	0.070	0.080	-0.237**	0.088
Secondary schools	-0.093	0.061	-0.006	0.072	-0.019	0.064	-0.161*	0.072
Percent student mobility	-0.036	0.030	-0.020	0.035	-0.020	0.031	-0.016	0.035
PD days devoted to design team	0.022	0.031	0.070	0.038	-0.022	0.032	-0.005	0.038
Years Implementing	0.036	0.030	-0.008	0.036	0.019	0.032	0.025	0.036
Resources index (range 1–5)	0.024	0.031	0.011	0.036	0.028	0.032	0.098**	0.036
Cincinnati	-0.138	0.087	-0.582**	0.101	-0.338**	0.090	-0.232*	0.102
Dade	-0.123	0.145	-0.253	0.173	-0.413**	0.150	-0.286	0.173
Kentucky	0.280*	0.118	-0.019	0.139	0.158	0.123	0.398**	0.138
Philadelphia	-0.006	0.116	-0.510**	0.137	-0.117	0.121	-0.321*	0.138
San Antonio	-0.706**	0.118	-0.835**	0.136	-0.461**	0.121	-0.626**	0.135
Washington	-0.340*	0.134	-0.872**	0.157	0.142	0.138	-0.311	0.158
Sample Size								
Teachers	1,848		1,827		1,661		1,842	
Schools	104		104		104		104	
Variance Components								
Variance between schools (τ)	0.179		0.261		0.113		0.270	
Proportion explained by model	0.888		0.816		0.823		0.815	
Variance within schools (σ²)	0.823		0.743		0.889		0.720	
Proportion explained by model	0.188		0.226		0.258		0.225	

Notes: *significant at .05 level; **significant at .01 level.

DESCRIPTION OF STANDARDIZED TESTS USED BY VARIOUS JURISDICTIONS

CALIFORNIA ACHIEVEMENT TEST SERIES, FORM E

The California Achievement Test (CAT) is a norm- and criterion-referenced achievement test for students in kindergarten through 12th grade, developed by CTB/McGraw-Hill. Form E was published in 1985 and assesses student achievement across the following subject areas (although content varies by grade level): reading, language, spelling, mathematics, and study skills, with optional coverage of science and social studies. Two newer versions of the CAT (the fourth and fifth editions) have been published since the publication of Form E back in 1985; however, the CAT assessment data referenced in this report are from Form E.

COMPREHENSIVE TEST OF BASIC SKILLS, FOURTH EDITION

The Comprehensive Test of Basic Skills (CTBS) is a norm- and criterion-referenced achievement assessment for students in kindergarten through 12th grade, developed by CTB, a Macmillan/McGraw-Hill Company. The fourth edition of the test was developed between the years 1984 and 1989. The CTBS is made up of 11 testing levels that measure student achievement across the following subject areas: mathematics, study skills, science, and social studies. The CTBS is available in three configurations: the Benchmark Battery, the Survey Battery, and the Complete Battery. The Benchmark Battery and the Survey Battery are solely norm-referenced assessments (where Survey is a shortened version of Benchmark), whereas the Complete Battery also includes a criterion-referenced section.

The CTBS/4 was nationally standardized separately for both spring and fall administrations in 1988 using a stratified random sample of 156,000 (spring) and 167,000 (fall) K–12 students drawn from public, Catholic private, and non-Catholic private schools. The test drew on a wide variety of curriculum and existing assessment instruments in order to identify broad concepts common to all curricula. This information was used to ensure that the entire test was not content specific and to formulate broadly applicable criterion for the criterion-referenced portion of the exam. A newer version of the CTBS, known as TerraNova, was normed in 1996. However, the CTBS assessment data referenced in this report are from the older version of this test, the CTBS/4.

IOWA TEST OF BASIC SKILLS, FORMS K & L

The Iowa Test of Basic Skills (ITBS) is a norm-referenced achievement test for students in kindergarten though 8th grade, developed by the Iowa Testing Program at the University of Iowa and published as part of the Riverside 2000 Integrated Assessment Program by the Riverside Publishing Company. Forms K and L of the ITBS were published in 1994. The ITBS is made up of 10 levels.

Levels 5 and 6 are intended for administration to students in kindergarten and 1st grade with no time limit. These levels are only published in one length, known as the Complete Battery. The Complete Battery covers listening, vocabulary, language, and mathematics with optional sections for reading and word analysis. Levels 5 and 6 are only available in one form, Form K.

Levels 7 and 8 are intended for administration to students in 1st through 3rd grade with no time limit. These levels are published in three lengths, known as the Survey Battery, the Core Battery, and the Complete Battery. The Survey Battery is the shortest, containing a section each for reading, language, and mathematics, with an optional section for math computation. The Core Battery is in the middle, containing a section each for listening, vocabulary, reading, language, mathematics concepts, and mathematics problems, with optional sections for word analysis and mathematics computation. The Complete Battery is the longest, containing social studies, science, and sources of information sections—in addition to all the sections included in the Core Battery. Levels 7 and 8 (all three batteries) are published in two equivalent forms, Form K and Form L.

Levels 9–14 are intended for administration to students in 3rd through 9th grade. These levels are also published in three lengths, the Survey Battery, the Core Battery, and the Complete Battery. The Survey Battery contains a section each for reading, language, and mathematics, with an optional section for math computation. The Core Battery contains a section each for vocabulary, reading comprehension, spelling, capitalization, punctuation, usage and expression, math concepts and estimation, math problem solving and data interpretation, and math computation. The Complete Battery contains social studies, science, maps and diagrams, and reference materials sections—in addition to all the sections included in the Core Battery. Levels 8–14 (all three batteries) are published in two equivalent forms, Form K and Form L.

Forms K and L of the Test of Achievement and Proficiency (TAP) were normed (in a joint norming program with the ITBS) in the spring and fall of 1992. The norming was conducted using a stratified random sample of public school districts, Catholic private schools, and other private schools. The spring sample included approximately 170,000 students, while the fall sample included approximately 100,000 students.

KENTUCKY INSTRUCTIONAL RESULTS INFORMATION SYSTEM

The Kentucky Instructional Results Information System (KIRIS) is a performance assessment developed by Advanced Systems for Measurement in Education on contract with the Kentucky Department of Education. The creation of this test was mandated by the Kentucky Education Reform Act (KERA) of 1990, which links school performance on standardized performance assessments to a system of rewards and sanctions. The KIRIS is intended to be a broad criterion-referenced performance assessment rather than a traditional multiple choice achievement test. It was decided that no previously developed assessment would fulfill these requirements; in order to develop the test and establish baseline performance for each school, the test was implemented for an interim period beginning in the 1991–1992 school year.

The KIRIS originally covered the following subject areas: mathematics, reading, science, social studies, and writing. Sections testing arts/humanities and living/vocational studies were added in 1995. The KIRIS is mandatory for all Kentucky State students, with very few exemptions, in the 4th, 8th, and 12th grades (although most 12th grade testing was moved to the 11th grade in 1995). The exam is made up of three components: the Traditional Assessment, the Performance Event, and the Portfolio Assessment.

The Transitional Assessment includes both multiple choice and open-ended questions across all of the tested subject areas. Although the exam was primarily intended to be a performance assessment, it was deemed necessary to include multiple choice questions as a "safety net" in case the open-ended questions failed to meet technical standards. The state concluded that the open-ended questions were technically satisfactory and decided to eliminate the multiple choice questions in 1995 (in the long term the state hoped to eliminate the Transitional Assessment altogether and rely exclusively on the remaining components). However, this decision was reversed in 1997 and multiple choice questions were re-added due to their technical importance in the areas of content validity, reliability, and score equating. The Transitional Assessment has 12 equivalent forms, each of which contain both questions that are common to all forms and questions that are unique to the specific form. The writing portion of the Transitional Assessment is an exception to the above, with only 9 forms, where the student must respond to 1 of 2 writing prompts. While the KIRIS is mandated in the 4th, 8th, and 11th grades, additional levels of the Transitional Assessment, known as the Continuous Assessment, are available for all grades if a school is interested in administering a schoolwide assessment.

The Performance Event requires each student to take part in a task that draws upon group and individual problem solving skills. Four performance events were developed in each content area. Students are given 50–60 minutes, depending on the grade, to complete the task.

The Portfolio Assessment requires each student to compile exemplary samples of his/her work into a folder throughout the school year. Originally, there was only a Portfolio Assessment in writing, but later a math portfolio was added. Originally, teachers graded their own student's portfolios, but it was discovered that the student's teacher gave significantly higher grades than did independent graders.

According to legislation, the KIRIS was intended to be both a norm- and criterion-referenced exam, but a norming has never been conducted. The tested curriculum was designed to gauge student performance across a wide variety of broadly defined educational goals; goals included specific content/skills requirements as well as the ability to complete certain cognitive processes. These goals were both developed by the State Board of Education and drawn from the criterion used in the National Assessment of Educational Progress (NAEP).

STANFORD ACHIEVEMENT TEST SERIES, EIGHTH AND NINTH EDITIONS

The Stanford Achievement Test Series is a norm-referenced achievement testing series developed by Harcourt Brace Educational Measurement. The Stanford Achievement Test Series consists of three components: the Stanford Early School Achievement Test (SESAT), the Stanford Achievement Test (SAT), and the Stanford Test of Academic Skills (TASK); together these components assess student achievement in reading, language arts, mathematics, science, and social science for students in kindergarten through 12th grade (although subject coverage varies according to grade level). The SESAT is made up of two levels that measure student achievement in kindergarten and the first half of 1st grade. The SAT is made up of 8 levels that measure student achievement from the second half of 1st grade through the end of 9th grade. Finally, the TASK is made up of three levels that measure student achievement from the beginning of 9th grade through college entry. All levels of the SAT and the TASK consist of two equivalent forms, while the SESAT only consists of a single form. Two editions of the Stanford Achievement Test Series are referenced in this report.

The eighth edition, referred to as the SAT/8 or the Stanford 8, is a traditional norm-referenced, multiple choice achievement test. The SAT/8 was norm-referenced in the spring and fall of 1988 using a randomly selected sample of schools/districts, with selection stratified by socioeconomic status, urbanicity, ethnicity, and public/private school type; approximately 175,000 students from 1,000 districts participated in the spring norming, although only 20 percent of invited schools/districts responded. Approximately 135,000 students participated in the fall norming, although only 30 percent of invited schools/districts responded. The eighth edition was published in 1989.

The ninth edition, referred to as the SAT/9 or the Stanford 9, is both a norm- and criterion-referenced achievement test, consisting of both free and fixed response items (each SAT/9 level is divided into a multiple choice and a free-response section; the test administrator has the choice of using either section as a stand-alone test or using both sections together). The SAT/9 was norm-referenced in the spring and fall of 1995 using a randomly selected sample of schools/districts, with selection stratified by socioeconomic status, urbanicity, ethnicity, and public/private funding. Approximately 250,000 students from 1,000 districts participated in the spring norming, although only 20 percent of invited schools/districts responded; approximately 200,000 students participated in the fall norming, although only 30 percent of invited schools/districts responded. The SAT/9 was criterion-referenced in 1995 using a panel of 200 educators who were gathered together in order to evaluate how well students of various performance levels should be expected to perform on the SAT/9. The ninth edition was published in 1996.

TEST OF ACHIEVEMENT AND PROFICIENCY, FORMS K AND L

The Test of Achievement and Proficiency (TAP) is a norm-referenced achievement test for students in high school, published as part of the Riverside 2000 Integrated Assessment Program by the Riverside Publishing Company. Forms K and L of the TAP were published in 1994. The TAP is made up of 4 levels.

Levels 15–18 are intended for administration to students in 9th through 12th grade. These levels are published in two lengths, the Survey Battery and the Complete Battery. The Survey Battery contains a section each for reading, language, and mathematics, with an optional section for math computation. The Complete Battery contains a section each for vocabulary, reading comprehension, written expression, math concepts and problem solving, social studies, science, and information processing, with an optional section for math computation. The TAP (both batteries) are published in two equivalent forms, Form K and Form L.

Forms K and L of the TAP were normed (in a joint norming program with the ITBS) in the spring and fall of 1992. The norming was conducted using a stratified random sample of public school districts, Catholic private schools, and other private schools. The spring sample included approximately 170,000 students, while the fall sample included approximately 100,000 students.

TEXAS ASSESSMENT OF ACADEMIC SKILLS

The Texas Assessment of Academic Skills (TAAS) is a norm- and criterion-referenced achievement assessment for students exiting high school or in 3rd–8th grade. Legislative action in the fall of 1990 required that the existing Texas Assessment of Minimum Skills (TEAMS) be replaced with a criterion-referenced testing program. Legislation additionally required the development of end-of-course tests to be administered after the completion of specific high school courses. The Student Assessment Division of the Texas Education Agency (TEA) was given the responsibility of creating the TAAS, which was created and is maintained with the help of several subcontractors, including Harcourt Brace Educational Measurement. Two forms of each battery exist, with a third Spanish form currently in development. Since the spring of 1994, the TAAS reading and mathematics assessments have been administered to students exiting high school or in 3rd–8th grade. Writing assessment began at the same time for students exiting high school or in 4th and 8th grade. In the spring of 1995, science and social studies assessments were added for grade 8 only. End-of-course assessments were implemented in Biology I and Algebra I in the spring of 1994 (although

Algebra I was subsequently revised and reintroduced in the spring of 1995).   End-of-course exams are currently in development for American History and English II.

The content development began with the Texas Essential Elements, defined by the State Board of Education. Test objectives were formulated by TEA staff members with the aid of advisory committees. These objectives were broad subject-specific educational themes that transcended the primary and secondary educational systems. These subject-specific objectives were then broken down into grade-specific instructional targets.

In addition to mandating that the TAAS be criterion-referenced, legislation also required that the TAAS be norm-referenced. The TEA contracted Harcourt Brace Educational Measurement to conduct the norming process. The norming was conducted by administering the Metropolitan Achievement Test, Seventh Edition (MAT/7) to a stratified random sample of Texas classrooms in the spring of 1996 and equating the TAAS to the MAT/7. The stratified sample targeted about 12,500 students per grade with a response rate of about 57 percent across all subject area components.

GRAPHS FOR READING SCORES FOR NAS SCHOOLS IN EVERETT, NORTHSHORE, AND SHORELINE DISTRICTS IN WASHINGTON

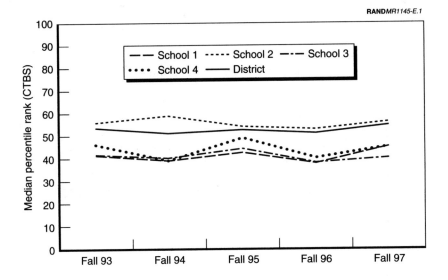

Figure E.1—Mean Percentile Reading Scores in Everett: NAS Schools
Compared to the District, Grade 4

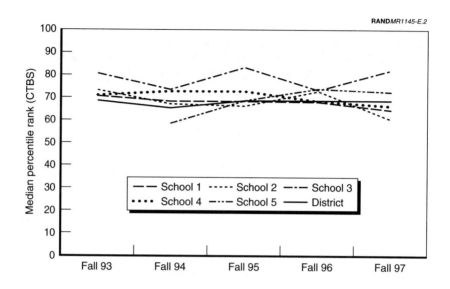

Figure E.2—Mean Percentile Reading Scores in Northshore: NAS Schools Compared to the District, Grade 4

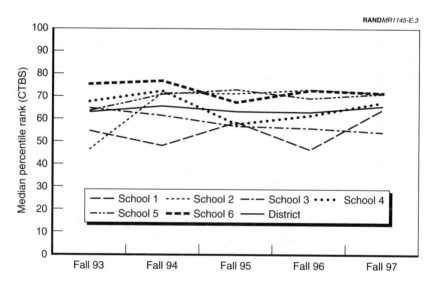

Figure E.3—Mean Percentile Reading Scores in Shoreline: NAS Schools Compared to the District, Grade 4

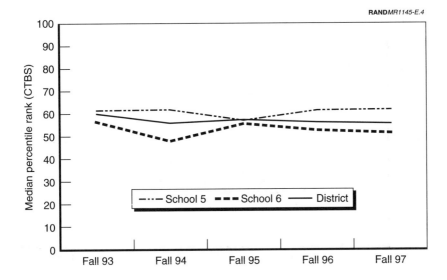

Figure E.4—Mean Percentile Reading Scores in Everett: NAS Schools
Compared to the District, Grade 8

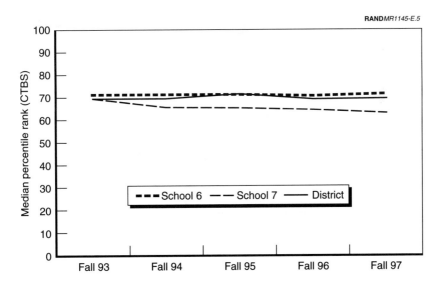

Figure E.5—Mean Percentile Reading Scores in Northshore: NAS Schools
Compared to the District, Grade 8

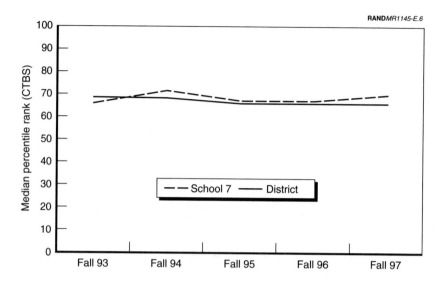

Figure E.6—Mean Percentile Reading Scores in Shoreline: NAS Schools Compared to the District, Grade 8

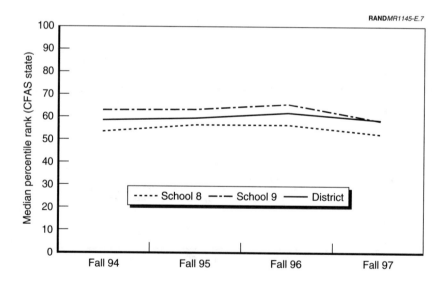

Figure E.7—Mean Percentile English/Language Arts Scores in Northshore: NAS Schools Compared to the District, Grade 11

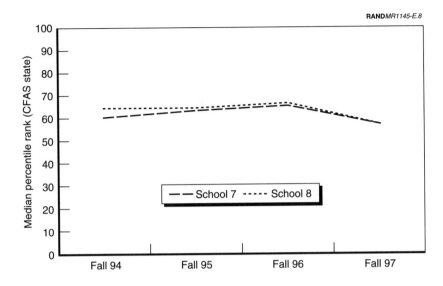

RAND*MR1145-E.8*

Figure E.8—Mean Percentile English/Language Arts Scores in Shoreline:
NAS Schools, Grade 11

RAND PRINCIPAL AND TEACHER QUESTIONNAIRES

Rand Teacher Survey of New American Schools: Spring 1998

RAND is conducting this survey to learn about your experiences with one of the New American Schools (NAS) designs. Completing it is voluntary, but the information you provide will be critical for understanding the impact of this reform across the nation.

RAND will keep your responses strictly *confidential*; no information that could be linked to you or your school will be released by RAND to any party except as required by law. RAND will retain and keep secure the names of teachers so that we can contact teachers for next year's survey.

Filling out the survey should take about **THIRTY MINUTES**. Please indicate which questions, if any, are unclear and briefly explain why.

After you are finished, please remove the label with your name on it, seal your completed survey in the attached envelope, and return it to the designated person in your school who will send the sealed surveys back to RAND.

THANK YOU, in advance, for your time, your honesty, and your input.

      RAND Education
      1333 H Street, NW
      Washington, DC 20005-4707
      (202) 296-5000
      Main Offices:
      1700 Main Street PO Box 2138
      Santa Monica, CA 90407-2138
      (310) 393-0411

I. IMPLEMENTATION OF DESIGN-BASED ASSISTANCE IN YOUR SCHOOL

1. What New American Schools (NAS) design is being implemented in your school?

   ⬭ Authentic Teaching, Learning, and Assessment for All Students (ATLAS)

   ⬭ Audrey Cohen (a.k.a. Purpose-Centered Education)

   ⬭ Co-NECT

   ⬭ Expeditionary Learning Outward Bound (ELOB)

   ⬭ Modern Red Schoolhouse

   ⬭ National Alliance for Restructuring Education (NARE) (a.k.a. America's Choice)

   ⬭ Roots & Wings

   ⬭ Other (please specify) _____

   ⬭ Don't know

2. How familiar are you with the NAS design team program in your school? *(circle one number)*

   Not at all familiar   1 2 3 4 5 6   Very familiar

3. This year, did the design team clearly communicate its program to school staff so that it could be well-implemented? *(circle one number)*

   No, not at all   1 2 3 4 5 6   Yes, definitely

4. To what extent does your school have the resources needed to implement the major elements of the design team program?

(mark one on each line)	No resources are available	Few are available	Some are available	Most are available	All are available
a. Design team materials to support instruction					
b. Availability of design team materials to further implement the design in your school					
c. Professional development for teachers					
d. Time for planning, collaboration, and development					
e. Staff or consultants to mentor, advise, and provide ongoing support					
f. Technology and connectivity					
g. Funds					
h. Funding flexibility					
i. Other resources (please specify) _____					

II. GENERAL PROGRAM ELEMENTS

5. To what extent do the following program elements describe your school? **(circle the number on each line that best describes your school now)**

(circle one number on each line)	Does not describe my school					Clearly describes my school	Don't Know
a. Teachers and others share in school decisionmaking and governance	1	2	3	4	5	6	7
b. Students are required on a regular basis to apply their learning in ways that directly benefit the community	1	2	3	4	5	6	7
c. Parents and community members are involved in the educational program	1	2	3	4	5	6	7
d. Most teachers in this school meet regularly with teachers in other schools to observe and discuss progress toward design team goals	1	2	3	4	5	6	7
e. Students are required by this school to make formal presentations to exhibit what they have learned before they can progress to the next level	1	2	3	4	5	6	7
f. Student assessments are explicitly linked to academic standards	1	2	3	4	5	6	7
g. Teachers develop and monitor student progress with personalized, individualized learning programs	1	2	3	4	5	6	7
h. Students frequently revise their work toward an exemplary final product	1	2	3	4	5	6	7
i. Student grouping is fluid, multi-age, OR multi-year	1	2	3	4	5	6	7
j. This school has specific activities aimed directly at reducing student absenteeism	1	2	3	4	5	6	7
k. Technology is an integrated classroom resource	1	2	3	4	5	6	7
l. The scope and sequence of the curriculum is organized into semester- or year-long themes	1	2	3	4	5	6	7
m. This school is part of a K–12 feeder pattern that provides integrated health and social services to improve student learning	1	2	3	4	5	6	7
n. Students engage in project-based learning for a significant portion of the school day (i.e., more than 1/3 of the time)	1	2	3	4	5	6	7
o. Students are organized into instructional groups using block scheduling for specific curricular purposes	1	2	3	4	5	6	7

(circle one number on each line)	Does not describe my school					Clearly describes my school	Don't Know
p. Teachers are continual learners and team members through professional development, common planning, and collaboration	1	2	3	4	5	6	7
q. Performance expectations are made explicit to students so that they can track their progress over time	1	2	3	4	5	6	7
r. Technology is used in this school to manage curriculum, instruction, and student progress	1	2	3	4	5	6	7
s. Students who are not progressing according to expectations are provided with extended days and/or tutors	1	2	3	4	5	6	7
t. Students frequently listen to speakers and go on field trips that specifically relate to the curriculum	1	2	3	4	5	6	7
u. Student assessments are used to reassign students to instructional groups on a frequent and regular basis	1	2	3	4	5	6	7
v. Consistent and coherent curriculum and performance standards have been established across the K–12 feeder patterns	1	2	3	4	5	6	7
w. There are formal arrangements within this school providing opportunities for teachers to discuss and critique their instruction with each other	1	2	3	4	5	6	7
x. This school has the authority to make budget, staffing, and program decisions	1	2	3	4	5	6	7
y. Students in this school are grouped by achievement levels into high, middle, and/or remedial instructional groups on a regular basis	1	2	3	4	5	6	7
z. Curriculum throughout this school emphasizes preparation for and relevance to the world of work (e.g., responsibility, collegiality, timeliness, and job-specific skills)	1	2	3	4	5	6	7
aa. A majority of teachers in this school stay with the same group of students for more than one year	1	2	3	4	5	6	7
bb. This school has a coordinator, facilitator, or resource specialist assigned on a full- or part-time basis	1	2	3	4	5	6	7
cc. Students are monitored according to annual performance targets established by the school as a whole	1	2	3	4	5	6	7

III. ACTIVITIES IN TARGET CLASS

Questions 6–10 ask for information about your teaching in a specific class, namely the group of students with whom you meet to teach a subject on a regular basis. We will refer to this class as the **TARGET CLASS** (please provide a full description such as language arts/reading; mathematics/ Algebra 2; history/U.S. History to 1865).

6. Name, Title, and Subject of your **TARGET CLASS**

   _____

7. How many hours per week does this class meet? _____ hours

8. Grade level of most of the students in the class _____

9. Number of students enrolled _____

10. Indicate about how much total time you spend during a *typical WEEK* doing each of the following with this **TARGET CLASS:** Because the categories are not mutually exclusive, the sum of time across categories need not sum to the total hours spent with the **TARGET CLASS** each week. *(mark one on each line)*

TYPICAL WEEK	none	5 min. to 30 min.	1 hour	2 hours	3 hours	4 hours	5 or more hours
a. Lecturing to the class as a whole							
b. Leading discussions							
c. Students working in small groups							
d. Drill and practice on basic facts, definitions, computations, skills, or procedures							
e. Providing instruction to individual students							
f. Conducting lab periods or other hands-on activities							
g. Students use class time for outside activities (field trips, library, community experiences, outside speakers, etc.)							
h. Problem-solving or research that requires organizing and integrating							
i. Maintaining order/keeping students on task/discipline							
j. Routine administrative tasks (attendance, announcements, etc.)							
k. Giving tests or quizzes that require brief responses (true/false, multiple-choice, short answer)							
l. Giving tests or quizzes that require extended responses (a sentence or more, demonstration, and/or graphic representation)							
m. Working independently on worksheets or in workbooks							

IV. IMPACT OF DESIGN-BASED ASSISTANCE

11. How satisfied are you with your students' progress *this school year* in the following areas?

(circle one number on each line)	Not satisfied					Very satisfied
a. Higher-order thinking	1	2	3	4	5	6
b. Understanding and use of subject area content	1	2	3	4	5	6
c. Elaborated oral and written communication	1	2	3	4	5	6
d. Order, discipline, and civil behavior	1	2	3	4	5	6
e. Ability to apply subject area content to new problems	1	2	3	4	5	6
f. Ability to work on academic tasks together in small groups	1	2	3	4	5	6
g. Ability to work independently	1	2	3	4	5	6
h. Student motivation to learn	1	2	3	4	5	6

12. On balance, to what extent has the NAS design team program had positive or negative effects on the following aspects of your work life during *this school year?*

(circle one number on each line)	Great deal of **negative** effect			**No Effect**			Great deal of **positive** effect
a. Your teaching	1	2	3	4	5	6	7
b. Your professional growth	1	2	3	4	5	6	7
c. Your job satisfaction	1	2	3	4	5	6	7
d. Your students' achievement	1	2	3	4	5	6	7
e. Your students' enthusiasm for learning	1	2	3	4	5	6	7
f. Your classroom curriculum	1	2	3	4	5	6	7
g. Your students' engagement in learning	1	2	3	4	5	6	7

13. How strongly do you support or oppose the NAS design team program in your school?

Strongly oppose	Somewhat oppose	Neither oppose nor support	Somewhat support	Strongly support
◯	◯	◯	◯	◯

13a. Please indicate the extent to which the following have changed in *the past 3 years* in your school.

(mark one on each line) THE PAST 3 YEARS	Greatly Improved	Somewhat Improved	Stayed about the Same	Somewhat Worsened	Greatly Worsened	Don't Know
a. Student behavior (order and discipline)						
b. The school's relationship with parents						
c. How the school relates to the community						
d. How students get along with students						
e. How teachers get along with students						
f. Student attendance						
g. The quality of curriculum						
h. The quality of instruction						
i. The quality of student academic performance						
j. How parents get along with teachers						
k. My commitment to the school						
l. Teachers learning from one another						
m. The quality of professional development						
n. Student engagement in learning						
o. My teaching effectiveness						

V. PARENT INVOLVEMENT & COMMUNITY RELATIONS

13b. How strongly do you agree or disagree with each of the following statements about your school?

(mark one on each line)	Strongly Disagree	Some-what Disagree	Some-what Agree	Strongly Agree
a. The principal encourages teachers to communicate regularly with parents.				
b. Parents are greeted warmly when they call or visit the school.				
c. Teachers work closely with parents to meet students' needs.				
d. Teachers and parents think of each other as partners in educating children.				
e. Parents have confidence in the expertise of the teachers.				
f. Staff at this school work hard to build trusting relationships with parents.				

VI. PROFESSIONAL DEVELOPMENT

13c. *During the past 12 months*, about how much time have you spent in professional development activities (sponsored by the New American Schools design team, your school, or district) devoted to the following topics?

(mark one on each line)	Hours spent in professional development				
THE PAST 12 MONTHS	None	1–4	5–8	9–24	24+
a. Alternative student assessment (performance-based, work sampling, etc.)					
b. Content standards					
c. Single subject area teaching (reading, mathematics, science, etc.)					
d. Teaching techniques (cooperative learning, constructivist classrooms, etc.)					
e. Student portfolio development and assessment					
f. Classroom management					
g. Educational technology					
h. Site-based management					

13d. For those professional development activities you participated in *during the last 12 months*, how much did those experiences affect your classroom practice?

(mark one on each line)	A Substantial Amount	A Moderate Amount	A Minimal Amount	None	Not Applicable— Did Not Attend
a. Alternative student assessment (performance-based, work sampling, etc.)					
b. Content standards					
c. Single subject area teaching (reading, mathematics, science, etc.)					
d. Teaching techniques (cooperative learning, constructivist classrooms, etc.)					
e. Student portfolio development and assessment					
f. Classroom management					
g. Educational technology					
h. Site-based management					

13e. Overall (on a scale from strongly agree to strongly disagree), the professional development activities sponsored by the NAS design team, your school, or district *during the past 12 months* have:

(mark one on each line) THE PAST 12 MONTHS	Strongly Disagree	Some- what Disagree	Some- what Agree	Strongly Agree
a. Been sustained and coherently focused, rather than short-lived and unrelated.				
b. Included enough time to think carefully about, try, and evaluate new ideas.				
c. Been closely connected to the design team's activities in my school.				
d. Included opportunities to work productively with colleagues in my school.				
e. Included opportunities to work pro- ductively with teachers from other schools.				
f. Deepened my understanding of the subject matter I teach.				
g. Led me to make changes in my teaching.				
h. Helped my school's staff work together better.				
i. Changed the way teachers talk about students in this school.				
j. Deepened my understanding of how students learn the subject matter I teach.				
k. Altered approaches to teaching in this school.				
l. Furthered my understanding of school- based management and the responsibili- ties involved.				
m. Advocated practices I do not believe in.				

13f. *In the last 12 months,* have you attended workshops or institutes specifically oriented toward the design team program activities?

Yes _____   No _____

14. *During the current school year,* how many additional hours per week outside of class did you devote, on average, to the NAS design team restructuring effort? _____ hours/week

15. Of this time, how many hours per week were <u>unpaid</u>? (unpaid refers to time after school or on weekends) _____ hours/week

16. On average *during the current school year,* how many hours per week have you spent by yourself preparing for your classes <u>during the regular school day</u>? _____ hours/week

17. On average *during the current school year,* how many hours per week have you spent with others in <u>common</u> planning time? _____ hours/week

VII. PERCEPTIONS AND ATTITUDES TOWARDS TEACHING

18. Do you agree or disagree with each of the following statements?

(mark one on each line)	Strongly Disagree	Somewhat Disagree	Somewhat Agree	Strongly Agree
a. Teachers in this school are evaluated fairly.				
b. The principal lets staff members know what is expected of them.				
c. The school administration's behavior toward the staff is supportive and encouraging.				
d. I am satisfied with my teaching salary.				
e. The level of student misbehavior (e.g., noise, horseplay or fighting in the halls, cafeteria or student lounge) in this school interferes with my teaching.				
f. Teachers participate in making most of the important educational decisions in this school.				
g. I receive a great deal of support from parents for the work I do.				
h. Necessary materials (e.g., textbooks, supplies, copy machine) are available as needed by the staff.				
i. The principal does a poor job of getting resources for this school.				
j. Routine duties and paperwork interfere with my job of teaching.				
k. My principal enforces school rules for student conduct and backs me up when I need it.				
l. The principal talks with me frequently about my instructional practices.				
m. Rules for student behavior are consistently enforced by teachers in this school, even for students who are not in their classes.				
n. Most of my colleagues share my beliefs and values about what the central mission of the school should be.				
o. The principal knows what kind of school he/she wants and has communicated it to the staff.				
p. There is a great deal of cooperative effort among the staff members.				
q. In this school, staff members are recognized for a job well done.				
r. I have to follow rules in this school that conflict with my best professional judgment.				

18a. There are many factors that may hinder or prevent students from achieving at high levels in school. To what extent do each of the following factors hinder *your students'* academic success?

(mark one on each line)	Greatly	Moderately	Slightly	Not at All
a. Lack of basic skills				
b. Inadequate prior student preparation in the subject areas				
c. Lack of student motivation				
d. Inadequate instructional materials				
e. Inadequate alignment of curriculum and standards				
f. Inadequate additional support for students who need it				
g. Student advancement to next grade without meeting promotion requirements				
h. High student mobility in and out of the school				
i. Poor student attendance				
j. Lack of coherent, sustained professional development for teachers				
k. Inadequate support from parents for students				
l. Lack of student discipline				

18b. To what extent do you agree or disagree with each of the following statements?

(mark one on each line)	Strongly Disagree	Somewhat Disagree	Somewhat Agree	Strongly Agree
a. My success or failure in teaching my students is due primarily to factors beyond my control rather than to my own efforts and ability.				
b. The attitudes and habits my students bring to my class greatly reduce their chances for academic success.				
c. Most of my students can learn with the school resources available to them.				

18c. *This school year*, how often have you had conversations with the colleagues at your school about:

(mark one on each line)	Less than once a month	Several times a month	Twice a week	Almost daily
a. What helps students learn best?				
b. Development of new curriculum?				
c. The goals of this school?				
d. Managing classroom behavior?				
e. Instructional strategies and approaches?				
f. Design team activities?				

18d. To what extent do you agree or disagree with each of the following statements?

(mark one on each line)	Strongly Disagree	Some-what Disagree	Some-what Agree	Strongly Agree
a. The principal has confidence in the expertise of the teachers.				
b. The principal takes a personal interest in the professional development of teachers.				
c. Teachers respect other teachers who take the lead in school improvement efforts.				
d. Teachers in this school trust each other.				
e. Teachers at this school respect those colleagues who are experts at their craft.				

VIII. TEACHER BACKGROUND

19. Prior to this year, how many years of experience have you had as a full-time teacher in this school?

_____ years

20. Prior to this year, how many years of experience have you had as a full-time teacher in other schools?

_____ years

21. Are you a member of this school faculty on

A full-time basis   ⬭

A part-time basis   ⬭

22. What is your primary affiliation with a single subject area department?

(mark only one)

a. No primary affiliation with a single subject (e.g., self-contained classroom)   ⬭

b. Special Education   ⬭

c. Reading/Language Arts/English   ⬭

d. History/Social Studies   ⬭

e. Math   ⬭

f. Science   ⬭

g. Art/Music   ⬭

h. Vocational Field   ⬭

i. Health/Physical Education   ⬭

j. English as a Second Language   ⬭

k. Bi-lingual Teacher   ⬭

l. Computer or Technology Teacher   ⬭

m. Counselor ⬭

n. Librarian ⬭

o. Other (please describe) ⬭

_____

23. Please mark the grade level of most of the students you teach in all classes.

(circle all that apply)

Pre-kinder-garten	kinder-garten	1	2	3	4	5	6	7	8	9	10	11	12
○	○	○	○	○	○	○	○	○	○	○	○	○	○

24. Your gender:

Male ⬭

Female ⬭

25. Which of the following categories best describes you?

American Indian or Alaskan Native ⬭

Asian or Pacific Islander ⬭

Hispanic, regardless of race ⬭

Black/African-American, not of Hispanic origin ⬭

White, not of Hispanic origin ⬭

Other (please write in)

_____

26. Your year of birth: 19 _____

27. Do you have a BA, BS, or some other four-year college degree?
Yes_____   No _____

28. If yes, what was your *major* subject area of study?

   _____

29. What was your college *minor* subject area of study?

   _____

30. If applicable, please mark and describe *all* advanced degrees you have earned.

		Major	Minor (if applicable)
a. Master's in education	◯	_____	_____
b. Master's in an academic subject	◯	_____	_____
c. Doctorate in education	◯	_____	_____
d. Doctorate in an academic subject	◯	_____	_____
e. Other degree	◯	_____	_____

If you were employed at this school last year and you changed your name (e.g., change in marital status), please **print** your former name in the space below. This is for statistical purposes only. Again, the information you provide will be kept strictly confidential. No teacher will be identified in results reported from this survey.

_____

Thank you for completing this questionnaire.

RAND PRINCIPAL PHONE INTERVIEW OF NEW AMERICAN SCHOOLS

SPRING 1998

School Name: _____

Principal Name: _____

Design Team Name: _____

Month/Day Interview Completed_____

Phone Number: _____

Interviewer Name: _____

(Cincinnati Public Schools, Dade County Public Schools, Memphis City Schools, the School District of Philadelphia, Pittsburgh Public Schools, San Antonio Independent School District, the State of Kentucky **OR** Washington Alliance for Better Schools), New American Schools (NAS), and RAND would like your help in gathering information about aids and impediments to school reform. Your input will help strengthen efforts to support your work. This year your school has continued its partnership with the New American Schools [ATLAS, Audrey Cohen, Co-NECT, ELOB, MRSH, National Alliance, or R&W] design team program. I would like to ask a number of questions about your early experiences with the design.

Before we begin, I'd like to make a couple of points. Today's conversation will focus on school reform and the New American Schools design; our interest is in general trends, not individual schools or educators. The information you provide will be kept strictly confidential. No information that could be linked to you or your school will be released by RAND to any party. Your participation in this interview is strictly voluntary and you may decline to participate or terminate the interview at any point. The interview will take about an hour. I will give you response options for each question, from which you may choose. However, feel free to elaborate on your answers as you wish.

Thank you, in advance, for your time and input.

A. PARTNERSHIP STATUS & ADOPTION OF THE DESIGN

0. Are you still a [ATLAS, Audrey Cohen, Co-NECT, ELOB, MRSH, National Alliance, or R&W] school this year?

                              (CIRCLE ONE)
                              No (0)   Yes (1)

    IF NOT: Are you implementing a different type of design?

                              No (0)   Yes (1)

    IF YES: Which design? (**SPECIFY** _____)

1. We are interested in the status of your partnership with [ATLAS, Audrey Cohen, Co-NECT, ELOB, MRSH, National Alliance, or R&W] this year.

    Would you say you are in:

    (CIRCLE ONE)

    1. an exploratory year, that is, the school hasn't committed to the design yet, Ë **GO TO QUESTION 3**

    2. a planning year, that is, the school has partnered with the design team and is planning for implementation next year, Ë **GO TO QUESTION 3**

    3. an initial implementation year for <u>part</u> of the school (a subset of the staff is implementing, e.g. a subset of teams, grades, a school-within-the-school),

    4. an initial implementation year for the <u>whole</u> school (all or most of the staff are working with the design),

    5. continuing implementation for part of the school, or

    6. continuing implementation for the whole school?

2. **If answer to Q1 is 3 through 6:** Including this year, how long has your school been implementing the design? (in years)

    _____ years **NOTE SOME LEGITIMATE (= 777) SKIPS POSSIBLE**

3. Approximately what percentage of your teachers is currently involved in [ATLAS, Audrey Cohen, Co-NECT, ELOB, MRSH, National Alliance, or R&W] activities in or out of the classroom?

    _____%

B. INFORMATION ABOUT YOUR SCHOOL

Now I would like to get some background information about your students, staff, and school to supplement the data provided by the district in the school profile reports.

4. We would like to know about how students came to be enrolled in your school this year. Please answer yes or no to each of the following. Were enrollments in your school determined by:

	WRITE YES OR NO
a. Residential assignment	
b. Busing or desegregation plan	
c. Parent choice with open enrollment and a non-specialized curriculum	
d. Parent choice with a theme or focus, for example, technology, school w/in a school, special needs, other magnet	

5. **ASK ONLY IF THE SCHOOL ACCEPTS ENROLLMENT BY PARENT CHOICE:** Did the number of families *requesting* enrollment in your school…

   CIRCLE ONE

   1. increase

   2. decrease, or

   3. remain about the same this year **compared to last year?**

   4. no policy of enrollment by parent choice

6. Did your school experience any of the following program disruptions this year? Did you have:

	WRITE YES OR NO
a. A new principal?	
b. Large turnover in teaching staff?	
c. Problematic relationships among school staff?	
d. Significant cuts in funding of needed programs?	
e. Problematic relationships with parents or community members?	
f. Any other significant program or school disruptions? (SPECIFY)_____	

7. **How many** businesses partnered with, adopted, or participated in the school by providing human resources, materials, and/or monetary assistance? We're looking for a formal, sustained partnership, not a one-time donor.

_____ #

IF RESPONDENT SAYS NO PARTNERS ‡ GO TO QUESTION 9

8. **ASK ONLY IF SCHOOL HAD PARTNERS:** How much impact did your school's business and community partnerships have on the day-to-day functioning of the school? Were there:

   CIRCLE ONE

   1. no effects

   2. very few positive effects

   3. some positive effects, or

   4. a great deal of positive effect?

Now I'm going to ask you the questions in Section 1 of the fax we sent you over the last few days, so you may want to consult those sheets. Did you receive this fax? Is it there in front of you?

If you have filled out the fax, would you like to simply read me the question numbers and responses?

9. What is your current school enrollment? _____

10. What is the average daily attendance rate for students in your school this year? (***Please give your best estimate*** and include both excused absences and unexcused absences in figuring this rate.)

_____%

11. On average, what percentage of your total student body enrolled at the beginning of the school year is still enrolled at the end of the school year?

_____% (please give your best estimate)

12. For the current school year, what percentage of your total student body was officially referred beyond the classroom level for disciplinary action? (Meaning, "sent to the principal's office") Do not count behavioral incidents for the same students on different occasions.

_____% (please give your best estimate)

13. About what percentage of your total student body is Limited English Proficient (LEP) or "Language Minority"?

_____% (please give your best estimate)

14. Approximately, what percentage of the total student body in your school receives the following special services? *(please give your best estimate)*

   a. Free or reduced-price school lunch   _____ %

   b. Remedial reading   _____ %

   (i.e., % of students who are in low ability reading classes and/or receive additional instructional support outside of regular classroom time.)

   c. Remedial math   _____ %

   (i.e., % of students who are in low ability math classes and/or receive additional instructional support outside of regular classroom time.)

   d. Bilingual education   _____ %

   e. English as a Second Language   _____ %

   f. Special education   _____ %

   g. Gifted and Talented education   _____ %

   h. Job training   _____ %

   Now I have a few questions that are not on the fax ...

15. Did your school receive any Title 1 funds for the 1997-98 academic year?

   No (0)   Yes (1)   **(CIRCLE ONE)**

IF NO ‡ GO TO Q16

IF YES, ASK:

15b. Could your school use these Title 1 funds for the **whole school?**

No (0)   Yes (1)   **(CIRCLE ONE)**

15c. Did you use any part of Title I funds for implementing the [ATLAS, Audrey Cohen, Co-NECT, ELOB, MRSH, National Alliance, or R&W] design?

No (0)   Yes (1)   **(CIRCLE ONE)**

16. How would you rate the academic ability of the students when they enter this school? Are they...

	(CIRCLE ONE)
much above the national norm	1
somewhat above the national norm	2
at the national norm	3
somewhat below the national norm	4
or much below the national norm	5

17. Now I would like to return to the fax to ask about suspensions and expulsions in your school this year. **So far this school year,** please estimate the number of students in your school who were removed from classroom instruction for academic or disciplinary reasons (temporarily or permanently).

How many were:	For academic or disciplinary reasons
a. suspended out of school	**(WRITE NUMBER)**
b. suspended in school	**(WRITE NUMBER)**
c. expelled	**(WRITE NUMBER)**

18. How many full-time <u>regular</u> classroom teachers do you have in your school? Please do not count teacher-aids, resource teachers, part-time staff, the librarian(s), or guidance counselors but do include the special education, physical education, music, and art teachers.

_____#

19. How many classroom teachers requested transfers out of your school in preparation for or during the year? Do not include leave of absence or termination.

_____#

20. What was your teacher retention rate?

    PROBE: 1. This is defined as the percent of classroom teachers who remained on the school payroll from June 1996 through September of 1997.

                        2. Please include all classroom teachers in your answer, even if they retired later in the year.

_____

(Typically will be number of teachers left/number of teachers in the school; interviewer can calculate after interview is complete)

Now we are done with the fax for the moment.

21. How well are curriculum and instruction of the [ATLAS, Audrey Cohen, Co-NECT, ELOB, MRSH, National Alliance, or R&W] design at your school aligned with the:

Cincinnati	*Were they?*	(CIRCLE NUMBER)
Ohio Proficiency Test *(Grades 4, 6, 9, 12)*	Not well aligned	1
	Somewhat aligned	2
	Well aligned	3
Stanford - 9 *(Grades 1, 3, 5, 7)*	Not well aligned	1
	Somewhat aligned	2
	Well aligned	3
Dade		
Stanford Achievement Test *(Grades 1 thru 9, 11)*	Not well aligned	1
	Somewhat aligned	2
	Well aligned	3
Florida Writing Assessment *(Grades 4, 8, 10)*	Not well aligned	1
	Somewhat aligned	2
	Well aligned	3
Memphis		
C.T.B.S. *(Grades 2 thru 8, 10)* (Comprehensive Test of Basic Skills part of TCAP [Tennessee Comprehensive Assessment Program – "tee-cap"]	Not well aligned	1
	Somewhat aligned	2
	Well aligned	3
Writing Assessment *(Grades 4, 8, 11)*	Not well aligned	1
	Somewhat aligned	2
	Well aligned	3
T.P.T. *(HS only)* (Tennessee Proficiency Test) – being phased out	Not well aligned	1
	Somewhat aligned	2
	Well aligned	3
TCAP/C.T.	Not well aligned	1
	Somewhat aligned	2
	Well aligned	3
Kentucky		
KIRIS	Not well aligned	1

| (Grades 4, 8, 11) | Somewhat aligned | 2 |
| | Well aligned | 3 |

Philadelphia

Stanford - 9 *(Grades 4, 8, 11)* (SAT-9)	Not well aligned	1
	Somewhat aligned	2
	Well aligned	3
P.S.S.A. *(Elementary, Middle, & High Schools)* (PA State Student Assessment)	Not well aligned	1
	Somewhat aligned	2
	Well aligned	3

Pittsburgh

I.T.B.S. (Iowa Test of Basic Skills)	Not well aligned	1
(Grades 1 thru 8)	Somewhat aligned	2
	Well aligned	3
P.S.S.A. *(Elementary, Middle, & High Schools)* (PA State Assessment)	Not well aligned	1
	Somewhat aligned	2
	Well aligned	3
New Standards *(Grades 4, 8, 10)*	Not well aligned	1
	Somewhat aligned	2
	Well aligned	3

San Antonio

TAAS *(Grades 3 thru 8)* Texas Assessment of Academic Skills	Not well aligned	1
	Somewhat aligned	2
	Well aligned	3

Washington

State 4th Assessment (i.e., Riverside Test)	Not well aligned	1
	Somewhat aligned	2
	Well aligned	3
C.T.B.S. *(Grades 4, 6, 8)* (Comprehensive Test of Basic Skills)	Not well aligned	1
	Somewhat aligned	2
	Well aligned	3
CFAS *(Grade 11)*	Not well aligned	1
	Somewhat aligned	2
	Well aligned	3

22. To what extent is each of the following matters a problem in your school? Indicate whether it is a serious problem, a moderate problem , a minor problem, or not a problem.

Mark (X) one box on each line	Serious	Moderate	Minor	Not a problem
A. Student tardiness				
B. Student absenteeism				
C. Teacher absenteeism				
D. Students cutting class				
E. Physical conflicts among students				
F. Robbery or theft				
G. Vandalism of school property				
H. Student pregnancy				
I. Student use of alcohol				
J. Student drug abuse				
K. Student possession of drugs				
L. Verbal abuse of teachers by students				

Interviewers: remind principals of response options

	Serious	Moderate	Minor	Not a problem
M. Student disrespect for teachers				
N. Students dropping out				
O. Student apathy				
P. Lack of academic challenge				
Q. Lack of parent involvement				
R. Parental alcoholism and/or drug abuse				

Interviewers: "Just a few more items, and we will complete this question."

	Serious	Moderate	Minor	Not a problem
S. Poverty				
T. Racial tension				
U. Students come to school unprepared to learn				
V. Poor nutrition				
W. Poor student health				
X. Student problems with the English language				
Y. Student's motivation to learn				

23. Please refer to question 23 in Section 2 of your fax sheet. How much influence do you feel each of the following has on how your performance is evaluated by your superiors? Please answer on a scale from 1 to 6, where **1** indicates **no influence**, and **6** indicates **a great deal of influence**.

KEY IN THE CIRCLED NUMBER	No Influence					Great Deal of Influence
a. How much do you feel the performance of your school's students on standardized tests has on how your performance is evaluated....	1	2	3	4	5	6
b. A good disciplinary environment in the school	1	2	3	4	5	6
c. Efficient administration	1	2	3	4	5	6
d. Parent or community reaction	1	2	3	4	5	6
e. Parent or community involvement in your school	1	2	3	4	5	6
f. Having a coherent school improvement plan with design-based assistance	1	2	3	4	5	6

C. IMPLEMENTATION EFFORTS

24. Other than the New American Schools design in your school, are you currently participating in any curriculum, instruction, or organizational reform efforts (e.g. Chicago Math, Reading Recovery, Coalition of Essential Schools, Different Ways of Knowing)?

_____

_____

_____

25. Please refer to question 25 on your fax sheet. How would you describe the availability of resources needed to implement the major elements of the [ATLAS, Audrey Cohen, Co-NECT, ELOB, MRSH, National Alliance, or R&W] design? Please consider "availability of resources" from any source (district, grants, business donors, New American Schools).

	No resources are available	Few are available	Some are available	Most are available	All are available
a. Design team materials to support instruction	1	2	3	4	5
b. Availability of design team materials to further implement the design in your school	1	2	3	4	5
c. Professional development for teachers	1	2	3	4	5
d. Time for planning, collaboration, and development	1	2	3	4	5
e. Staff or consultants to mentor, advise, and provide ongoing support	1	2	3	4	5
f. Technology and connectivity	1	2	3	4	5
g. Funds	1	2	3	4	5
h. Funding flexibility	1	2	3	4	5
i. Any other resources? SPECIFY _____ _____	1	2	3	4	5

26. How much <u>actual influence</u> do you think each of the following people and organizations has on allocating school funds? Please answer on a scale from 1 to 6, where **1** means **no influence** and **6** means **a great deal of influence**. This is question 26 on your fax sheet.

> **PROBE:** "Allocating school funds" means making budgetary decisions within your school, not deciding how much money your school gets in the first place.

CIRCLE ONE NUMBER IN EACH ROW	Allocating funds						
	No Influence					Great Deal of Influence	N/A
a. Superintendent	1	2	3	4	5	6	7
b. Central office administrators	1	2	3	4	5	6	7
c. Teachers at this school	1	2	3	4	5	6	7
d. Parents	1	2	3	4	5	6	7
e. Your school's board or governing board or site-based management council	1	2	3	4	5	6	7
f. Teachers' associations or unions	1	2	3	4	5	6	7
g. And you as the principal?	1	2	3	4	5	6	7

27. To what extent do you agree or disagree with the following statements regarding **your school**? Please answer on a scale from 1 to 6, where **1** indicates **strongly disagree** and **6** indicates **strongly agree**. This is question 27 on the fax.

KEY IN THE CIRCLED NUMBER	Strongly Disagree					Strongly Agree
a. Goals and priorities for this school are clear.	1	2	3	4	5	6
b. Bad attitudes that students develop about school and learning over the years are difficult or impossible to overcome in school.	1	2	3	4	5	6
c. Almost all students in this school are capable of mastering their coursework.	1	2	3	4	5	6
f. Staff members are involved in making decisions that affect them.	1	2	3	4	5	6
g. The teachers' union (or education association) and the school administration work together to improve the achieve ment of students in this school.	1	2	3	4	5	6
h. Staff members maintain high s tandards of performance for themselves.	1	2	3	4	5	6
i. The morale of staff members is low.	1	2	3	4	5	6
j. There is a great deal of cooperative effort among staff members.	1	2	3	4	5	6
k. We – the entire staff – solve problems **together**; we don't just talk about them.	1	2	3	4	5	6

28. To what extent do the following statements describe **your school**. On a scale of 1 to 6, where **1 does not describe your school**, and **6 clearly describes your school**. This question is number 28 on the fax.

KEY IN THE CIRCLED NUMBER	Does not de-scribe my school					Clearly de-scribes my school	Don't Know
a. There is conflict between teachers and administrators	1	2	3	4	5	6	7
b. Discipline is emphasized at this school	1	2	3	4	5	6	7
c. Students at this school place a priority on learning	1	2	3	4	5	6	7
e. Students are expected to do homework	1	2	3	4	5	6	7
f. Teacher morale is high	1	2	3	4	5	6	7
g. Teachers have a negative attitude about students	1	2	3	4	5	6	7
h. Deviation by students from school rules is not tolerated	1	2	3	4	5	6	7
i. Teachers take time to respond to students' individual needs	1	2	3	4	5	6	7

29. Were any of the following barriers to this year's implementation efforts? Please answer not at all, a little, a fair amount, or a great deal, to each of the following questions.

> **PROBE:** Would you say not at all, a little, a fair amount, or a great deal?

	Not at all	A little	A fair amount	A great deal
a. Did problems with state regulations impede your implementation efforts this year?	1	2	3	4
b. Did problems with district regulations impede your implementation efforts this year?	1	2	3	4
c. Did opposition from school staff impede your efforts?	1	2	3	4
d. Opposition from parents or other community members?	1	2	3	4
e. Inadequate training in the design?	1	2	3	4
f. Inadequate teacher education and experience in general?	1	2	3	4
h. Lack of alignment between the district/state mandated tests and the [ATLAS, Audrey Cohen, Co-NECT, ELOB, MRSH, National Alliance, or R&W] design?	1	2	3	4

30. Conversely, how much did the following things help your implementation efforts this year? Again, please answer not at all, a little, a fair amount, or a great deal, to each of the following questions.

   PROBE: Would you say not at all, a little, a fair amount, or a great deal?

	Not at all	A little	A fair amount	A great deal
a. Did support/mandates from the state help your implementation efforts this year?	1	2	3	4
b. Did support/mandates from the district help your implementation efforts this year?	1	2	3	4
c. Did support from other political actors (for example, the mayor, city council members) help your implementation efforts …	1	2	3	4
d. Did support from parents or community members help …	1	2	3	4
e. Did buy-in among school staff help …	1	2	3	4
f. Did staff development and follow-up help …	1	2	3	4
g. Did the capabilities of your school staff help …	1	2	3	4
i. Did additional financial support for the reform help your implementation efforts?	1	2	3	4

30a. Would you briefly elaborate on how state and district and school policies supported or inhibited implementation of the design this year?

   State:

   _____

   _____

   District:

   _____

   _____

   School:

   _____

   _____

D. YOUR TEACHING STAFF AND THEIR PROFESSIONAL DEVELOPMENT ACTIVITIES

We'd like to ask you some questions about your staff, specifically how teaching positions were filled in your school this year.

31. Did you fill any open teaching positions **over the past 12 months?**

     CIRCLE ONE

     NO (0)   Ë **GO TO QUESTION 32**

     (then rest is legitimate skips = 777)

     Yes (1)

     b. Did you have much hiring flexibility **over the past 12 months?**

     CIRCLE ONE

     No (0)   Yes (1)

     c. In selecting from the available pool of teachers **over the past 12 months**, did you consider the alignment between applicants' interests, experiences, and skills and the requirements of the [Audrey Cohen, ATLAS, Co-NECT, ELOB Modern Red Schoolhouse, National Alliance, or Roots & Wings] design?

     No (0)   Yes (1)

32. How much <u>actual influence</u> do you think each of the following people and organizations has on whom your school hires as new full-time teachers? Please answer on a scale from 1 to 6, where 1 means **no influence** and 6 means **a great deal of influence**. This is question 32 on your fax sheet.

CIRCLE ONE NUMBER IN EACH ROW	Hiring New Full-Time Teachers						
	No In-fluence					Great Deal of In-fluence	N/A
a. How much influence does the <u>superintendent</u> have on whom your school hires…	1	2	3	4	5	6	7
b. Central office administrators	1	2	3	4	5	6	7
e. Your school's board or governing board or site-based management council	1	2	3	4	5	6	7
c. Teachers at this school	1	2	3	4	5	6	7
d. Parents (not including those parents on the school governing board, for example.)	1	2	3	4	5	6	7
f. Teachers' associations or unions	1	2	3	4	5	6	7
g. And you as the principal?	1	2	3	4	5	6	7

We would now like to ask you some questions about the professional development experiences of your teachers.

33. In general, how many days of professional development did the typical teacher in your school receive? Please count professional development that occurred during the summer in preparation for the school year as well as training during the year.

_____ # of days

34. Of these professional development days, how many were specifically related to the [ATLAS, Audrey Cohen, Co-NECT, ELOB, MRSH, National Alliance, or R&W] design?

_____ # of days

35. What is your reaction to the professional development that your staff has received **this current school year** as it related to the [ATLAS, Audrey Cohen, Co-NECT, ELOB, MRSH, National Alliance, or R&W] design?

_____

_____

_____

36. In what areas do staff need more training?

_____

_____

_____

Now we are going to return to the questions we faxed to you.

E. PARENT INVOLVEMENT

Now I have some questions about parent involvement for which I would like you to refer to Section 3 of your fax.

37. For what percent of your total student body, did a parent or guardian attend one or more official conferences during the current school year? This is question 37 on the fax.

_____ %

38. Since the beginning of the current school year, about <u>how many</u> students' parents have you or your administrative staff spoken or met with regarding their <u>child's behavior</u>? **Administrative staff** here refers to the principal, vice principal, and school counselor.

_____ # number

(If principal gives percentage, try to pin down a number; otherwise repeat the total enrollment of school and say "*x% of this number?*")

How about regarding their <u>academic performance</u>?

_____ # number

39. How many parent volunteers participated in the instructional program, administrative support of the school, fundraising activities, and/or extracurricular activities during the current

school year?   Please include parents who are **active** on leadership councils, PTA, volunteer in helping teachers in classrooms, and other activities.

_____ # number

40. How much impact did parent and other volunteers, those not sponsored by businesses or community organizations, have on the instructional program in your school? Were there:

> **CIRCLE ONE**
>
> 1. no effects
>
> 2. very few positive effects
>
> 3. some positive effects, or
>
> 4. a great deal of positive effect?

F. EARLY IMPACT

Now I have just a few more questions, and we will be done.

41. Many principals say they have some teachers who are very resistant to making changes to their instruction. If you have such teachers, how would you rate the [ATLAS, Audrey Cohen, Co-NECT, ELOB, MRSH, National Alliance, or R&W] design so far as a tool for encouraging them to make positive changes in their instruction? Has it been:

> **CIRCLE ONE**
>
> 1. Not very useful
>
> 2. Somewhat useful
>
> 3. Moderately useful
>
> 4. Very useful
>
> 5. Have no such teachers

42. On balance, to what extent has the [ATLAS, Audrey Cohen, Co-NECT, ELOB, MRSH, National Alliance, or R&W] design team had positive or negative effects on the following aspects in your school during the current school year? Please answer on a scale

from 1 to 7, where **1** indicates a great deal of **negative** effect, and **7** indicates a great deal of **positive** effect; so **4** indicates **no effect** (question 43 on the fax). What effect has the design had on:

KEY IN CIRCLED NUMBER	Great deal of negative effect			No effect			Great deal of positive effect
b. Your professional growth	1	2	3	4	5	6	7
c. Your job satisfaction	1	2	3	4	5	6	7
h. Your capacity to be an active instructional leader	1	2	3	4	5	6	7
i. Your capacity to be a good administrator	1	2	3	4	5	6	7

43. How strongly do you support or oppose the [ATLAS, Audrey Cohen, Co-NECT, ELOB, MRSH, National Alliance, or R&W] design in your school? Do you …

> **CIRCLE ONE**
> 1. Strongly oppose
> 2. Somewhat oppose
> 3. Neither oppose nor support
> 4. Somewhat support
> 5. Strongly support

G. PRINCIPAL'S PROFESSIONAL BACKGROUND

44. How long have you been a principal in this school, including this year? _____ years

45. How many years were you a principal *before* serving in this school? _____years

46a. Do you have any comments about the impact of the [ATLAS, Audrey Cohen, Co-NECT, ELOB, MRSH, National Alliance, or R&W] design in your school?

_____

_____

_____

b. Any comments about the <u>professional development</u> of your teachers related to the design?

_____

_____

_____

c. Are there any further <u>resource or funding</u> issues related to the design?

_____

_____

_____

d. Any <u>testing and accountability</u> issues related to the design?

_____

_____

_____

Do you have any questions about the interview today or RAND's data collection in general?

We will send you the published report on last year's results, but unfortunately it won't be available until this summer. We will send your school a copy in September. We will also send you a report from this year's data as soon as it becomes available.

Thank you for taking the time to respond to our questions. I hope you have a good day.

American Association of School Administrators (1995). *Great Expectations: Understanding the New Title I.* Washington, DC: Author.

Ball, D. L., E. Camburn, D. K. Cohen, and B. Rowan (1998). "Instructional Improvement and Disadvantaged Students." University of Michigan, unpublished manuscript.

Berends, M. (2000). "Teacher-Reported Effects of New American Schools' Designs: Exploring Relationships to Teacher Background and School Context." *Educational Evaluation and Policy Analysis,* 22(1), 65–82.

Berends, M. (1999). *Assessing the Progress of New American Schools: A Status Report.* Santa Monica, CA: RAND, MR-1085-ED.

Berends, M., and S. Bodilly (Forthcoming). "New American Schools' Scale-Up Phase: Lessons Learned to Date." In S. Stringfield, A. Datnow, and S. Yonezawa, eds., *Scaling Up Designs for Educational Improvement.* Baltimore, MD: Johns Hopkins University Press.

Berends, M., D. W. Grissmer, S. N. Kirby, and S. Williamson (1999). "The Changing American Family and Student Achievement Trends." *Review of Sociology of Education and Socialization,* 23, 67–101.

Berends, M., and B. King (1994). "A Description of Restructuring in Nationally Nominated Schools: Legacy of the Iron Cage?" *Educational Policy,* 8(1), 28–50.

Berends, M., and S. N. Kirby (2000). "Analyzing State Assessment Data Within the Context of the Federal Evaluations of Title I and Comprehensive School Reform Demonstration (CSRD) Programs." Washington, DC: RAND.

Berends, M., S. N. Kirby, S. Naftel, and J. S. Sloan (In Review). *The Status of Standards-Based Reforms in Title I Schools: First-Year Findings from the National Longitudinal Study of Schools.* Santa Monica, RAND, DRU-2262-EDU.

Berman, P. and M. McClaughlin (1978). *Federal Programs Supporting Educational Change, Vol. VII: Factors Affecting Implementation and Continuation.* Santa Monica, CA: RAND, R-1589/7.

Bodilly, S. J. (1996). *Lessons from New American Schools Development Corporation's Demonstration Phase.* Santa Monica, CA: RAND.

Bodilly, S. J. (1998). *Lessons from New American Schools' Scale-up Phase: Prospects for Bringing Designs to Multiple Schools.* Santa Monica, CA: RAND, MR-1777-NAS.

Bodilly, S. J. (Forthcoming). *New American Schools' Concept of Break the Mold Designs: How Designs Evolved over Time and Why.* Santa Monica, CA: RAND.

Bodilly, S. J., and M. Berends (1999). "Necessary District Support for Comprehensive School Reform." In G. Orfield and E. H. De Bray, eds., *Hard Work for Good Schools: Facts Not Fads in Title I Reform.* Boston , MA: The Civil Rights Project, Harvard University, pp. 111–119.

Bodilly, S. J., S. Purnell, K. Ramsey, and C. Smith (1995). *Designing New American Schools: Baseline Observations on Nine Design Teams.* Santa Monica, CA: RAND, MR-598-NASDC.

Borman, K. M., P. W. Cookson, Jr., A. R. Sadovnik, and J. Z. Spade, eds. (1996). *Implementing Educational Reform: Sociological Perspectives on Educational Policy.* Norwood, N.J.: Ablex Publishing Corporation.

Bratton, S. E., S. P. Horn, and S. P. Wright (1996). *Using and Interpreting Tennessee's Value-Added Assessment System: A Primer for Teachers and Principals.* Knoxville, TN: Value-Added Research and Assessment Center, University of Tennessee.

Bryk, A. S., and M. E. Driscoll (1988). "The High School as Community: Contextual Influence and Consequences for Students and Teachers." Madison, WI: National Center on Effective Secondary Schools, Wisconsin Center for Education Research, University of Wisconsin-Madison.

Bryk, A. S., and S. W. Raudenbush (1992). *Hierarchical Linear Models: Applications and Data Analysis Methods.* Newbury Park, CA: Sage Publications.

Bryk, A. S., V. Lee, and P. Holland (1993). *Catholic Schools and the Common Good.* Cambridge, MA: Harvard University.

Bryk, A. S., S. W. Raudenbush, and R. T. Congdon (1996). *HLM: Hierarchical Linear and Nonlinear Modeling with the HLM/2L and HLM/3L Programs.* Chicago, IL: Scientific Software International.

Bryk, A. S., P. B. Sebring, D. Kerbow, S. Rollow, and J. Q. Easton (1998a). *Charting Chicago School Reform: Democratic Localism as a Lever for Change.* Boulder, CO: Westview.

Bryk, A. S., Y. M. Thum, J. Q. Eaton, and S. Luppescu (1998b). *Academic Productivity of Chicago Public Elementary Schools.* Chicago, IL: Consortium on Chicago School Research.

Burstein, L., L. McDonnell, J. VanWinkle, T. H. Ormseth, J. Mirocha, and G. Guiton (1995). *Validating National Curriculum Indicators.* Santa Monica, CA: RAND, MR-658-NSF.

Coleman, J. S., E. Q. Campbell, C. J. Hobson, J. McPartland, A. M. Mood, F. D. Weinfeld, and R. L. York (1966). *Equality of Educational Opportunity.* Washington, DC: U.S. Government Printing Office.

Comer, J. P., and N. M. Haynes (1999). "The Dynamics of School Change: Response to the Article, 'Comer's School Development Program in Prince George's County, Maryland: A Theory-Based Evaluation by Thomas D. Cook et al.'" *American Educational Research Journal,* 36(3), pp. 599–607.

Cook, T. D., F. N. Habib, M. Phillips, R. A. Settersten, S. C. Shagle, and S. M. Degirmencioglu (1999). "Comer's School Development Program in Prince George's County, Maryland: A Theory-Based Evaluation." *American Educational Research Journal*, 36(3), pp. 543–597.

Cook, T. D., H. D. Hunt, and R. F. Murphy (1998). "Comer's School Development Program in Chicago: A Theory-Based Evaluation." Northwestern University, unpublished manuscript.

Darling-Hammond, L. (1988). "Policy and Professionalism." In A. Lieberman, ed., *Building a Professional Culture in Schools*. New York: Teachers College Press.

Darling-Hammond, L. (1995). *Policy for Restructuring*. In A. Lieberman, ed., *The Work of Restructuring Schools: Building from the Ground Up*. New York: Teachers College Press, pp. 157–175

Darling-Hammond, L. (1997). *The Right to Learn: A Blueprint for Creating Schools that Work*. San Francisco: Jossey Bass.

Datnow, A., and S. Stringfield (1997). *School Effectiveness and School Improvement* 8(1).

Desimone, L. (2000). *Making Comprehensive School Reform Work*. New York: ERIC Clearinghouse on Urban Education, Teachers College.

Edmonds, R. R. (1979). "Effective Schools for the Urban Poor." *Educational Leadership*, 37, 15–24.

Elmore, R. F., and R. Rothman, eds. (1999). *Testing, Teaching, and Learning: A Guide for States and School Districts*. Committee on Title I Testing and Assessment, National Research Council. Washington, DC: National Academy Press.

Epstein, J. (1985). "Home and School Connections in Schools of the Future: Implications of Research on Parent Involvement." *Peabody Journal of Education*, 62(2), 18–41.

Epstein, J. (1992). "School and Family Partnerships." in M. Alkin, ed., *Encyclopedia of Educational Research, 6th Edition*. MacMillan: New York, New York, pp. 1139–1151.

Fullan, M. (1982). *The Meaning of Educational Change.* New York: Teachers College Press.

Fullan, M. G. (1991). *The New Meaning of Educational Change.* New York: Teachers College Press.

Furhman, S. H., and G. W. Ritter (1998). "External School Reform Providers and Accountability." Graduate School of Education, University of Pennsylvania, unpublished manuscript.

Gamoran, A. (1987). "The Stratification of High School Learning Opportunities," *Sociology of Education,* 60, 135–155.

Gamoran, A. (1992). "The Variable Effects of High School Tracking." *American Sociological Review,* 57, 812–828.

Gamoran, A., and M. Berends (1987). "The Effects of Stratification in Secondary Schools: Synthesis of Survey and Ethnographic Research." *Review of Educational Research,* 57, 415–435.

Gamoran, A., and R. Dreeben (1986). "Coupling and Control in Educational Organizations." *Administrative Science Quarterly,* 31, 612–632.

Gamoran, A., M. Nystrand, M. Berends, and P. C. LePore (1995). "An Organizational Analysis of the Effects of Ability Grouping." *American Educational Research Journal,* 32, 687–715.

Garet, M. S., B. F. Birman, A. C. Porter, L. Desimone, B. Herman, with K. S. Yoon (1999). *Designing Effective Professional Development: Lessons from the Eisenhower Program.* Washington, DC: U.S. Department of Education.

Glennan, T. K., Jr. (1998). *New American Schools after Six Years.* Santa Monica, CA: RAND, MR-945-NASDC.

Grissmer, D. W., and A. Flanagan (1998). *Exploring Rapid Achievement Gains in North Carolina and Texas.* Washington, DC: National Education Goals Panel.

Grissmer, D. W., S. N. Kirby, M. Berends, and S. Williamson (1994). *Student Achievement and the Changing American Family.* Santa Monica, CA: RAND, MR-488-LE.

Hall, G. E., S. Hord, and T. Griffin (1980). "Implementation at the School Building Level: The Development and Analysis of Nine Mini-Case Studies." Paper presented at the American Education Research Association Annual Meeting.

Hallinan, M. T. (1994). "Tracking: From Theory to Practice." *Sociology of Education*, 67(2), 79–83.

Henke, R. R., S. P. Choy, S. Geis, and S. P. Groughman (1996). *Schools and Staffing in the United States: A Statistical Profile, 1993–1994*. Washington, DC: National Center for Education Statistics, U.S. Department of Education, NCES 96-124.

Herman, R., D. Aladjem, P. McMahon, E. Masem, I. Mulligan, A. S. O'Malley, S. Quinones, A. Reeve, and D. Woodruff (1999). *An Educators' Guide to Schoolwide Reform*. Arlington, VA: Educational Research Service.

Hess, A.G. (1995). *Restructuring Urban Schools: A Chicago Perspective*. New York: Teachers College.

Jencks, C. S., M. Smith, H. Acland, M. J. Bane, D. Cohen, H. Gintis, B. Heyns, and S. Michelson (1972). *Inequality: A Reassessment of the Effect of Family and Schooling in America*. New York, NY: Basic Books.

Jennings, J. F. (1996). "Travels Without Charley." *Phi Delta Kappan*, 78, 11–16.

Jennings, J. F. (1998). *Why National Standards and Tests? Politics and the Quest for Better Schools*. Thousand Oaks, CA: Sage Publications.

Keltner, B. (1998). *Resources for Transforming New American Schools: First Year Findings*. Santa Monica: RAND, IP-175.

King, J. A. (1994). "Meeting the Needs of At-Risk Students: A Cost-Analysis of Three Models." *Educational Evaluation and Policy Analysis*, 16(1), 1–19.

King, J. A. (1999). "Making Economically-Grounded Decisions about Comprehensive School Reform Models: Considerations of Costs, Effects, and Contexts." Paper presented at the National

Invitational Conference on Effective Title I Schoolwide Program Implementation, Laboratory for Student Success at Temple University Center for Research in Human Development and Education, May 10–11, Arlington, VA.

Kirby, S. N., M. Berends, S. Naftel, and J. S. Sloan (In Review). *Comprehensive School Reform Demonstration (CSRD) Schools: Early Findings on Implementation.* Santa Monica, CA: RAND.

Koretz, D. M. (1996). "Using Student Assessments for Educational Accountability." In E. A. Hanushek and D. W. Jorgenson, eds., *Improving America's Schools: The Role of Incentives.* Washington, DC: National Academy Press, pp. 171–196.

Koretz, D. M., and S. I. Barron (1998). *The Validity of Gains in Scores on the Kentucky Instructional Results Information System (KIRIS).* Santa Monica, CA: RAND, MR-1014-EDU.

Lee, V. E., and A. S. Bryk (1989). "A Multilevel Model of the Social Distribution of High School Achievement." *Sociology of Education,* 62(3), 172–192.

Lee, V. E., A. S. Bryk, and J. B. Smith (1993). "The Organization of Effective Secondary Schools." *Review of Research in Education,* 19, 171–267.

Lee, V. E., and J. B. Smith (1995). "Effects of High School Restructuring and Size on early Gain in Achievement and Engagement." *Sociology of Education,* 68(4), 241–270.

Lee, V. E., and J. B. Smith (1997). "High School Size: Which Works Best and for Whom?" *Educational Evaluation and Policy Analysis,* 19(3), 205–227.

Levin, H. M. (1991). *Learning from Accelerated Schools.* Pew Higher Education Research Program, Policy Perspectives. Philadelphia: Pew Charitable Trusts.

Lortie, D. (1970). *School Teacher.* Chicago, IL: University of Chicago Press.

Louis, K. S., and H. M. Marks (1998). "Does Professional Community Affect the Classroom? Teachers' Work and Student Experiences in Restructuring Schools." *American Journal of Education* 106(4), 532–575.

Louis, K. S., and M. B. Miles (1990). *Improving the Urban High School: What Works and Why.* New York: Teachers College Press.

McLanahan, S., and G. Sandefur (1994). *Growing Up with a Single Parent: What Hurts, What Helps.* Cambridge, MA: Harvard University Press.

McLaughlin, M. W. (1990). "The RAND Change Agent Study Revisited: Macro Perspectives and Micro Realities." *Educational Researcher,* 19(9), 11–16.

McLaughlin, M. W. (1991). "Learning from Experience: Lessons from Policy Implementation." In A. R. Odden, ed., *Education Policy Implementation.* Albany, NY: State University of New York Press, pp. 185–195.

McLaughlin, M. W., and D. D. Marsh (1978). "Staff Development and School Change." *Teachers College Record,* 80(1), 69–94.7

Meyer, R. H. (1996). "Value-Added Indicators of School Performance." In E. A. Hanushek and D. W. Jorgenson, eds., *Improving America's Schools: The Role of Incentives.* Washington, DC: National Academy Press, pp. 197–224.

Miller, M, M. Rollefson, M. Garet, M. Berends, N. Adelman, L. Anderson, & K. Yamashiro (2000). *Summary and Implications from a Conference on Student Achievement and the Evaluation of Federal Programs: A Working Paper.* Washington, DC: American Institutes for Research.

Mitchell, Karen (1996). *Reforming and Conforming: NASDC Principals Discuss School Accountability Systems.* Santa Monica, CA: RAND, MR-716-NASDC.

Montjoy, R. and L. O'Toole (1979). "Toward a Theory of Policy Implementation: An Organizational Perspective." *Public Administration Review,* 465–476.

Murphy, J. (1992). *Restructuring Schools: Capturing and Assessing the Phenomena.* New York: Teachers College Press.

New American Schools Development Corporation (1991). *Designs for a New Generation of American Schools: Request for Proposals.* Arlington, VA: Author.

New American Schools Development Corporation (1997). *Bringing Success to Scale: Sharing the Vision of New American Schools.* Arlington, VA: NAS.

New American Schools Development Corporation (1999). *New American Schools: An Update to the Board of Directors.* Presentation to the NAS Board of Directors, unpublished document. Arlington, VA: NAS.

Newman, F. M., and G. G. Wehlage (1995). *Successful School Restructuring.* Madison, WI: Center on Organization and Restructuring of Schools, Wisconsin Center on Education Research, University of Wisconsin-Madison.

Newmann, F. M, and Associates, eds. (1996). *Authentic Achievement: Restructuring Schools for Intellectual Quality.* San Francisco: Jossey Bass.

Newmann, F. M., R. A. Rutter, and M. S. Smith (1989). "Organizational Factors that Affect School Sense of Efficacy, Community, and Expectations." *Sociology of Education,* 51(4), 221–238.

Nunnery, J. A. (1998). "Reform Ideology and the Locus of Development Problem in Educational Restructuring: Enduring Lessons from Studies of Educational Innovation." *Education and Urban Society,* 30(3), 277–295.

Oakes, J. (1994). "More than Misapplied Technology: A Normative and Political Response to Hallinan on Tracking." *Sociology of Education,* 67(2), 84–88.

Oakes, J., A. Gamoran, and R. N. Page (1992). "Curriculum Differentiation: Opportunities, Outcomes, and Meanings." In P. W. Jackson, ed., *Handbook of Research on Curriculum.* New York: Macmillan, pp. 570–608.

Odden, A. (1997). *How to Rethink School Budgets to Support School Transformation.* Arlington, VA: New American Schools.

Orr, M. (1998). "The Challenge of School Reform in Baltimore: Race, Jobs, and Politics." In C. N. Stone, ed., *Changing Urban Education.* Lawrence, KS: University Press of Kansas, pp. 93–117

Parsons, T. (1959). "The School Class as a Social System: Some of Its Functions in American Slociety." *Harvard Educational Review,* 29, 297–318.

Perrow, C. (1986). *Complex Organizations: A Critical Essay, 3rd Edition.* New York: Random House.

Powell, A. G., E. Farrar, and D. K. Cohen (1985). *The Shopping Mall High School: Winners and Losers in the Educational Marketplace.* Boston: Houghton Mifflen.

Pressman, J. L., and A. Wildavsky (1973). *Implementation.* Berkeley, CA: University of California Press.

Purkey, S. C., and M. S. Smith (1983). "Effective Schools: A Review." *The Elementary School Journal,* 83(4), 427–452.

Purnell, S., and P. Hill (1992). *Time for Reform.* Santa Monica, CA: R-4234-EMC.

Rose, L. C., and A. M. Gallup (1999). "The 31st Annual Phi Delta Kappa/Gallup Poll Of the Public's Attitudes Toward the Public Schools." *Phi Delta Kappan,* 81(1), 41–56.

Rosenholtz, S. J. (1985). "Effective Schools: Interpreting the Evidence." *American Journal of Education,* 93, 352–388.

Ross, S. M., M. Alberg, and J. Nunnery (1999a). "Selection and Evaluation of Locally Developed Versus Externally Developed Schoolwide Programs." In G. Orfield and E. H. DeBray, eds., *Hard Work for Good Schools: Facts not Fads in Title I Reform.* Boston, MA: The Civil Rights Project, Harvard University, pp. 147–158.

Ross, S. M., W. L. Sanders, S. P. Wright, and S. Stringfield (1998). "The Memphis Restructuring Initiative: Achievement Results for Years 1 and 2 on the Tennessee Value-Added Assessment

System (TVAAS)." University of Memphis, unpublished manuscript.

Ross, S., A. Troutman, D. Horgan, S. Maxwell, R. Laitinen, and D. Lowther (1997). "The Success of Schools in Implementing Eight Restructuring Designs: A Synthesis of First Year Evaluation Outcomes." *School Effectiveness and School Improvement,* 8(1), 95–124.

Ross, S. M., L. W. Wang, W. L. Sanders, S. P. Wright, and S. Stringfield (1999b). "Two- and Three-Year Achievement Results for the Tennessee Value-Added Assessment System for Restructuring Schools in Memphis." Center for Research in Educational Policy, University of Memphis, unpublished manuscript.

Rossi, P. H., and H. E. Freeman (1993). *Evaluation: A Systemic Approach.* Newbury Park, CA: Sage Publications.

Sanders, W. L., and S. P. Horn (1994). "The Tennessee Value-Added Assessment System (TVAAS): Mixed-Model Methodology in Educational Assessment." *Journal of Personnel Evaluation in Education,* 8, 299–311.

Sanders, W. L., and S. P. Horn (1995). "Educational Assessment Reassessed: The Usefulness of Standardized and Alternative Measures of Student Achievement as Indicators for the Assessment of Educational Outcomes." *Educational Policy Analysis Archives,* 3(6).

Sarason, S. B. (1996). "Foreword." In D. E. Muncy and P. J. McQuillan, eds., *Reform & Resistance in Schools and Classrooms: An Ethnographic View of the Coalition of Essential Schools.* New Haven, CT: Yale University Press, pp. vii–viii.

Scriven, M. (1980). *The Logic of Evaluation.* Iverness, CA: Edgepress.

Shadish, W. R., T. D. Cook, and L. C. Leviton (1995). *Foundations of Program Evaluation: Theories of Practice.* Thousand Oaks, CA: Sage Publications.

Singer, J. D. (1998). "Using SAS PROC MIXED to Fit Multilevel Models, Hierarchical Models, and Individual Growth Models." *Journal of Educational and Behavioral Statistics*, 24(4), 323–355.

Sizer, T. R. (1984). *Horace's Compromise: The Dilemma of the American High School.* Boston: Houghton Mifflen.

Sizer, T. R. (1992). *Horace's School: Redesigning the American High School.* New York: Houghton Mifflin.

Slavin, R. E. (1987). "Ability Grouping and Student Achievement in Elementary Schools: A Best-Evidence Synthesis." *Review of Educational Research*, 57, 293–336.

Slavin, R. E. (1990). "Achievement Effects of Ability Grouping in Secondary Schools: A Best-Evidence Synthesis." *Review of Educational Research*, 60, 471–499.

Smith, L., S. Ross, M. McNelis, M. Squires, R. Wasson, S. Maxwell, K. Weddle, L. Nath, A. Grehan, and T. Buggey (1998). "The Memphis Restructuring Initiative: Analyses of Activities and Outcomes that Impact Implementation Success." *Education and Urban Society*, 30(3), 296–325.

Smith, M. S., and B. W. Scoll (1995). "The Clinton Human Capital Agenda." *Teachers College Record*, 96(3), 389–404.

Smith, M. S., B. W. Scoll, and J. Link (1996). "Research-Based School Reform: The Clinton Administration's Agenda." In E. A. Hanushek and D. W. Jorgenson, eds., *Improving America's Schools: The Role of Incentives.* Washington, DC: National Academy Press, pp. 9–27.

Stringfield, S., and A. Datnow, eds. (1998). *Education and Urban Society* 30(3).

Stringfield, S., M. A. Millsap, and R. Herman (1997). *Special Strategies for Educating Disadvantaged Children: Findings and Policy Implications of a Longitudinal Study.* Washington, DC: U.S. Department of Education.

Stringfield, S., S. Ross, and L. Smith, eds. (1996). *Bold Plans for School Restructuring: The New American Schools Designs.* Mahwah, NJ: Lawrence Erlbaum Associates.

Sykes, G. (1990). "Fostering Teacher Professionalism in Schools." In R. F. Elmore, ed., *Restructuring Schools: The Next Generation of Educational Reform.* San Francisco: Jossey-Bass, pp. 59–96.

Tyack, D., and L. Cuban (1995). *Tinkering Toward Utopia: A Century of Public School Reform.* Cambridge, MA: Harvard University Press.

U.S. Department of Education (1993). *Improving America's Schools Act of 1993: The Reauthorization of the Elementary and Secondary Education Act and Other Amendments.* Washington, DC: U.S. Department of Education.

U.S. Department of Education (1999). *Promising Results, Continuing Challenges: The Final Report of the National Assessment of Title I.* Washington, DC: U.S. Department of Education.

Wallerstein, J. S., and S. Blakeslee (1995). *The Good Marriage.* New York: Warner Books.

Weatherly, R., and M. Lipsky (1977). "Street Level Bureaucrats and Institutional Innovation: Implementing Special Education Reform." *Harvard Education Review,* 47(2), 171–197.

Wise, A. E. (1989). "Professional Teaching: A New Paradigm for the Management of Education." In T. J. Sergiovanni and J. H. Moore, eds., *Schooling for Tomorrow: Directing Reforms to Issues that Count.* Boston: Allyn and Bacon.

Wong, K. K. and S. Meyer (1998a). *An Overview of Title I Schoolwide Programs: Federal Legislative Expectations.* Philadelphia, PA: Mid-Atlantic Regional Education Laboratory at Temple University Center for Research in Human Development and Education.

Wong, Kenneth, and Stephen Meyer (1998b). "Title I School-Wide Programs: A Synthesis of Findings from Recent Evaluation." *Educational Evaluation and Policy Analysis,* 20(2), 115–136.